Simulation Using Personal Computers

Professor John M. Carroll *BSIE*
Dr. Eng. Sci.

Department of Computer Science
The University of Western Ontario
London, Canada

PRENTICE-HALL, INC.
Englewood Cliffs, New Jersey 07632

Library of Congress Cataloging-in-Publication Data

Carroll, John Millar.
    Simulation using personal computers.

    Bibliography: p.
    Includes index.
    1. Digital computer simulation.   2. Microcomputers.
I. Title.
QA76.9.C6557 1987   003   86-12208
ISBN 0-8359-6924-X

Editorial/production supervision and
    interior design: Lori L. Baronian
Cover design: Ben Santora
Manufacturing buyer: Ed O'Dougherty

Printed in the United States of America

10 9 8 7 6 5 4 3 2

ISBN 0-8359-6924-X 025

PRENTICE-HALL INTERNATIONAL (UK) LIMITED, *London*
PRENTICE-HALL OF AUSTRALIA PTY. LIMITED, *Sydney*
PRENTICE-HALL CANADA INC., *Toronto*
PRENTICE-HALL HISPANOAMERICANA, S.A., *Mexico*
PRENTICE-HALL OF INDIA PRIVATE LIMITED, *New Delhi*
PRENTICE-HALL OF JAPAN, INC., *Tokyo*
PRENTICE-HALL OF SOUTHEAST ASIA PTE. LTD., *Singapore*
EDITORA PRENTICE-HALL DO BRASIL, LTDA., *Rio de Janeiro*

To Billie with love

Contents

Preface

I have always considered computers to be fun, computer programming to be more fun, and computer simulation to be the most fun of all. I built my first computer hardware, a cascaded decade counter, in 1945.

I wrote my first program, machine language, of course, in 1953; and took my first programming course in 1959 (written in SOAP II). In 1964 I quit my job as managing editor of *Electronics* magazine to teach scientific programming (Lewiz) and data processing (Gecom) to industrial engineering students, at a 50% pay cut. In 1968, I joined the then new department of computer science at the University of Western Ontario, where I taught computer simulation as well.

I never experienced the real joy of programming until 1978 when I acquired a TRS-80 model I personal computer and no longer had to run hat in hand to ensconced computer-center bureaucrats to get computing time or disk space.

I am impatient with computer science teachers who take the fun out of computing with abstract and arcane mathematical incantations, burdensome loads of make-work, and highly opinionated but never validated notions about programming style—no more GOTOs, lots of comments, albeit meaningless ones, and indentation to the nth power. I am also impatient with bright, upwardly mobile kids who see a degree in computer science as a passport to a lifestyle of cross-country skiing, cheese fondues, and BMWs; and live for the day when they collect their sheepskins and no longer have any damned programs to write.

I am saddened each year as we turf out one or two of the keenest and most innovative programmers because their programming style didn't please some politically well positioned instructor, or because they failed a math course that has little or no relevance to their work.

This book is intended to put some of the fun back into programming. If you work through it while sitting at your personal computer, you'll learn the essentials of computer simulation. Every principle is introduced by a program whose results are reported as graphically as I was able to make them. You can copy my programs or write your own. There may be bugs in my programs; if not now, they'll be there when the typesetters get through with them. Anyway, it's all part of the learning experience; and consider how much satisfaction you'll have when you prove you're a better programmer than I am.

You don't have to put off using this book until you take a third, fourth, or fifth year course in simulation. This book would go well with a first year computer course. Everything you need to know is explained as you go along and the exercises are a lot more fun than the dust-dry assignments you find so boring. Working through this book will put you well on your way to successfully writing and debugging the 200 odd programs you will have to write before computer programming really becomes second nature to you and your first inclination when you have a problem to solve, or nothing better to do, is to sit down at the keyboard, fire up your PC, and do some creative programming.

The first eight chapters deal pretty much with waiting lines or queues and you might get the idea that all simulation was good for was predicting how long the line outside a theatre or sporting event is likely to be. Well, the simulation of waiting lines is an important part of this art. They are truly pervasive in our society where contention for ever diminishing stores of resources becomes keener every year on all levels from interpersonal relationships to superpower feuds. And waiting lines often exist within systems where their presence is not immediately evident.

In Chapter Ten I try to put the uses of simulation into perspective by discussing some of the simulation projects I have managed in the past twenty years (Chapter Nine was written by a former student of mine. It describes a simulation language he wrote—GPSS for microcomputers).

I'd like to tell you what my graduate students did last year to show the breadth of this subject:

Bill wrote a program simulating one terminal of the US Ocean Surveillance Information System, which was a main-frame (i.e., a "big" computer) simulation. A microcomputer version of it is described in Chapter Eight.

Ashok wrote the household simulator described in Chapter Ten. It used census data to predict the size and composition of households years into the future.

Milan rewrote the police patrol simulator described in Chapter Ten (a main-frame simulation) to make a training simulator for police dispatchers and commanders. It now runs on an IBM/AT personal computer.

Laurie simulated an Ethernet local area network in the physiology research laboratory. Among other things it tells how many word-processing users can be allowed to work at any given time without causing undesired loss of information from data-collection stations to which living subjects are connected.

Nelson carried out an investigation of the US Data Encryption Standard to see whether statistical tests could detect any suspicious patterns in the composition of the Substitution Boxes that might suggest that the National Security Agency had inserted "trap doors" that would make the DES easy to break. He didn't find any. Formally, he found that at the 95% level of confidence he could not reject the hypothesis that the S-boxes were randomly chosen permutations.

Kathy designed a simulator to test evacuation paths in a day-care center. This simulation runs on a microcomputer. It does incorporate waiting lines: when children line up at the exits. The user can type in the description of any day-care center and the simulator will show how a given set of evacuation rules would work. It will even show how to modify the rules in case the fire cuts off one or more escape routes.

CHAPTER ONE

Getting Started in Simulation

A simulation is a procedure in which one system is substituted for another system that it resembles in certain important aspects. As an example, consider a model airplane suspended in a wind tunnel where it is used to simulate a full-sized plane moving through the atmosphere so engineers can study its aerodynamic characteristics. As is the case with most simulations, this one enables the persons conducting the simulation to learn about the real system. They can do this without having to build and fly a full-sized plane. This saves time and money and avoids the risk of flying an unproven aircraft.

There are many other reasons for using simulated systems to study real ones. The real ones may not exist; the airplane represented by the model in the wind tunnel may only be in the first stages of design.

It may be too expensive to work with the real system; perhaps the experiments we are contemplating would damage it. In the real system, the changes we want to study may take place too slowly or too fast to be observed conveniently. When simulating the propagation of plant species on the shoreline of Lake Huron, we study events occurring over a period of 400 years. When simulating nuclear reactions, we study events taking place in millionths of a second.

There are some algorithms (that is, specific problem-solving methodologies) that require random choices to be made. A random-selection routine may be included in packages for Factor Analysis, Linear Programming, or the Project Evaluation and Review Technique.

Most important of all, the very act of studying a real system may change it and render our observations about it invalid. Half a century ago at the Hawthorne Works of the Western Electric Company near Chicago, engineers wanted to find out whether changing working conditions would increase worker productivity. In one experiment, they increased workplace illumination in stages and observed that productivity went up. Then, just to make sure that there was a genuine cause-and-effect relationship, they reduced the illumination in stages. Surprisingly, productivity continued to increase. This situation has become known as the "Hawthorne Effect." As near as anyone can make out, productivity increased mainly because the workers were so pleased that somebody was taking an interest in them that they worked their hearts out. But, as far as the engineers were concerned, the process of observation had contaminated the results.

In 1924, German physicist Werner Heisenberg expressed somewhat the same idea when he formulated his "Uncertainty Principle." Among other things, it asserted that one cannot observe the location of a subatomic particle without changing its momentum, nor can one observe its momentum without altering its position.

COMPUTER SIMULATION

The cheapest, most versatile, and convenient kind of simulation is one that is carried out within a computer. We are talking specifically about "discrete, stochastic, digital" simulation. It is discrete because it proceeds in steps; stochastic because the element of chance is introduced by use of pseudorandom number generators, and digital because the computers used are digital. (Nearly all computers are digital today, but years ago most computers were analog in nature; and they were widely used in certain kinds of simulation—but that is another story.)

SIMULATION WITH PERSONAL COMPUTERS

The advent of the personal computer has dispelled one of the principal drawbacks of computer simulation; that is, that the programs can sometimes take a long time to develop significant results. This can be a problem when you have to share a computer with other people; or, even worse, if you have to pay for computer time by the minute. However, with a personal computer, you can start the program before you go to bed; the results will be there in the morning. Nobody will be upset with you, and it won't cost a cent.

This book will introduce you to simulation on personal computers by giving a step-by-step description of programs that illustrate important concepts in simulation. Most of the programs were written on a Texas Instruments Professional computer running under the Microsoft Disk Operating System (MS/DOS). They are written in Microsoft's version of the BASIC programming language (MS/BASIC). BASIC stands for Beginners' All-purpose Symbolic Instruction

Code; it was invented at Dartmouth College in the early 1960s. BASIC is today the most widely used programming language, especially in the personal computing field. The programs that do not use bit-level graphics will run on any personal computer that is compatible with the IBM-PC. This includes the TI, the Zenith/Heath personal computers, and many more. I shall assume that you have already done some programming in BASIC.

In this chapter, I want to accomplish these goals:

1. Show how to use random numbers to simulate a process.
2. Review BASIC programming.
3. Show how to interact with a user by menus.
4. Introduce two concepts of structured programming: typing of variables, and modular design.
5. Tell how to generate pseudorandom numbers.

I shall do this by belaboring a very simple program used for teaching on the grade-school level. Even if you're not a grade-school teacher or the parent of a grade-school child, it may hold some interest for you. Computers are becoming better regarded as teaching tools, especially to give rapid tuition in the use of complex programs such as Database Management Systems.

ARITHMETIC DRILL AND PRACTICE

The first program we shall examine is one I wrote to help my granddaughters with their elementary arithmetic. I regard this program as a simulation in which the computer takes the part of the teacher, who assigns problems, corrects the students' work, and encourages them in their efforts. Some people might call this kind of program Computer-Aided Learning (CAL) or Computer-Assisted Instruction (CAI); I wouldn't argue. It just goes to emphasize the extensive scope of simulation as a technique. It takes in CAL/CAI, some numerical computation methods, some video games, and much more.

Operation of the Program

Here's how the program operates. It introduces itself and asks the student to type his or her first name. Then the program addresses the student by name and announces that it has some math questions for the student to work out. The student is instructed to enter answers and afterward press either the <ENTER> or the <RETURN> key. The student is then told to press either <ENTER> or <RETURN> to advance the program.

The program asks whether the student wishes to add, subtract, multiply, or divide; and the student is told to type 1 for "add," 2 for "subtract," 3 for

```
                    HELLO THERE
       I'M YOUR TI PROFESSIONAL COMPUTER
          PLEASE TYPE YOUR FIRST NAME ? JACK




 ** JACK **

 HERE ARE SOME MATH QUESTIONS FOR YOU TO WORK OUT.

 ENTER YOUR ANSWERS THEN PRESS <ENTER> OR <RETURN>

 WHEN YOU ARE READY, PRESS <ENTER> OR <RETURN> TO CONTINUE?

 DO YOU WANT TO: ADD, SUBTRACT, MULTIPLY OR DIVIDE?
 TO ADD, TYPE 1; SUBTRACT, 2; MULTIPLY, 3; DIVIDE, 4? 1
```

FIGURE 1–1 Introduction, instructions, and menu for arithmetic drill-and-practice program.

"multiply," and 4 for "divide." If the student types any character except 1, 2, 3, or 4, the program will refuse it and ask the student to enter a correct number (1, 2, 3, or 4). This way of presenting alternative choices is called a "menu." Figure 1–1 shows the introduction, instruction, and menu.

The operation of addition entails adding a variable quantity called TERM1%, an integer (whole number) in the range 1 to 100; to TERM2%, an integer in the range from 1 to 1,000. Variable TERM2% is selected so that it is always greater than TERM1%. The character "%" is a type-declaration symbol. It signifies that the character type of these two variables is "integer." Figure 1–2 shows a correct and an incorrect addition.

Subtraction entails subtracting TERM1% from TERM2%.
Multiplication entails multiplying TERM1% by TERM2%.

Division entails dividing TERM2% by TERM1%. Here is where the requirement that TERM1% always exceed 1 pays off, since division by zero is a big "no-no" in computing (the product of 1/0 and any number is undefined in mathematics).

The student is told to round off the quotient of TERM2% divided by TERM1% to two decimal places. That is, if the third decimal place of the quotient is five or more, the student is supposed to increase the value in the second decimal place by one.

```
** ADDITION **

   6  +  60  = ?
? 66
RIGHT !!!!!

WANT MORE? TYPE <YES/Y> OR <NO/N>? Y

DO YOU WANT TO: ADD, SUBTRACT, MULTIPLY OR DIVIDE?
TO ADD, TYPE 1; SUBTRACT, 2; MULTIPLY, 3; DIVIDE, 4? 1
```

```
** ADDITION **

   55  +   238  = ?
? 292
WRONG !!
THE RIGHT ANSWER IS   293

WANT MORE? TYPE <YES/Y> OR <NO/N>? Y

DO YOU WANT TO: ADD, SUBTRACT, MULTIPLY OR DIVIDE?
TO ADD, TYPE 1; SUBTRACT, 2; MULTIPLY, 3; DIVIDE, 4? 2
```

FIGURE 1–2 Correct and incorrect examples of addition.

The problems are presented in the following form (the type-declaration symbols are not shown on the display):

TERM1 + TERM2 = ?
TERM2 − TERM1 = ?
TERM1 × TERM2 = ? or
TERM2 / TERM1 = ?

If student types in the correct answer, the program displays: "RIGHT !!!!!" If the answer is wrong, the program displays: "WRONG !!" and then proceeds to display the correct answer.

The student is now asked, "Want more?" and instructed to type <YES> or <Y> to get another question; or to type <NO> or <N> to finish the exercise. If the student types anything else, the program will refuse it and prompt for a correct answer.

At the end of the exercise, the program divides the number of correct answers by the total number of questions presented. The resulting decimal is rounded up to two places and reported as an integer percentage (that is, multiplied by 100).

Structure of the Program

The program is divided into a Main Program and eight subroutines. Figure 1–3 is a complete listing of all 86 statements in the program.

FIGURE 1–3 Complete listing of arithmetic drill-and-practice program.

```
LIST -200
10 ' THIS PROGRAM PROVIDES DRILL AND PRACTICE IN ELEMENTARY ARITHMETIC
20 '
30 CLS: LOCATE 10,36: PRINT "HELLO THERE"
40 PRINT "                         I'M YOUR TI PROFESSIONAL COMPUTER"
50 INPUT "                         PLEASE TYPE YOUR FIRST NAME "; FIRSTNAME$
60 '
70 CLS: PRINT" ** "FIRSTNAME$" **"
80 PRINT:PRINT"HERE ARE SOME MATH QUESTIONS FOR YOU TO WORK OUT."
90 PRINT:PRINT"ENTER YOUR ANSWERS THEN PRESS <ENTER> OR <RETURN>"
100 PRINT:PRINT"WHEN YOU ARE READY, PRESS <ENTER> OR <RETURN> TO CONTINUE";
110 INPUT X
120 '
130 GOSUB 230  ' CALCULATE ALL THE RIGHT ANSWERS
140 PRINT:PRINT:PRINT "DO YOU WANT TO: ADD, SUBTRACT, MULTIPLY OR DIVIDE?"
150 FLAG$=""  ' RESET COMMAND FLAG
160 INPUT "TO ADD, TYPE 1; SUBTRACT, 2; MULTIPLY, 3; DIVIDE, 4"; FLAG$
165 IF FLAG$="1" OR FLAG$="2" OR FLAG$="3" OR FLAG$="4" THEN 170 ELSE 150
170 CODE%=VAL(FLAG$) ' CONVERT COMMAND FLAG TO A COMMAND CODE
180 ON CODE% GOSUB 390,470,550,630  ' SELECT STUDENT PROBLEM
190 '
200 FLAG$="" ' RESET COMMAND FLAG
Ok



LIST 210-400
210 PRINT:INPUT "WANT MORE? TYPE <YES/Y> OR <NO/N>"; FLAG$
215 IF FLAG$="NO" OR FLAG$="N" OR FLAG$="YES" OR FLAG$="Y" THEN 220 ELSE 200
220 IF FLAG$="NO" OR FLAG$="N" THEN 820 ELSE 130
230 '
240 ' RANDOMIZATION AND CALCULATION SUBROUTINE
250 RANDOMIZE TIME ' SEED THE RANDOM NUMBER GENERATOR
260 ' FROM THE REAL TIME CLOCK
270 ' THIS ROUTINE CALCULATES THE RIGHT ANSWERS
280 NUMBER%=NUMBER%+1     ' THIS STEP COUNTS TOTAL TRIES
290 TERM1%=INT(RND*100)+1 ' TERM1 IS A RANDOM INTEGER FROM 1 TO 100
300 TERM2%=INT(RND*1000)+1 ' TERM2 IS A RANDOM INTERGER FROM 1 TO 1000
310 ' TERM 1 MUST BE LESS THAN TERM2
320 IF TERM1%>=TERM2% OR TERM1%=0 THEN 290 ' GET ANOTHER PAIR OF RANDOM NUMBERS
330 ADD%=TERM1%+TERM2%  ' ADDITION
340 SUBT%=TERM2%-TERM1%  ' SUBTRACTION
350 MULT#=TERM1%*TERM2%  ' MULTIPLICATION
360 DIVD!=INT(((TERM2%/TERM1%)+.005)*100)/100 ' DIVISION
370 ' THE QUOTIENT IS ROUNDED UP TO TWO DECIMAL PLACES
380 RETURN
390 '
400 ' STUDENT ADDITION SUBROUTINE
Ok


Ok
LIST 410-600
410 CORRECT=ADD% ' SAVE THE RIGHT ANSWER
```

```
420 CLS:PRINT:PRINT:PRINT"** ADDITION **"
430 PRINT:PRINT:PRINT" "TERM1%" + "TERM2%" = ? "
440 INPUT ANS%
450 IF ANS%=ADD% THEN GOSUB 720 ELSE GOSUB 770
460 RETURN
470 '
480 ' STUDENT SUBTRACTION SUBROUTINE
490 CORRECT=SUBT% ' SAVE RIGHT ANSWER
500 CLS:PRINT:PRINT:PRINT"** SUBTRACTION **"
510 PRINT:PRINT:PRINT" "TERM2%" - "TERM1%" = ? "
520 INPUT ANS%
530 IF ANS%=SUBT% THEN GOSUB 720 ELSE GOSUB 770
540 RETURN
550 '
560 ' STUDENT MULTIPLICATION SUBROUTINE
570 CORRECT=MULT# ' SAVE THE RIGHT ANSWER
580 CLS:PRINT:PRINT:PRINT"** MULTIPLICATION **"
590 PRINT:PRINT:PRINT" "TERM1%" X "TERM2%" = ? "
600 INPUT ANS#
Ok


Ok
LIST 610-800
610 IF ANS#=MULT# THEN GOSUB 720 ELSE GOSUB 770
620 RETURN
630 '
640 ' STUDENT DIVISION SUBROUTINE
650 CORRECT=DIVD! ' SAVE RIGHT ANSWER
660 CLS:PRINT:PRINT:PRINT"** DIVISION **"
670 PRINT "<<ROUND OFF YOUR ANSWERS TO 2 DECIMAL PLACES>>"
680 PRINT:PRINT:PRINT" "TERM2%" / "TERM1%" = ? "
690 INPUT ANS!
700 IF ANS!=DIVD! THEN GOSUB 720 ELSE GOSUB 770
710 RETURN
720 '
730 ' CORRECT ANSWER SUBROUTINE
740 RIGHT%=RIGHT%+1 ' INCREMENT COUNT OF RIGHT ANSWERS
750 PRINT "RIGHT !!!!! "
760 RETURN
770 '
780 ' WRONG ANSWER SUBROUTINE
790 PRINT "WRONG !!"
800 PRINT "THE RIGHT ANSWER IS "CORRECT
Ok


Ok
LIST 810-
810 RETURN
820 '
830 ' EXIT SUBROUTINE
840 SCORE%=INT((RIGHT%/NUMBER%)*100+.5)
850 PRINT:PRINT "YOUR SCORE IS "SCORE%
860 END
Ok
```

FIGURE 1-3 (continued)

The Main Program handles most of the dialogue between the student and the computer, and it calls up the subroutines. The principal parts of the Main Program are:

Program introduces itself and asks the student's first name (statements 30–50).
Addresses the student by name and gives basic instructions (statements 70–110).

Calls a subroutine to calculate the right answer, gets the student's choice of arithmetic operation, and calls the appropriate subroutine to implement it (statements 130–180).

Gets the student's choice of whether to continue or quit (statements 200–220). In the former case, it recycles to statement 130; in the latter case, it calls the Exit Subroutine.

The subroutines are: (1) Randomization and Calculation, (2) Student Addition, (3) Student Subtraction, (4) Student Multiplication, (5) Student Division, (6) Correct Answer, (7) Wrong Answer, and (8) Exit.

1. The Randomization and Calculation Subroutine (statements 240–380) contains these parts:

   >> It "seeds" the random-number generator (statements 250–260)—more about this later.

   >> Counts the total number of questions that have been asked (statement 280).

   >> Chooses appropriate values for TERM1% and TERM2% (statements 290–320)—more about this later.

   >> Calculates the right answer for addition (statement 330).

   >> Calculates the right answer for subtraction (statement 340).

   >> Calculates the right answer for multiplication (statement 350).

   >> Calculates the right answer for division (statement 360)—more about this later.

2. Student Addition Subroutine (statements 400–460) stores the correct answer for addition, displays the question, accepts the student's answer, and branches to the Correct Answer or Wrong Answer Subroutine, depending upon whether the student's answer was right or wrong.

3. Subtraction Subroutine (statements 480–540) is directly analogous to the Student Addition Subroutine.

4. Student Multiplication Subroutine (statements 560–620) is directly analogous to the Student Addition Subroutine.

5. Student Division Subroutine (statements 640–710) is analogous to the Student Addition Subroutine except that it instructs the student to round the answer up to two decimal places.

6. Correct Answer Subroutine (statements 730–760) increments the count of right answers and displays the "Right !!!!!" message.

7. Wrong Answer Subroutine (statements 780–810) displays the "Wrong !!" message and the correct answer.

8. Exit Subroutine (statements 830–860) calculates the student's score, displays it, and terminates the program.

Meaning of the Program Variables

The following variables are used in this program:

**FIRSTNAME$** a string (alphanumeric) variable used to hold the first name of the user. The symbol "$" is another type-declaration symbol; it denotes a string variable.

X a dummy variable "INPUT" when either the <ENTER> or <RETURN> key is pressed to advance the program.

FLAG$ a string variable used to hold menu choices. It is reset to <NULL>, signified by "" before a choice is made. When selecting arithmetic operations, the contents can be 1, 2, 3, or 4. When selecting "CONTINUE" or "QUIT," the contents can be YES or Y, or NO or N. It is generally preferable to use a string variable to give commands to a program rather than a numeric variable. One reason is that a string variable can be reset to null, and then any printable character or sequence of characters can be used as a command; a number must be reset to zero, and this precludes us from using zero as a command symbol.

CODE% the numerical equivalent of the string values 1, 2, 3, or 4 created by using the function VAL(FLAG$). CODE% transfers control to the selected subroutine by means of the command "ON CODE% GOSUB 390, 470, 550, 630".

NUMBER% an integer representing the total number of math questions presented.

TERM1% an integer greater than 0 and less than 101; it assumes the role of the addend in addition, the minuend in subtraction, the multiplier in multiplication, and the divisor in division.

TERM2% an integer greater than 0 and less than 1001, and always greater than TERM1%; it assumes the role of the augend in addition, the subtrahend in subtraction, the multiplicand in multiplication, and the dividend in division.

ADD% the actual sum in addition.

SUBT% the actual difference in subtraction.

MULT# the actual product in multiplication. The type-declaration symbol "#" signifies that this variable is a double-precision real variable. This kind of type declaration is used here to preserve integer format despite the fact that it is possible that a product may exceed 32767, the upper size limit for an integer in this version of BASIC.

DIVD! the actual quotient in division, it is always rounded up to two decimal places. Here the type-declaration symbol "!" signifies that it is a single-precision real variable. This allows for the fact that decimals will be obtained in quotients.

CORRECT a data location used to store the actual answer corresponding to the arithmetic operation chosen by the student. It is declared by default to be a single-precision real variable because it may have to hold integers (ADD% and SUB%), double-precision real variables (MULT#), and single-precision real variables (DIVD!). However, no tests for equality can be made with CORRECT; it is used for display purposes only.

ANS% the answer entered by the student when doing addition, subtraction, or multiplication.

ANS! the answer entered by the student when doing division, it is rounded up to two decimal places; hence its type-declaration symbol shows it to be a single-precision real variable.

RIGHT% an integer representing the number of correct answers.

SCORE the student's grade on the exercise. It is the quotient of RIGHT% divided by NUMBER%, rounded up by first multiplying by 100 then adding 0.5, and made into an integer by using the function INT(Argument)—where "Argument" is a general term for any number you want to make into an integer.

Program Implementation

There are two important steps in this program. The first is central to the subject of simulation; the second is crucial to making an arithmetic drill-and-practice program work.

Central to the subject of simulation is the process of generating random numbers. Indeed, the fact that this program can tirelessly generate different arithmetic problems without repeating itself (unless you run the program for a very long time indeed) is what makes it a simulation of a live teacher rather than a substitute for an exercise book in which the problems are all set down in advance.

In subsequent chapters, you will learn many things about random numbers; for now, it is sufficient to say that they are supposed to possess two attributes: (1) the chance of producing any number in the range of interest is identical to that of producing any other number, and (2) the appearance or nonappearance of any number in no way affects the chance of the appearance or nonappearance of any other number.

We are going to get our random numbers by using a function called RND that is built into the BASIC programming subsystem. It produces random numbers in the form of single-precision real variables in the range 0 to 1. Practically speaking, they are decimals having 7 or fewer digits (usually 6). To see how it works, RUN this program (see Figure 1–4):

```
10 CLS
20 FOR I = 1 TO 100
30 PRINT RND;
40 NEXT I
```

Notice that we produced a few odd-looking numbers, such as 5.532474E-02. This is an example of exponential, or so-called "scientific," notation. It is

```
THIS PROGRAM PRINTS 100 RANDOM NUMBERS
BETWEEN ZERO AND ONE


 .1213501   .651861   .8688611   .7297625   .798853   7.369805E-02   .4903128
 .4545189   .1072496   .9505102   .7038703   .5318641   .9711614   .3209329   .9561278
 .9345151   .5349368   .5644215   .6712188   .7025723   .7407752   .6668768   .4539406
 .3341433   .156853   .7362702   .5428795   .425969   5.544812E-02   .7682681
 .5135362   .564048   .7410649   .6618574   .23145   .4642614   .1285592   .4849701
 5.532474E-02   .3629986   .5712636   .9901088   .290153   .6577815   .9391122
 .379971   .8903414   .7978898   .9467658   .3230751   .412836   .4249863   .7317363
 .2193842   .2202465   .7637411   .6825126   .7159321   .9339718   .2624577   .5166851
 .4724479   .137325   .4836971   .6090706   .1769807   .3286581   .244903   .5698376
 .8115254   .1244871   9.027124E-03   7.263118E-02   .1676467   .7126173   .525154
 .9326978   .6121049   .555268   .7191259   .4350108   .1024807   .3421974   .8341678
 .9123946   .4527998   .1938278   .8215128   .5736507   .8491585   .1143708   .9810265
 .5816818   .6153483   .6949517   .8518325   .3816174   .2284811   6.673521E-02
 .3529371
Ok




Ok
LIST
10 CLS
20 PRINT "THIS PROGRAM PRINTS 100 RANDOM NUMBERS "
30 PRINT "BETWEEN ZERO AND ONE "
40 PRINT: PRINT
50 FOR I = 1 TO 100
60 PRINT RND;
70 NEXT I
Ok
```

FIGURE 1–4 Generation of pseudo-random numbers in the range zero to one.

the way BASIC displays very small or very large numbers. The E-02 (characteristic) represents the base number 10 raised to the -2 power, or .01, and is to be multiplied by the rest of the number (mantissa). Very simply, you move the decimal point N places to the left for a negative exponent $(E-N)$ and N places to the right for a positive exponent $(E+N)$. In this case, the value is .05532474.

We do not want numbers in the range 0 to 1; we want numbers in the range 1 to 100. However, so we can see changes take place within the sequence of 100 numbers we are displaying, let's employ one of the principles of simulation and multiply by 10 instead of 100. RUN this program (see Figure 1–5):

```
10 CLS
20 FOR I = 1 TO 100
30 PRINT RND*10;
40 NEXT I
```

```
THIS PROGRAM PRINTS 100 RANDOM NUMBERS
BETWEEN ZERO AND TEN

 1.213501   6.51861   8.688611   7.297625   7.98853   .7369805   4.903128   4.545189
 1.072496   9.505102   7.038703   5.318641   9.711614   3.209329   9.561278   9.345151
 5.349367   5.644214   6.712188   7.025723   7.407752   6.668768   4.539406   3.341433
 1.56853   7.362702   5.428796   4.259691   .5544811   7.682681   5.135362   5.640479
 7.410649   6.618574   2.3145   4.642615   1.285592   4.849701   .5532473   3.629986
 5.712636   9.901087   2.90153   6.577815   9.391123   3.79971   8.903415   7.978898
 9.467657   3.230751   4.12836   4.249863   7.317363   2.193842   2.202465   7.637411
 6.825126   7.159322   9.339718   2.624577   5.166851   4.724479   1.37325   4.836971
 6.090706   1.769807   3.286581   2.44903   5.698376   8.115254   1.244871
 9.027124E-02   .7263118   1.676467   7.126174   5.25154   9.326979   6.121049
 5.55268   7.191259   4.350107   1.024807   3.421974   8.341679   9.123946   4.527998
 1.938278   8.215128   5.736507   8.491585   1.143708   9.810266   5.816818   6.153484
 6.949518   8.518325   3.816174   2.284811   .6673521   3.529371
Ok




Ok
LIST
10 CLS
20 PRINT "THIS PROGRAM PRINTS 100 RANDOM NUMBERS "
30 PRINT "BETWEEN ZERO AND TEN "
40 PRINT: PRINT
50 FOR I = 1 TO 100
60 PRINT RND * 10;
70 NEXT I
Ok
```

FIGURE 1–5 Generation of pseudo-random numbers in the range zero to ten.

We are still generating decimal numbers, and we want whole numbers, or integers. We can correct this defect by using the INT or "integerize" function of the BASIC language. RUN this program (see Figure 1–6):

```
10 CLS
20 FOR I = 1 TO 100
30 PRINT INT(RND*10);
40 NEXT I
```

Notice now that the numbers lie in the range 0 to 9 and not in the range 1 to 10. This is because the INT function just chops off the decimal part of a number. If we used this subroutine in our arithmetic drill-and-practice program, we would get an error message every time we tried to divide by 0. To fix things, RUN this program (Figure 1–7):

```
10 CLS
20 FOR I = 1 TO 100
30 PRINT INT(RND*10)+1;
40 NEXT I
```

```
THIS PROGRAM PRINTS 100 RANDOM INTEGERS
BETWEEN ZERO AND NINE

1  6  8  7  7  0  4  4  1  9  7  5  9  3  9  9  5  5  6  7  7  6  4  3  1  7
5  4  0  7  5  5  7  6  2  4  1  4  0  3  5  9  2  6  9  3  8  7  9  3  4  4
7  2  2  7  6  7  9  2  5  4  1  4  6  1  3  2  5  8  1  0  0  1  7  5  9  6
5  7  4  1  3  8  9  4  1  8  5  8  1  9  5  6  6  8  3  2  0  3
Ok
```

```
Ok
LIST
10 CLS
20 PRINT "THIS PROGRAM PRINTS 100 RANDOM INTEGERS "
30 PRINT "BETWEEN ZERO AND NINE "
40 PRINT: PRINT
50 FOR I = 1 TO 100
60 PRINT INT(RND * 10);
70 NEXT I
Ok
```

FIGURE 1–6 Generation of pseudorandom integers in the range zero to nine.

To obtain TERM1%, we multiply RND by 100, apply the INT function to convert the result to integer form, and add 1. To obtain TERM2%, we multiply RND by 1,000, apply the INT subroutine to convert the result to integer form, and add 1. Then we test to be sure that TERM2% is larger than TERM1%. If it isn't, we loop back and pick two other random numbers and try again until it is.

RUN the last program twice and compare the two sequences of integers. They are both the same! If we were to incorporate this subroutine in our drill-and-practice program, we would produce the same sequence of TERM1%:TERM2% pairs every time we ran it, diminishing its value as a tool for instruction. This is because every random-number generator has to contain a starting number called the "seed." The seed is built into the random function of the programming language. Unless you change the seed when you generate a sequence of random numbers, you will get the same sequence every time.

These random number sequences are finite in length but they are very long; so one way to reseed a random-number generator is to preexercise it. You could set up a loop:

FOR I = 1 to NUMBER: R = RND: NEXT I

```
THIS PROGRAM PRINTS 100 RANDOM INTEGERS
BETWEEN ONE AND TEN
TYPE RUN NUMBER ? 1

 2  7  9  8  8  1  5  5  2 10  8  6 10  4 10  10  6  6  7  8  8  7  5  4  2
 8  6  5  1  8  6  6  8  7  3  5  2  5  1  4  6 10  3  7 10  4  9  8 10  4
 5  5  8  3  3  8  7  8 10  3  6  5  2  5  7  2  4  3  6  9  2  1  1  2  8  6
10  7  6  8  5  2  4  9 10  5  2  9  6  9  2 10  6  7  7  9  4  3  1  4
Ok


THIS PROGRAM PRINTS 100 RANDOM INTEGERS
BETWEEN ONE AND TEN
TYPE RUN NUMBER ? 2

 2  7  9  8  8  1  5  5  2 10  8  6 10  4 10  10  6  6  7  8  8  7  5  4  2
 8  6  5  1  8  6  6  8  7  3  5  2  5  1  4  6 10  3  7 10  4  9  8 10  4
 5  5  8  3  3  8  7  8 10  3  6  5  2  5  7  2  4  3  6  9  2  1  1  2  8  6
10  7  6  8  5  2  4  9 10  5  2  9  6  9  2 10  6  7  7  9  4  3  1  4
Ok




Ok
LIST
10 CLS
20 PRINT "THIS PROGRAM PRINTS 100 RANDOM INTEGERS "
30 PRINT "BETWEEN ONE AND TEN "
40 INPUT "TYPE RUN NUMBER ";X
50 PRINT: PRINT
60 FOR I = 1 TO 100
70 PRINT INT(RND * 10) + 1;
80 NEXT I
Ok
```

FIGURE 1-7 Generation of pseudo-random integers in the range one to ten without re-seeding the generator.

And use an INPUT NUMBER statement to decide how far into the sequence to go for each execution of the program.

An easier way to seed the random-number generator is to use the built-in function RANDOMIZE. It automatically requests you to provide as a seed, an integer in the range -32768 to 32767. For best—that is, "most nearly random"—results, these seed values should themselves be random numbers.

Now, even though you can generate true random numbers by consulting a book, published in 1955 by the RAND (Research and Development) Corporation called *One Million Random Numbers and 100,000 Normal Deviates*, or by rolling six special ten-sided Japanese dice that have a different digit inscribed on each face, it is a nuisance to have to do so and then keep feeding those random seed numbers to the program.

If you become really involved in simulation, you may want to purchase a hardware generator of true random numbers. It is a circuit board that can fit into one of the unused slots of your personal computer. The circuit consists of a pulse oscillator feeding into a counter. The oscillator is started and stopped in a completely random manner by pulses from a small and harmless radioactive source. The random numbers are the numbers of oscillator pulses counted between start-stop pulses from the source. The card cost about $600 in 1985. Remember, however, that if you want to repeat an experiment, you have to make a file of the random numbers you use, because no two sequences are ever alike.

A way to get different pseudorandom number sequences is to make a call to the computer's internal clock. You can do this by writing the code RAN-DOMIZE TIME, where TIME simply calls the current value of the computer's real-time clock (as contrasted with any simulated-time clocks). RUN this program twice (Figure 1–8):

```
10 CLS
20 RANDOMIZE TIME
30 FOR I = 1 TO 100
40 PRINT INT(RND*10) +1;
50 NEXT I
```

FIGURE 1–8 Generation of pseudorandom integers in the range one to ten with reseeding of the generator.

```
THIS PROGRAM PRINTS 100 RANDOM INTEGERS
BETWEEN ONE AND TEN
AND RE-SEEDS THE RANDOM NUMBER GENERATOR
TYPE RUN NUMBER ? 1

 6  6  2  9  8  8 10  8  7  6  2  1  7  8  5  8  2  3  5  8  6  2  6  7  9  1
 9  7  5  1  8  9  5  4  6  3 10  9  3  2  1  3  9  3 10  9  6  3  7  9  8  2
 8  9  3  5  1 10  2  8  4  3  9  3  6  7  8  6  9  3 10  3  3  6  1  3  2  6
 6  6 10  4  5  6  5  5  3  4  1  5  1  2  4  3  2  2 10  4 10  8
Ok


THIS PROGRAM PRINTS 100 RANDOM INTEGERS
BETWEEN ONE AND TEN
AND RE-SEEDS THE RANDOM NUMBER GENERATOR
TYPE RUN NUMBER ? 2

 4  6  3  6  9  9  9 10  9  8  3  5  4  1  5  1  6  7  2 10  5  8  2  9 10  6
10  8  6  4  5  4  9  5  8  7 10  1  4  2  6  1  9  6  8  2  6  5  5  1  2  8
 1  5  4  1  2  4 10 10  9  6  8  3  7  1  6  1  6  1  4  1  3  6  4  3  1  3
 4  9  4  4  4  4  8  9  8  9  8  3  7  1  8  2 10  7  5  2  2  8  4
Ok



Ok
LIST
10 CLS
20 PRINT "THIS PROGRAM PRINTS 100 RANDOM INTEGERS "
30 PRINT "BETWEEN ONE AND TEN "
40 PRINT "AND RE-SEEDS THE RANDOM NUMBER GENERATOR"
50 INPUT "TYPE RUN NUMBER ";X
60 PRINT: PRINT
70 RANDOMIZE TIME
80 FOR I = 1 TO 100
90 PRINT INT(RND * 10) + 1;
100 NEXT I
Ok
```

This is the way things were under MS/DOS 1.0. Under MS/DOS 2.12 or higher, TIME is not available. Instead we have to work with a system variable called TIME$ that displays real time in the form HH:MM:SS. We can obtain TIME in its old form by inserting this line of code:

```
TIME=VAL(RIGHT$(TIME$,2))+VAL(MID$(TIME$,4,2))
   +VAL(LEFT$(TIME$,2))
```

Now, about the operation of division: Although it is easy to compare to integers for equality, it is theoretically impossible to compare two real numbers for equality (that is, numbers with nonzero values to the right of the decimal point). If you wish to make such a comparison, you must specify exactly how many decimal places you are going to allow.

For this reason, we specify two decimal places of accuracy. We instruct the student to enter answers that way, and we internally multiply our quotients by 100, integerize them, then divide them by 100.

Furthermore, to ensure consistency between the student's answers and the program's answers, we must explicate the rounding convention: We shall increase the value of the number in the second decimal place by 1 if the value of the number in the third decimal place is 5 or more. We implement this rule by instructing the student to input answers in this form; we implement the rule on the part of the computer by adding .005 to the quotient before doing any part of the integerization procedure. The addition of .005 will always increase the value of the second decimal place if the value of the third decimal place is 5 or more. The integerization procedure then merely throws away all decimal places to the right of the second place irrespective of their value.

EVALUATING INTEGRALS

One of the first practical uses of computer simulation was evaluating elliptical integrals in several dimensions. This work played a central role in the development of nuclear weapons in the mid-1950s. The task involved finding the area bounded by several surfaces having highly complex shapes. This task defied solution by analytical means.

We shall illustrate the principle employed by using simulation to find an approximate value for PI. Let's imagine a quarter circle inscribed within a unit square. The area of the square is 1×1, or 1. The area of the inscribed unit quarter circle is given by:

$$A = PI \times R^2 / 4 = PI / 4$$

We are going to approximate the area of the circle by throwing dots randomly onto the square and counting how many fall within the quarter circle. The approximate area of the quarter circle is then:

A = COUNT / POINTS

where POINTS is the total number of dots thrown at the square and COUNT is the number of dots falling within the quarter circle. This program does it for us:

```
10 ' TITLE: EVALUATING PI BY SIMULATION
20 CLS: RANDOMIZE TIME
30 INPUT "ENTER TOTAL NUMBER OF POINTS"; POINTS
40 FOR I = 1 TO POINTS
50 X = RND: Y = RND
60 IF SQR (X^2 + Y^2) <= 1 THEN COUNT = COUNT + 1
70 NEXT I
80 AREA = COUNT / POINTS
90 PRINT "APPROXIMATE VALUE OF PI IS " 4 * AREA
100 END
```

Statement 50 selects the horizontal (X) and vertical (Y) coordinates of a point in the square bounded by the lines

Y = 0, Y = 1, and X = 0, X = 1

Statement 60 determines whether or not the point lies within the quarter circle; that is, whether the line from the origin (0,0) is less than or equal to the radius (1). Statement 90 evaluates PI in terms of the area of the quarter circle as determined by simulation.

The results of several simulation runs are:

Number of Points	Value of PI
10	3.20
100	2.92
1,000	3.07
10,000	3.16
100,000	3.14

This is a poor way to evaluate PI. It takes a very long (in fact, an exponentially long) time to converge on a value with useful precision. There are better ways to evaluate PI, of course (one algorithm is based on a famous problem called Buffon's Needle). The point of this exercise is to demonstrate how simulation can be used to find areas or volumes. It is not as economical as analytic methods, or even other numerical methods (such as the Trapezoid Rule); but it can be used when these other methods, for one reason or another, cannot be used. Incidentally, the code name of the project in which this technique was used was "Monte Carlo"; since then, all applications of simulations have sometimes been called Monte Carlo methods. (Actually, the Monte Carlo project focused upon reducing the variance of the estimates of the values of definite elliptical integrals.)

SUMMARY

In this chapter we have defined simulation in general, and computer simulation in particular, and suggested several reasons why simulation is so widely used. We have shown some of the advantages of using personal computers for simulation.

We have used a Computer Aided Learning sequence to illustrate some of the tools of simulation. These include:

1. Generation of random-number sequences, including the procedure of seeding the random-number generator.
2. Conducting a dialogue with a computer program. This may include: use of menus to present alternative choices, use of alphanumeric command strings, and use of "guard" statements to prevent the user from entering undefined command sequences.
3. Structuring a computer program so that the main program contains user–computer dialogue and control sequences, while the actual work of the program is done by subroutines called from the main program.
4. The definition and type declaration of all program variables for easy reference by the programmer; this and the preceding attribute of structuring the program make programs easy to modify, and most simulation programs require a great deal of modification before they accurately represent the real system under study.
5. We have shown some of the problems involved in comparing numeric values within a computer and some ways to attack these problems; this is a key feature in simulation programs.

Our final example showed how simulation can be used to perform the calculus operation of integration; that is, finding the area under a curve. This was one of the first accomplishments of computer simulation.

In the next chapter, we shall illustrate the use of random processes in a computer game, another popular kind of simulation. Then, after a closer look at the process of generating both random and pseudo- (false) random sequences, we shall introduce the most widely used forms of experimental simulation.

CHAPTER TWO

Playing Games with Simulation

A common pejorative observation by theoreticians is that simulationists are just playing games. I gladly acknowledge that simulationists play games; in fact, one of the pleasures of simulation is that the whole field is a game. In this chapter, we are going to play some typical games. Games have an important place in the world of simulation. Many computer systems come with a "game package" as part of the software to entice users into becoming familiar with system commands and operating procedures. Programmers of games are the highest-paid members of our profession (with six-figure incomes in some cases). Unlike other programmers, who may get sued for using their own work out of context, these programmers get substantial royalties. Sober-sided students and instructors are, of course, free to skip this chapter.

CLIMB THE LADDER

You may have watched the popular television game show "The Price is Right." In one of its subgames, the contestant's answers are depicted by an Alpine yodeler climbing an incline at a rate determined by the magnitude of the sum of the prices he or she has guessed. At some point, the sum may exceed a maximum unknown to the contestant; the yodeler then appears to fall over a precipice at the top of the incline, signifying that the contestant has exceeded the maximum and therefore lost the game.

In "Ladder," the incline is constructed using the byte graphics capability of MS/BASIC. Let's regard the screen as a 25-by-80 matrix with the upper-left-hand corner having the coordinates 1, 1 and the lower-right-hand corner having the coordinates 25, 80. Our incline starts at 23, 46, and the precipice is at 1, 69. A complete listing of the 35 statements of the program is shown in Figure 2–1.

The player is asked to press the <RETURN> key to climb. Each time the player presses the key, the incline grows by a random number in the range 1 to 23. If the first random number is 23, the player has 23 added to the overall score and the first round of play terminates with the player's being proclaimed the winner. See Figure 2–2 for a winning round.

If the player goes over the cliff, the entire count, which, of course, exceeds 23, is subtracted from the player's score (see Figure 2–3).

If the player chooses to quit climbing before going over the cliff, the player wins and the score is equal to the rung of the ladder occupied when <QUIT> was pressed. This is what happened in Figure 2–2.

There is a "guts and glory" component of this game. Suppose the player climbs five rungs on the first try. If he or she quits, the score is +5. If the player presses <RETURN> for another ascent and climbs, say, six rungs more, the total score is (5 + 6) × 2, or 22; that is, the number of rungs climbed in that round *times the number of ascents in the round*.

In the program, statement 10 seeds the random-number generator from the real-time clock. Statements 20–30 start a round of play; they reset C$, the command flag, to null; set SUM, the rung counter, to zero; set S, the ascent counter, to zero; and set N to 23, forming a 23-rung ladder. The command

FIGURE 2–1 Program listing for "Climb the Ladder."

```
10 CLS
15 '
20 RANDOMIZE
30 C$="":CLS
35 PRINT: PRINT
40 PRINT"********** WELCOME TO 'CLIMB THE LADDER' **********"
45 PRINT: PRINT: PRINT
50 PRINT"WHEN '?' APPEARS, TYPE 'RETURN' TO CLIMB; 'Q' TO QUIT."
60 PRINT:PRINT
70 N=25:SUM=0:S=0
80 INPUT C$
90 IF C$="Q" THEN 220
100 R=INT(RND*24)+1
110 SUM=SUM+R:S=S+1
120 IF SUM>24 THEN 210
130 IF SUM=24 THEN 220
140 Y=N-R
150 FOR I=N TO Y STEP -1
160 LOCATE I,46-I
170 PRINT CHR$(220)
180 NEXT I
190 N=Y
200 GOTO 80
205 S=0: SK=SK-SUM: PRINT: PRINT
210 PRINT"OOPS!!!! YOU FELL OFF!!!! YOUR SCORE IS "SK
215 GOTO 230
220 C$="":SK=SK+SUM*S:PRINT:PRINT
225 PRINT"YOU WIN!!!! YOUR SCORE IS "SK:S=0:GOTO 230
230 PRINT:PRINT:PRINT:INPUT;"WANT MORE? TYPE 'Y'";C$
240 IF C$="Y" THEN 30 ELSE END
```

```
*************** WELCOME TO 'CLIMB THE LADDER' *************

WHEN 'QUESTION-MARK' APPEARS, TYPE 'RETURN' TO CLIMB;'Q' TO QUIT
```

```
                                                   *
                                                  *
                                                 *
                                                *
                                               *
                                              *
YOU WIN!!!! YOUR SCORE IS  76                *
                                            *
WANT MORE? TYPE 'Y'? Y                      *
                                           *
                                          *
                                         *
                                        *
                                       *
                                      *
                                     *
                                    *
                                   *
```

FIGURE 2-2 Instructions; and the display of a good climb.

KEY OFF gets rid of the function key menu that may be displayed on line 25 of your screen.

Statements 40–150 are a dialogue with the computer. The player is welcomed to the game and told to press <RETURN> to ascend the ladder and <Q> to quit the round. When <Q> is pressed, control is transferred to the "WIN" subroutine along with the cumulative score left over from the last round of play. Statement 80 is a timing loop that gives the player an opportunity to read the legend before statements 90 and 110 blank it out. The blanking out is done so the game display will not be interrupted.

Statement 160 generates a random number in the range 1 to 23; statement 170 computes the number of rungs climbed and the number of ascents

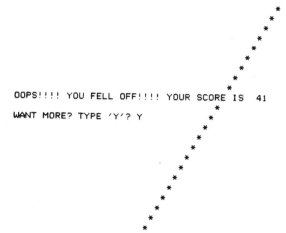

FIGURE 2–3 Climb in which the
player falls over
the precipice.

```
OOPS!!!! YOU FELL OFF!!!! YOUR SCORE IS   41

WANT MORE? TYPE 'Y'? Y
```

in the current round. Statements 180 and 190 set "WIN" or "LOSS" flags depending upon whether the first random number drawn is exactly 23 (WIN) or if the cumulative number of rungs climbed has exceeded 23 (LOSS).

In statement 200, quantity Y is the complement of R and reflects the fact that the top of the ladder is actually at line 1 on the screen. Statements 210–250 print the ladder, and statement 260 sets ladder height N to the height attained in the current ascent. In statements 270 and 280, flags transfer control to either the "WIN" or the "LOSS" subroutine.

In the "LOSS" subroutine (statements 300–310), the rungs "climbed" in the current round (always more than 23) are subtracted from the player's score in the game. In the "WIN" subroutine (statements 320–330), the rungs climbed in the current round are multiplied by the number of ascents in the current round and added to the player's cumulative score in the game. Both subroutines display the player's score.

Statement 340 asks whether the player wants to continue the game and loops back to statement 20 if the answer is "Y"; otherwise the game ends.

In the program shown here, the rungs of the ladder are depicted by asterisks; if your personal computer has sufficient graphics capability, you may want to depict them using CHR$(220). "ASCII" character #220 is a huge square; but it doesn't print out on my printer.

BUZZ-WORD GENERATOR

The next program is called "U–2–A–GURU." It slyly pokes fun at the sheeplike mentality of some computer scientists who go ape over the latest fad from Switzerland, the Netherlands, or wherever. Who knows—it could make you rich and famous, or at least win you some favorable recognition at the next departmental wine-and-cheese party. Figure 2–4 is a listing of the 30 statements of this program.

Statements 10 to 110 tell you that with this program, a sweat shirt three sizes too big, and a scraggly beard or granny glasses or both, depending on gender and/or preference, you too can become a guru.

Statements 120 to 220 load three ten-component vectors with string constants. The first two contain adjectives; the last contains nouns.

Statements 230 and 300 set up a WHILE-WEND loop; if we're going to be gurus, we might as well start off by banishing the despicable GOTO statement. This loop terminates when it recognizes string-constant <Q> in location Flag$. It gets there if, in statement 290, the user presses <Q> to end this madness.

Statement 240 is a FOR-NEXT loop that selects an index into each of the three vectors using the RND function. Statement 250 creates a string variable

FIGURE 2–4 Program listing for the buzzword generator "U–2–A–GURU."

```
Ok
LIST -200
10  ' U-2-A-GURU
20  '
30  ' COMPUTER SCIENCE BUZZWORD GENERATOR
40  ' ALL YOU NEED IS:
50  '  (1) A SCRAGGLY BEARD (OR GRANNY GLASSES)
60  '  (2) A SWEATSHIRT THREE SIZES TOO LARGE
70  '  (3) THIS PROGRAM
80  ' AND YOU CAN ILLUMINATE,
90  ' PONTIFICATE, AND
100 'INTELLECTUALLY MASTURBATE.
110 '
120 CLS: RANDOMIZE TIME
130 DATA ABSTRACT,ASYNCHRONOUS,DISTRIBUTED,FAULT-TOLERANT,INTEGRATED
140 DATA INTERACTIVE,NORMALIZED,OPTIMIZED,REAL-TIME,STRUCTURED
150 DATA COGNITIVE,CONVOLUTED,INVERTED,NON-LINEAR,RECURSIVE
160 DATA RELATIONAL,STOCHASTIC,SYSTOLIC,TESSELATED,UNDECIDABLE
170 DATA ALGORITHM,ARCHITECTURE,AUTOMATA,DATABASE,INTERFACE
180 DATA NETWORK,PARADIGM,REPRESENTATION,SIMULATION,SYNTAX
190 FOR I=1 TO 10: READ ADJECTIVE1$(I): NEXT I
200 FOR I=1 TO 10: READ ADJECTIVE2$(I): NEXT I
Ok


Ok
LIST 200-
200 FOR I=1 TO 10: READ ADJECTIVE2$(I): NEXT I
210 FOR I=1 TO 10: READ NOUN$(I): NEXT I
220 '
230 WHILE FLAG$<>"Q"
240   FOR I=1 TO 3:IX(I)=INT(RND*10)+1: NEXT I
250   DISPLAY$="THE "+ADJECTIVE1$(IX(1))+" "+ADJECTIVE2$(IX(2))+" "
      +NOUN$(IX(3))+"."
260   LOCATE 13,15: PRINT "
270   LOCATE 10,15: PRINT "TODAY'S ACADEMIC FAD IS: "
280   LOCATE 13,15: PRINT DISPLAY$
290   LOCATE 16,15: INPUT "PRESS <Q> TO END THIS MADNESS"; FLAG$
300 WEND
Ok
```

Display$ that is the concatenation of the three selected strings with appropriate spacing and punctuation. Statements 260 to 280 display the results, identifying them as "today's academic fad."

For example, the random numbers 5, 6, 2 generate the message:

INTEGRATED RELATIONAL ARCHITECTURE

4, 7, 1 generates:

FAULT-TOLERANT STOCHASTIC ALGORITHM

And on and on and on, through 1,000 possible master's-thesis topics. Figure 2–5 shows two more outputs from the program.

Incidentally, all computer scientists are not humorless or self-important. Our resident systems guru (our systems programmer) installed this program on the faculty UNIX system, so that it delivers its latest academic fad every time a user signs on.

TODAY'S ACADEMIC FAD IS:

THE REAL-TIME NON-LINEAR ARCHITECTURE.

PRESS <Q> TO END THIS MADNESS?

TODAY'S ACADEMIC FAD IS:

THE DISTRIBUTED CONVOLUTED DATABASE.

PRESS <Q> TO END THIS MADNESS?

FIGURE 2–5 Two "academic fads" produced by the buzzword generator.

WHEEL GAMES

The next program is called "LANTICTY." I wrote it for a friend who likes to visit the casinos in Atlantic City. It combines two popular wheel games: roulette and wheel-of-fortune. It worked so well for him that he developed a two-person system for playing roulette with it and claims he has made at least a $20 profit on every trip since.

Roulette

There are 38 numbers around the periphery of a roulette wheel. A play of the game ends when a bouncing metal ball is trapped in a numbered pocket as the rotating wheel slows down. The numbers are 00, 0, 1, . . . 36. The numbers 1, 3, 5, 7, 9, 12, 14, 16, 18, 19, 21, 23, 25, 27, 30, 32, 34, and 36 are colored red. The rest are colored black, except 0 and 00, which are green. You can bet on numbers for a payoff of 35 to 1; on red or black for even money; or on odd/even also for even money. Observe that the value of a bet on the field of numbers—that is, return times odds—is $(35+1) \times 1/38$, or .947. The value of a bet on red/black is $(1+1) \times 18/38$, or .947.

This program has 135 lines of code. They are listed in Figure 2–6. However, we are going to forego a boring line-by-line description of it and

```
Ok
LIST -200
10 '
20 ' INITIALIZATION
30 '
40 RANDOMIZE TIME
50 DIM ROULT$(38),RED$(18),BLACK$(18),WHEEL$(54)
60 FOR I=1 TO 38:READ ROULT$(I):NEXT I
70 FOR I=1 TO 18:READ RED$(I):NEXT I
80 FOR I=1 TO 18:READ BLACK$(I):NEXT I
90 FOR I=1 TO 54:READ WHEEL$(I):NEXT I
100 CONTROL$=""
110 '
120 ' INTRODUCTION & SIZE OF BANKROLL
130 '
140 CLS:LOCATE 10,20
150 PRINT "***  WELCOME TO 'LANTIC CITY  ***"
160 PRINT:INPUT " PLEASE ENTER THE AMOUNT OF YOUR BANKROLL";CAPITAL
170 '
180 ' CHOICE OF GAME -- ROULETTE/WHEEL-OF-FORTUNE
190 '
200 CLS:LOCATE 10,20
Ok


Ok
LIST 210-400
210 PRINT "*** SELECT YOUR GAME ***"
220 CHOICE$=""
230 PRINT:INPUT" TYPE: R='ROULETTE', OR W='WHEEL-OF-FORTUNE'";CHOICE$
240 IF CHOICE$="R" THEN 270
250 IF CHOICE$="W" THEN 660 ELSE 220
```

FIGURE 2–6 Program listing for the wheel games "Lanticty."

```
260 '
270 REM *** ROULETTE
280 '
290 ' SELECT NUMBERS 00-36 OR RED/BLACK; PLACE BET
300 '
310 WHILE CONTROL$<>"Q"
320 CLS:LOCATE 10,20
330 PRINT "*** PLACE YOUR BET ***"
340 GAME$=""
350 WHILE GAME$<>"1" AND GAME$<>"2"
360 PRINT:INPUT"TYPE <1> TO PLAY NUMBERS; TYPE <2> FOR RED/BLACK";GAME$
370 PRINT:NUMBR$="":RETN$=""
380 IF GAME$="1" THEN INPUT"TYPE THE NUMBER YOU HAVE CHOSEN";NUMBR$
390 IF GAME$="2" THEN INPUT"TYPE THE COLOR YOU HAVE CHOSEN";RETN$
400 WEND
Ok



Ok
LIST 410-600
410 AMOUNT=0:PRINT:INPUT " TYPE THE AMOUNT YOU WISH TO BET";AMOUNT
420 '
430 ' DETERMINE OUTCOME OF PLAY
440 '
450 NBASE=38
460 GOSUB 960
470 RANDB$="GREEN"
480 FOR I=1 TO 18
490 IF ROULT$(RESULT)=RED$(I) THEN RANDB$="RED"
500 IF ROULT$(RESULT)=BLACK$(I) THEN RANDB$="BLACK"
510 NEXT I
520 '
530 ' REPORT OUTCOME
540 '
550 PRINT " THE BALL STOPPED ON "ROULT$(RESULT)" WHOSE COLOR IS "RANDB$
560 PAYOFF=0:IF RANDB$=RETN$ THEN PAYOFF=AMOUNT:GOSUB 1290
570 IF ROULT$(RESULT)=NUMBR$ THEN PAYOFF=AMOUNT*35:GOSUB 1290
580 IF PAYOFF=0 THEN GOSUB 1250
590 '
600 ' CONTINUE OR QUIT
Ok



Ok
LIST 610-800
610 '
620 PRINT:INPUT" TYPE <Q> TO QUIT"; CONTROL$
630 WEND
640 GOSUB 1030
650 '
660 REM *** WHEEL-OF-FORTUNE
670 '
680 WHILE CONTROL$<>"Q"
690 '
700 ' CHOOSE NUMBER <1,2,5,10,20,45>; PLACE BETS
710 '
720 CLS:LOCATE 10,20
730 PRINT "*** PLACE YOUR BET ***"
740 NUMBR$="":AMOUNT=0
750 PRINT:INPUT " TYPE THE NUMBER YOU HAVE CHOSEN";NUMBR$
760 PRINT:INPUT " TYPE THE AMOUNT YOU WISH TO BET";AMOUNT
770 '
780 ' DETERMINE OUTCOME OF PLAY
790 '
800 NBASE=54
Ok
```

FIGURE 2–6 (continued)

```
Ok
LIST 810-1000
810 GOSUB 960
820 '
830 ' REPORT OUTCOME
840 '
850 PAYOFF=0
860 PRINT " THE WHEEL STOPPED ON "WHEEL$(RESULT)
870 IF WHEEL$(RESULT)=NUMBR$ THEN PAYOFF=AMOUNT*VAL(WHEEL$(RESULT)):GOSUB 1290
880 IF PAYOFF=0 THEN GOSUB 1250
890 '
900 ' CONTINUE OR QUIT
910 '
920 PRINT:INPUT" TYPE <Q> TO QUIT";CONTROL$
930 WEND
940 GOSUB 1030
950 '
960 REM *** RANDOM-NUMBER SUBROUTINE
970 '
980 RESULT=INT(NBASE*RND)+1
990 RETURN
1000 '
Ok


Ok
LIST 1010-1170
1010 REM *** FINISH-UP ROUTINE
1020 '
1030 CLS:LOCATE 10,20
1040 IF CAPITAL <0 THEN 1060
1050 PRINT "YOU ARE LEAVING WITH $"CAPITAL". DO YOU REQUIRE A CAB?":END
1060 DEBT=ABS(CAPITAL)
1070 PRINT "YOU OWE US $"DEBT". DO YOU LIKE TO WALK?":END
1080 '
1090 REM *** ROULETTE ARRAY (38)
1100 '
1110 DATA"0","2","14","35","23","4","16","33","21","6","18","31","19","8","12"
1120 DATA"29","25","16","27","00","1","13","36","24","3","15","34","22","5","17"
1130 DATA "32","20","7","11","30","26","9","22"
1140 REM *** ROULETTE RED  (18)
1150 DATA "14","23","16","21","18","19","12","25","27","1","36","3","34","5",
     "32","7","30","9"
1160 REM *** ROULETTE BLACK (18)
1170 DATA "2","35","4","33","6","31","8","29","10","13","24","15","22","17",
     "20","11","26","28"
Ok


Ok
LIST 1171-
1171 '
1180 REM *** WHEEL-OF-FORTUNE ARRAY   (54)
1181 '
1190 DATA "1","5","2","1","10","1","2","5","1","2","1","45"
1200 DATA "1","2","1","5","2","1","10","1","5","1","2","1"
1210 DATA "20","1","2","1","5","2","1","10","1","2","5","1"
1220 DATA "2","1","45","2","5","2","1","2","1","10","1","2"
1230 DATA "1","2","1","20","1","2"
1240 '
1250 'EVALUATION
1260 '
1270 PRINT:PRINT  " SORRY, YOU LOSE.":CAPITAL=CAPITAL-AMOUNT
1280 PRINT " YOU HAVE $"CAPITAL"LEFT.":RETURN
1290 PRINT:PRINT " YOU WIN $"PAYOFF:CAPITAL=CAPITAL+PAYOFF
1300 PRINT " YOU HAVE $"CAPITAL"LEFT."
1310 RETURN
Ok
```

FIGURE 2–6 (continued)

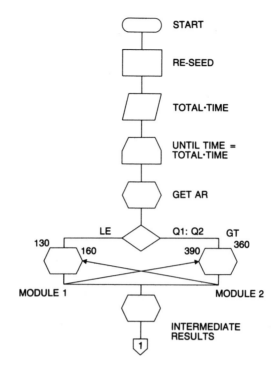

START

RE-SEED

TOTAL·TIME

UNTIL TIME =
TOTAL·TIME

GET AR

LE   Q1: Q2   GT

130   360
160   390

MODULE 1   MODULE 2

INTERMEDIATE
RESULTS

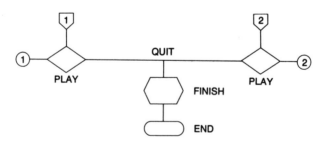

QUIT

PLAY   PLAY

FINISH

END

FIGURE 2–7   Flow chart of "Lanticty."

instead look at its logic flow chart. The logic flow chart is shown in Figure 2–7.

The first symbol is an oval (computer people sometimes call it a bologna, an apt characterization of some programs), signifying "start." The next is a processing element (rectangle) that initializes the program. It seeds the random-number generator and reads in the complete roulette array, the roulette array of red numbers, the roulette array of black numbers, and the wheel-of-fortune array.

```
        ***  WELCOME TO 'LANTIC CITY  ***
  PLEASE ENTER THE AMOUNT OF YOUR BANKROLL? 20
```

FIGURE 2–8 Player is welcomed to the casino; declares his bankroll; and elects to play Roulette.

```
            ***  SELECT YOUR GAME  ***
  TYPE: R='ROULETTE', OR W='WHEEL-OF-FORTUNE'? R
```

The next block is an input element (parallelogram), and it accepts from the keyboard the size of the player's bankroll in dollars. Then there is a decision element (lozenge), signifying that the player must type either "R" to select roulette or "W" to select wheel-of-fortune. Both the roulette and wheel-of-fortune subprograms are encapsulated in WHILE-WEND loops that terminate when the player types "Q" in response to an invitation to quit.

Figure 2–8 illustrates the start of a round of play. The player is welcomed to the casino, declares a bankroll of $20, and elects to play roulette.

The next element in the roulette subprogram is a decision about whether to play the field of numbers or to play red/black. It is implemented by a WHILE-WEND loop to guard against improper responses. The player is asked to select a number or a color depending upon the mode of play he or she has elected; these choices are depicted as input elements (parallelograms). Irrespective of mode selection, the player is next asked to input the amount of his or her bet.

Play is simulated in the "determine outcome" (RESULT) processing element (rectangle) by passing 38 as the multiplier to the random-number-generator subroutine, shown as a hexagon. Color is set to green in the event that either 0 or 00 comes up. The random number is indexed into the red and black arrays in a FOR-NEXT loop to determine whether the color should be changed.

The "report outcome" (REPORT) block compares the randomly generated number or color with that selected by the player, multiplies by the appropriate payoff factor, and displays the result on the screen. Control is then transferred to an evaluation subroutine at one of two entry points, depending upon whether the player has won or lost. Winnings are added to the player's bankroll; losses are subtracted.

In Figure 2–9, the player first bets $10 on number 35 and loses when the wheel stops on 0. Then the player bets $10 on black and wins $10 when the wheel stops on number 10, black.

```
            *** PLACE YOUR BET ***

TYPE <1> TO PLAY NUMBERS; TYPE <2> FOR RED/BLACK? 1

TYPE THE NUMBER YOU HAVE CHOSEN? 35

 TYPE THE AMOUNT YOU WISH TO BET? 10
 THE BALL STOPPED ON 0 WHOSE COLOR IS GREEN

 SORRY, YOU LOSE.
 YOU HAVE $ 10 LEFT.

 TYPE <Q> TO QUIT?
```

FIGURE 2–9 Roulette player loses on numbers and wins on colors.

```
            *** PLACE YOUR BET ***

TYPE <1> TO PLAY NUMBERS; TYPE <2> FOR RED/BLACK? 2

TYPE THE COLOR YOU HAVE CHOSEN? BLACK

 TYPE THE AMOUNT YOU WISH TO BET? 10
 THE BALL STOPPED ON 35 WHOSE COLOR IS BLACK

 YOU WIN $ 10
 YOU HAVE $ 20 LEFT.

 TYPE <Q> TO QUIT? Q


                  YOU ARE LEAVING WITH $ 20 . DO YOU REQUIRE A CAB?
Ok
```

FIGURE 2–10 Player leaves the casino with a positive (or zero) bankroll.

The player may type "Q" to quit, in which case control is transferred to a "finish-up" subroutine. If the player has money left (or a zero balance), the house asks if he or she desires a cab (see Figure 2–10); a player who owes money to the house is asked if he or she likes to walk—a subtle hint to pay up if the player wants to continue walking (The player would find it difficult to walk on two broken legs).

Wheel-of-Fortune

There are 54 numbers around the periphery of the wheel-of-fortune. They are distributed as follows:

        23 1s
        16 2s
         7 5s
         4 10s
         2 20s

```
            ***  WELCOME TO 'LANTIC CITY  ***

PLEASE ENTER THE AMOUNT OF YOUR BANKROLL?  10
```

FIGURE 2-11 Player is welcomed to the casino; declares his bankroll; and elects to play Wheel-of-Fortune.

```
            ***  SELECT YOUR GAME  ***

TYPE:  R='ROULETTE',  OR  W='WHEEL-OF-FORTUNE'?  W
```

You pick a number, and if the ball falls on it, you get a payoff of 45, 20, 10, 5, 2, or 1 to 1. Observe that the values of the bets are:

$$(1 + 1) \times 23/54 = .853$$
$$(1 + 2) \times 16/54 = .889$$
$$(1 + 5) \times 7/54 = .778$$
$$(1 + 10) \times 4/54 = .815$$
$$(1 + 20) \times 2/54 = .778$$
$$(1 + 45) \times 1/54 = .853$$

The wheel-of-fortune subprogram is much like roulette. The player is asked to select a number and place a bet. The "determine outcome" processing block passes the multiplier 54 to the random-number subroutine. The random number is used to index into the wheel-of-fortune array and thus obtain the simulated stopping point for the ball, which is also the payoff multiplier.

In Figure 2-11, the player is welcomed to the house, declares a bankroll of $10, and elects to play wheel-of-fortune.

The "report outcome" block displays the results on the screen and calls the evaluation subroutine that adjusts the amount of the player's bankroll, depending upon whether he or she lost or won, and by how much. The termination routine is the same as in the case of roulette. In Figure 2-12, the player first bets on number/payoff 20 and loses his or her bankroll. Then, playing with the house's money, he or she bets on number/payoff 45 and loses again. In Figure 2-13, we see the player leaving, having been given a subtle hint to pay up or else.

```
                *** PLACE YOUR BET ***

TYPE THE NUMBER YOU HAVE CHOSEN? 20

TYPE THE AMOUNT YOU WISH TO BET? 10
THE WHEEL STOPPED ON 1

SORRY, YOU LOSE.
YOU HAVE $ 0 LEFT.

TYPE <Q> TO QUIT?
```

FIGURE 2–12 Player loses twice at Wheel-of-Fortune.

```
                *** PLACE YOUR BET ***

TYPE THE NUMBER YOU HAVE CHOSEN? 45

TYPE THE AMOUNT YOU WISH TO BET? 10
THE WHEEL STOPPED ON 10

SORRY, YOU LOSE.
YOU HAVE $-10 LEFT.

TYPE <Q> TO QUIT?
```

```
            YOU OWE US $ 10 . DO YOU LIKE TO WALK?
Ok
```

FIGURE 2–13 Player leaves the casino in debt to the house.

COMPUTER CLUE

The last random-number game in this sampling of computer games is a version of the popular Parker Brothers board game Clue. It differs from it in two important aspects: It is played against the computer instead of head-to-head with other players, and it is not a board game.

You probably recall that the original game simulates the plot of a classic English murder mystery. The game board simulates an English country house populated with stock characters out of Agatha Christie. There are six suspects, six murder weapons, and nine rooms in which the crime can be committed. To win, a player must move into the room that is the scene of the crime and correctly announce "whodunit" and with which weapon.

The correct triple combination of suspect–weapon–room is established at the start of the game by blind draws from decks of 6 suspect cards, 6 weapon cards, and 9 room cards. The three cards are sealed in an envelope. In addition, all players get an equal share of the remaining card triples so each one knows at least one combination that is not correct. There are elements of both skill and luck involved in maneuvering one's playing piece over the two-dimensional board in response to successive rolls of the dice so as to cover all the rooms before the other players do. Each player is given a status board to record and thus eliminate the incorrect solutions. Even though no one knows the correct solution, together the players are able to eliminate all incorrect ones.

In the computer game, the correct triple combination is selected by random-number draws. There is no playing board, so a substitution of skills is made. We take away the manual status board and substitute an electronic one, a screen display of the incorrect triples the player has already guessed. Figure 2–14 is a complete listing of the program (125 statements).

The player starts out with a free look at the status display that reveals one incorrect triple, and is awarded 300 points. Each wrong guess costs the

```
Ok
LIST -200
10 '
20 ' THIS PROGRAM SIMULATES THE POPULAR GAME OF "CLUE" (C-CIRCLE PARKER BROS.)
30 ' THE GAME IS PLAYED AGAINST THE COMPUTER, NOT "HEAD-TO-HEAD"
40 '
50 'TITLE PANEL
60 '
70 CLS: LOCATE 1,1: FOR I=1 TO 80: PRINT "*";:NEXT I
80 LOCATE 1,1: FOR I=1 TO 19: PRINT "*":NEXT I
90 FOR I=1 TO 19: LOCATE 1+I,80: PRINT "*":NEXT I
100 LOCATE 20,1: FOR I=1 TO 80: PRINT "*";:NEXT I
110 LOCATE 5,26: PRINT "WELCOME TO 'COMPUTER CLUE II'"
120 LOCATE 9,19: PRINT "COPYRIGHT C-CIRCLE BY JOHN M. CARROLL 1984"
130 LOCATE 13,30: PRINT "ALL RIGHTS RESERVED"
140 LOCATE 22,1: INPUT "TYPE <RETURN> OR <ENTER> TO CONTINUE ";X
150 '
160 ' INTRODUCTORY PANEL
170 '
180 CLS: LOCATE 1,1: FOR I=1 TO 80: PRINT "*";:NEXT I
190 LOCATE 1,1: FOR I=1 TO 19: PRINT "*":NEXT I
200 FOR I=1 TO 19: LOCATE 1+I,80: PRINT "*":NEXT I
Ok


Ok
LIST 210-400
210 LOCATE 20,1: FOR I=1 TO 80: PRINT "*";:NEXT I
220 LOCATE 5,21: PRINT "***** RULES OF COMPUTER CLUE II *****"
230 LOCATE 8,26: PRINT "EACH GUESS COSTS 10 POINTS "
240 LOCATE 11,17: PRINT "EACH LOOK AT THE 'STATUS BOARD' COSTS 5 POINTS"
250 LOCATE 14,29: PRINT "A PERFECT SCORE IS 300"
260 LOCATE 22,1: INPUT "TYPE <RETURN> OR <ENTER> TO CONTINUE ";X
270 '
280 ' HOUSEKEEPING MODULE
290 '
300 DIM SUSPECT.NAME$(6), SUSPECT.ARRAY$(6)
310 DIM ROOM.NAME$(9), ROOM.ARRAY$(9)
320 DIM WEAPON.NAME$(6), WEAPON.ARRAY$(6)
330 '
340 ' READ CLUE NAMES
350 '
360 FOR I = 1 TO 6: READ SUSPECT.NAME$(I): NEXT I
370 DATA "COLONEL MUSTARDSEED ","PROF. PLUMCAKE       "
380 DATA "SCARLETT O'HORROR   ","MR. GREENSLEEVES     "
390 DATA "MRS. WHITEFISH      ","MRS. PETCOCK         "
400 '
Ok
```

FIGURE 2–14 Program listing for "Computer Clue II."

```
Ok
LIST 410-600
410 FOR I=1 TO 9: READ ROOM.NAME$(I): NEXT I
420 DATA "KITCHEN          ","LIVING ROOM      ","DINING ROOM      "
430 DATA "BEDROOM          ","DEN              ","PATIO            "
440 DATA "GAME ROOM        ","LIBRARY          ","BALLROOM         "
450 '
460 '
470 FOR I=1 TO 6: READ WEAPON.NAME$(I): NEXT I
480 DATA "REVOLVER         ","PIPE WRENCH      "
490 DATA "CHANDELIER       ","GARROTE          "
500 DATA "BLACKJACK        ","BUTCHER'S KNIFE  "
510 '
520 ' COPY CLUES & THEIR CODES FOR FUTURE REFERENCE
530 '
540 CLS: LOCATE 1,1: FOR I=1 TO 80: PRINT "*";:NEXT I
550 LOCATE 1,1: FOR I=1 TO 19: PRINT "*":NEXT I
560 FOR I=1 TO 19: LOCATE 1+I,80: PRINT "*":NEXT I
570 LOCATE 20,1: FOR I=1 TO 80: PRINT "*";:NEXT I
580 LOCATE 3,17: PRINT "***** THESE ARE YOUR CLUES & THEIR CODES *****"
590 FOR I=1 TO 6: LOCATE 4+I,4: PRINT SUSPECT.NAME$(I) I: NEXT I
600 FOR I=1 TO 9: LOCATE 4+I,30: PRINT ROOM.NAME$(I) I: NEXT I
Ok
```

```
Ok
LIST 610-800
610 FOR I=1 TO 6: LOCATE 4+I,55: PRINT WEAPON.NAME$(I) I:NEXT I
620 LOCATE 16,16: PRINT "TYPE <SHIFT-PRINT> OR <SHIFT-F12> TO MAKE A COPY"
630 LOCATE 22,1: INPUT "TYPE <RETURN> OR <ENTER> TO CONTINUE ";X
640 '
650 ' GENERATE THE CORRECT SOLUTION & AN INITIAL GUESS FOR THE PLAYER
660 '
670 DIM SOLUTION(3)
680 RANDOMIZE TIME
690 SOLUTION(1)=INT(RND*6+1)
700 INDEX=INT(RND*6+1)
710 IF INDEX <> SOLUTION(1) THEN SUSPECT.ARRAY$(INDEX)="X" ELSE 700
720 SOLUTION(2)=INT(RND*9+1)
730 INDEX=INT(RND*9+1)
740 IF INDEX <> SOLUTION(2) THEN ROOM.ARRAY$(INDEX)="X" ELSE 730
750 SOLUTION(3)=INT(RND*6+1)
760 INDEX=INT(RND*6+1)
770 IF INDEX <> SOLUTION(3) THEN WEAPON.ARRAY$(INDEX)="X" ELSE 760
780 '
790 ' MAIN CONTROL SWITCH
800 '
Ok
```

```
Ok
LIST 810-1000
810 C$=""
820 CLS: LOCATE 10,17: INPUT "TYPE <0> TO VIEW 'STATUS BOARD; <1> TO GUESS";C$
830 IF C$="0" THEN 850
840 IF C$="1" THEN 980 ELSE 810
850 '
860 ' DISPLAY THE "STATUS BOARD"
870 '
880 PENALTY=PENALTY+5
890 CLS: PRINT ">>>"
900 FOR I=1 TO 6:LOCATE I,4:PRINT I" "SUSPECT.NAME$(I) SUSPECT.ARRAY$(I):NEXT I
910 PRINT ">>>"
920 FOR I=1 TO 9:LOCATE 6+I,4: PRINT I" "ROOM.NAME$(I) ROOM.ARRAY$(I): NEXT I
930 PRINT ">>>"
940 FOR I=1 TO 6:LOCATE 15+I,4:PRINT I" "WEAPON.NAME$(I) WEAPON.ARRAY$(I)
950 NEXT I
```

FIGURE 2–14   (continued)

```
960 LOCATE 23,1: INPUT "PRESS <RETURN> OR <ENTER> TO CONTINUE ";X
970 GOTO 810
980 '
990 ' ACCEPT THE PLAYER'S GUESS AND DISPLAY IT
1000 '
Ok



1010 PENALTY=PENALTY+10
1020 C$=""
1030 CLS: LOCATE 5,6
1040 INPUT "TYPE THE CODE NUMBERS OF YOUR GUESSES: <SUSPECT>, <ROOM>, <WEAPON> "
; SUSPECT, ROOM, WEAPON
1050 LOCATE 10,27: PRINT SUSPECT.NAME$(SUSPECT) "DID IT"
1060 LOCATE 13,31: PRINT "IN THE "ROOM.NAME$(ROOM)
1070 LOCATE 16,31: PRINT "WITH A "WEAPON.NAME$(WEAPON)
1080 IF SUSPECT<>SOLUTION(1) THEN SUSPECT.ARRAY$(SUSPECT)="X"
1090 IF ROOM<>SOLUTION(2) THEN ROOM.ARRAY$(ROOM)="X"
1100 IF WEAPON<>SOLUTION(3) THEN WEAPON.ARRAY$(WEAPON)="X"
1110 LOCATE 22,1: INPUT "PRESS <RETURN> OR <ENTER> TO CONTINUE ";X
1120 GOTO 1130
1130 '
1140 ' TEST WHETHER OR NOT THE PLAYER'S GUESS IS CORRECT
1150 '
1160 IF SUSPECT=SOLUTION(1) AND ROOM=SOLUTION(2) AND WEAPON=SOLUTION(3)
     THEN 1170 ELSE 810
1170 '
1180 ' REPORT THAT PLAYER'S GUESS IS CORRECT & TERMINATE A ROUND OF PLAY
1190 '
1200 CLS: LOCATE 5,19: PRINT "CONGRATULATIONS, YOU HAVE SOLVED THE CASE!"
Ok

Ok
LIST 1210-
1210 LOCATE 10,32: PRINT "YOUR SCORE IS " 315-PENALTY
1220 LOCATE 15,18: PRINT "TYPE <RETURN> OR <ENTER> TO END THIS ROUND"
1230 LOCATE 20,21: INPUT "THEN PRESS <F2> TO PLAY ANOTHER ROUND ";X
1240 PRINT: PRINT
1250 END
Ok
```

FIGURE 2–14 (continued)

player 10 points, and each look at the status board costs 5 points. The player tries to get the highest possible score—300.

The first panel welcomes the player to "Computer Clue" and contains a copyright notice (see Figure 2–15).

The introductory panel (also Figure 2–15) sets out the rules of the game: cost of a guess, cost to view the status board, and value of a perfect game.

The housekeeping module dimensions the suspect, room, and weapon arrays. Each category has two arrays associated with it. One holds the name; the other is initially blank but holds an "X" after the name has been incorrectly guessed.

The next module reads the names of the suspects:

Colonel Mustardseed
Professor Plumcake
Mr. Greensleeves

```
****************************************************************************
*                                                                          *
*                                                                          *
*                                                                          *
*                    WELCOME TO 'COMPUTER CLUE II'                         *
*                                                                          *
*                                                                          *
*                                                                          *
*                COPYRIGHT C-CIRCLE BY JOHN M. CARROLL 1984                *
*                                                                          *
*                                                                          *
*                                                                          *
*                         ALL RIGHTS RESERVED                             *
*                                                                          *
*                                                                          *
*                                                                          *
*                                                                          *
*                                                                          *
*                                                                          *
****************************************************************************
TYPE <RETURN> OR <ENTER> TO CONTINUE ?




****************************************************************************
*                                                                          *
*                                                                          *
*                                                                          *
*                    ***** RULES OF COMPUTER CLUE II *****                 *
*                                                                          *
*                                                                          *
*                       EACH GUESS COSTS 10 POINTS                        *
*                                                                          *
*                                                                          *
*              EACH LOOK AT THE 'STATUS BOARD' COSTS 5 POINTS             *
*                                                                          *
*                                                                          *
*                      A PERFECT SCORE IS 300                             *
*                                                                          *
*                                                                          *
*                                                                          *
*                                                                          *
*                                                                          *
****************************************************************************
TYPE <RETURN> OR <ENTER> TO CONTINUE ?
```

FIGURE 2–15 Copyright notice and rules of the game.

Scarlett O'Horror
Mrs. Whitefish
Mrs. Petcock

and the rooms:

kitchen
bedroom
game room
living room
den
library

     dining room
     patio
     ballroom

and the weapons:

     revolver
     chandelier
     blackjack
     pipe wrench
     garrote
     butcher's knife

    The next panel, shown in Figure 2–16, invites the player to use the screen print utility to copy the list of clues (SHIFT-PRINT for TI computers; SHIFT-F12 for Heath/Zenith computers). The suspects and weapons are numbered 1 to 6; the rooms are numbered 1 to 9. The reason for copying the panel is that the player will be required to enter guesses as sequences of three numbers and will need to refer to the panel.

FIGURE 2–16 Schedule of clues and master control switch.

```
************************************************************************
*                                                                    *
*              ***** THESE ARE YOUR CLUES & THEIR CODES *****         *
*                                                                    *
*   COLONEL MUSTARDSEED  1     KITCHEN        1     REVOLVER       1  *
*   PROF. PLUMCAKE       2     LIVING ROOM    2     PIPE WRENCH    2  *
*   SCARLETT O'HORROR    3     DINING ROOM    3     CHANDELIER     3  *
*   MR. GREENSLEEVES     4     BEDROOM        4     GARROTE        4  *
*   MRS. WHITEFISH       5     DEN            5     BLACKJACK      5  *
*   MRS. PETCOCK         6     PATIO          6     BUTCHER'S KNIFE 6  *
*                              GAME ROOM      7                       *
*                              LIBRARY        8                       *
*                              BALLROOM       9                       *
*                                                                    *
*                                                                    *
*          TYPE <SHIFT-PRINT> OR <SHIFT-F12> TO MAKE A COPY          *
*                                                                    *
*                                                                    *
*                                                                    *
************************************************************************
TYPE <RETURN> OR <ENTER> TO CONTINUE ?




              TYPE <0> TO VIEW 'STATUS BOARD; <1> TO GUESS?
```

The next routine generates the correct solution by choosing a random integer in the range 1–6, another in the range 1–9, and a third in the range 1–6 after the generator has been reseeded by the real-time clock. The routine chooses another set of numbers and tests to make sure they all differ from the correct solution. The first set is stored in a three-component solution vector. The second set is used to index into the category arrays and mark a solution with X's; this is the player's initial and free guess.

The main control switch (see Figure 2–16) allows the player to choose to inspect the status board <0>; the first look is free. Or the player can guess <1>.

The status board, shown in Figure 2–17, lists the suspects' names and

FIGURE 2–17   Program status board and results of a guess at the solution.

```
>>> 1   COLONEL MUSTARDSEED
    2   PROF. PLUMCAKE          X
    3   SCARLETT O'HORROR
    4   MR. GREENSLEEVES
    5   MRS. WHITEFISH
    6   MRS. PETCOCK
>>> 1   KITCHEN
    2   LIVING ROOM
    3   DINING ROOM
    4   BEDROOM
    5   DEN                     X
    6   PATIO
    7   GAME ROOM
    8   LIBRARY
    9   BALLROOM
>>> 1   REVOLVER
    2   PIPE WRENCH             X
    3   CHANDELIER
    4   GARROTE
    5   BLACKJACK
    6   BUTCHER'S KNIFE

PRESS <RETURN> OR <ENTER> TO CONTINUE ?




TYPE THE CODE NUMBERS OF YOUR GUESSES: <SUSPECT>, <ROOM>, <WEAPON> ? 1,1,1



COLONEL MUSTARDSEED DID IT

IN THE KITCHEN

WITH A REVOLVER



PRESS <RETURN> OR <ENTER> TO CONTINUE ?
```

```
          CONGRATULATIONS, YOU HAVE SOLVED THE CASE!
```
FIGURE 2–18 Congratulatory display when a player wins the game.

```
                    YOUR SCORE IS   240



          TYPE <RETURN> OR <ENTER> TO END THIS ROUND



              THEN PRESS <F2> TO PLAY ANOTHER ROUND ?
```

the array, with *X*'s to denote incorrect choices; likewise for rooms and weapons. The player types <RETURN> or <ENTER> to go back to the main control switch.

If the player chooses to guess, he or she must enter a set of three numbers denoting choice of suspect, room, and weapon. If all choices are correct, the program branches to the report routine that congratulates the player, displays the score, and invites the player to start another round by pressing the proper function key for RUN. If the guess is incorrect, the program returns to the main control switch. Figure 2–17 shows a guess; Figure 2–18 is the congratulatory panel, which appears after a correct guess.

The perceptive reader will notice that there is an easy way to win at Computer Clue. Since only the *incorrect* choices are marked with an *X*, any choice made by the player that is not so marked is correct. Thus the player can incrementally ascertain the parts of the solution rather than having to guess the three parts at one time. This kind of attack can be helpful in breaking cryptograms and guessing other people's computer passwords!

```
*****************************************************************************
*
*
*
*              ***** WELCOME TO 'SPYCATCHER' *****
*
*                   COPYRIGHT C-CIRCLE 1984
*
*                     BY JOHN M. CARROLL
*
*                    ALL RIGHTS RESERVED
*
*
*
*
*
*
*****************************************************************************
              >>TYPE <RETURN> OR <ENTER> TO CONTINUE ?
```
FIGURE 2–19 Title panel for "Spycatcher."

```
    ***** THESE ARE YOUR CLUES *****

    PRESS [SHIFT/F12] TO MAKE A COPY


1    1                      2    2                   3    3
4    4                      5    5                   6    BLUE
7    GREEN                  8    IVORY               9    RED
10   YELLOW                 11   BEARD               12   GOATEE
13   LONG-HAIR             14   MUSTACHE            15   SIDEBURNS
16   BOMB                  17   KNIFE               18   PISTOL
19   RIFLE                 20   SHOTGUN             21   BOMBER
22   COMPUTER              23   FRIGATE             24   MISSILE
25   RADAR                 26   BULGARIAN           27   CZECH
28   HUNGARIAN             29   POLE                30   RUSSIAN
31

    ***** MAKE A COPY; THEN TYPE 'ENTER' TO SEE NARRATIVE CLUES?
```

FIGURE 2-20 Possible entries for the game solution board. Entry 31 will cancel a previous
bad choice.

SPY-CATCHER

The last game is one I regard as my premier program in this area. Most people
find it to be a lot of fun even though it doesn't have anything to do with random
numbers. I tried it on some real spy-catchers I taught in a course called "Computers for Investigators" (the students were from the Naval Investigative Service,
Army Counter-Intelligence Corps, Secret Service, and U.S. Marshal Service),
and it really held their interest.

Figure 2-19 is the usual title panel. Figure 2-20 is a list of "clues" that
must be entered in their proper places on the game board. Figure 2-21 lists
what we know about five spies who live next door to one another.

FIGURE 2-21 What we know about five spies who live next door to each other.

```
1. THERE ARE FIVE HOUSES.
2. THE HUNGARIAN LIVES IN THE RED HOUSE.
3. THE SPY IN THE THIRD HOUSE WEARS A GOATEE.
4. THE POLE IS TRYING TO STEAL PLANS FOR A FRIGATE.
5. THE CZECH IS ARMED WITH A RIFLE.
6. THE RUSSIAN LIVES IN THE FIRST HOUSE.
7. THE SPY WITH THE BOMB IS TRYING TO STEAL PLANS FOR A MISSILE.
8. THE SPY WEARING THE BEARD IS ARMED WITH A SHOTGUN.
9. THE SPY IN THE YELLOW HOUSE HAS A KNIFE.
10. THE SPY WEARING SIDEBURNS LIVES IN THE YELLOW HOUSE.
11. THE RUSSIAN LIVES NEXT DOOR TO THE BLUE HOUSE.
12. THE BULGARIAN HAS A MUSTACHE.
13. THE GREEN HOUSE IS IMMEDIATELY LEFT OF THE IVORY HOUSE.
14. A KNIFE IS HIDDEN IN THE HOUSE NEXT TO THE SPY WHO IS
    TRYING TO STEAL PLANS FOR A RADAR.
15. THE SPY TRYING TO STEAL PLANS FOR A BOMBER LIVES NEXT
    DOOR TO THE HOUSE WHERE A PISTOL IS HIDDEN.
16. THE SPY TRYING TO STEAL PLANS FOR A BOMBER LIVES NEXT DOOR
    TO THE SPY TRYING TO STEAL PLANS FOR A RADAR.
17. THE RED HOUSE IS ON THE BLUE HOUSE'S RIGHT.
18. THE SPY TRYING TO STEAL A BOMBER LIVES IN THE GREEN HOUSE.
--> WHICH SPY HAS LONG-HAIR?
--> WHO IS TRYING TO STEAL PLANS FOR A COMPUTER?
    ***** MAKE A COPY; THEN TYPE 'ENTER' TO CONTINUE?
```

```
            FORMAT FOR SOLUTION BOARD

   THESE ARE THE COLUMN DESIGNATIONS:
!     1      !     2      !     3      !     4      !     5      !     6      !
!            !            !            !            !           !            !
!HOUSE NUMBER!HOUSE COLOR !DESCRIPTION !WEAPON      !OBJECTIVE  !NATIONALITY !
!            !            !            !            !           !            !

   EACH LINE [I.E. 1, 7, 13, 19 & 21] DESIGNATES A HOUSE

   ENTER SQUARE NUMBER AND CLUE NUMBER (I.E. 'CONTENTS') WHEN PROMPTED
   ENTER 'SQUARE = 31' TO ESCAPE PROGRAM.
   ENTER 'CONTENTS = 31' TO ERASE A BAD CHOICE.


   ***** MAKE A COPY; THEN TYPE 'ENTER' TO CONTINUE?
```

FIGURE 2–22 Format for the game solution board and instructions for playing the game.

Figure 2–22 is the format of the game board. Figure 2–23 is the game board with all the easy entries filled in. Figure 2–24 is the source code listing. The game is an exercise in using the process of elimination, and I'll leave the rest of the solution to you.

SUMMARY

In this chapter we have seen examples of how a random-number generator can function as the heart of five games. The first was called Climb the Ladder, and involved some elementary computer graphics. The second was a buzz-word

FIGURE 2–23 Game solution board with the easy choices filled in.

```
1             ! 2            ! 3            ! 4            ! 5            ! 6
ENTER SQUARE NUMBER?                        !              !              !
1             !              !              !              !              ! RUSSIAN
              !              !              !              !              !
--------------!--------------!--------------!--------------!--------------!--------------
7             ! 8            ! 9            ! 10           ! 11           ! 12
              !              !              !              !              !
2             ! BLUE         !              !              !              !
              !              !              !              !              !
--------------!--------------!--------------!--------------!--------------!--------------
13            ! 14           ! 15           ! 16           ! 17           ! 18
              !              !              !              !              !
3             !              ! GOATEE       !              !              !
              !              !              !              !              !
--------------!--------------!--------------!--------------!--------------!--------------
19            ! 20           ! 21           ! 22           ! 23           ! 24
              !              !              !              !              !
4             !              !              !              !              !
              !              !              !              !              !
--------------!--------------!--------------!--------------!--------------!--------------
25            ! 26           ! 27           ! 28           ! 29           ! 30
5             !              !              !              !              !
```

```
Ok
LIST -200
10 X=0
20 GOSUB 1280
30 LOCATE 5,22:PRINT "***** WELCOME TO 'SPYCATCHER' *****"
40 LOCATE 7,29:PRINT "COPYRIGHT C-CIRCLE 1984"
50 LOCATE 9,31:PRINT "BY JOHN M. CARROLL"
60 LOCATE 11,30:PRINT "ALL RIGHTS RESERVED"
70 GOSUB 1340
80 CLS
90 LOCATE 5,16
100 PRINT"***** THESE ARE YOUR CLUES *****"
110 LOCATE 7,16: PRINT"PRESS [SHIFT/F12] TO MAKE A COPY"
120 PRINT:PRINT
130 DIM CLUE$(31),NARRATIVE$(25)
140 FOR I=1 TO 31:READ CLUE$(I):NEXT I
150 FOR I=1 TO 31:PRINT I" "CLUE$(I),:NEXT I
160 PRINT:PRINT
170 INPUT"    ***** MAKE A COPY; THEN TYPE 'ENTER' TO SEE NARRATIVE CLUES";X
180 FOR I=1 TO 23:READ NARRATIVE$(I):NEXT I
190 CLS
200 FOR I=1 TO 23:PRINT NARRATIVE$(I):NEXT I
Ok


210 INPUT"    ***** MAKE A COPY; THEN TYPE 'ENTER' TO CONTINUE";X
220 CLS
230 LOCATE 5,23:PRINT "FORMAT FOR SOLUTION BOARD"
240 PRINT:PRINT
250 PRINT"    THESE ARE THE COLUMN DESIGNATIONS:"
260 PRINT
270 PRINT"!    1    !    2    !    3    !    4    !    5    !
 6    !"
280 PRINT"!         !         !         !         !         !
     !"
290 PRINT"!HOUSE NUMBER!HOUSE COLOR !DESCRIPTION !WEAPON    !OBJECTIVE    !NATI
ONALITY !"
300 PRINT"!         !         !         !         !         !
     !"
310 PRINT
320 PRINT"    EACH LINE [I.E. 1, 7, 13, 19 & 21] DESIGNATES A HOUSE"
330 PRINT:PRINT
340 PRINT"    ENTER SQUARE NUMBER AND CLUE NUMBER (I.E. 'CONTENTS') WHEN PROMPT
ED"
350 PRINT"    ENTER 'SQUARE = 31' TO ESCAPE PROGRAM."
360 PRINT"    ENTER 'CONTENTS = 31' TO ERASE A BAD CHOICE."
370 PRINT:PRINT
Ok


380 INPUT"    ***** MAKE A COPY; THEN TYPE 'ENTER' TO CONTINUE";X
390 CLS
400 GOSUB 490
410 LOCATE 2,1:PRINT"                                        "
420 LOCATE 2,1:INPUT;"ENTER SQUARE NUMBER";L
430 IF L>30 THEN 480
440 LOCATE 2,1:PRINT"                                        "
450 LOCATE 2,1:INPUT;"ENTER CONTENTS";X
460 ON L GOSUB 660,670,680,690,700,710,720,730,740,750,760,770,780,    790,800,8
10,820,830,840,850,860,870,880,890,900,910,920,930,    940,950
470 GOTO 410
480 CLS:END
490 CLS
```

FIGURE 2–24 Source code listing of "Spycatcher."

```
500   FOR I=5 TO 20 STEP 5
510   FOR J=1 TO 80
520   LOCATE I,J
530   PRINT"-"
540   NEXT J,I
550   FOR I=1 TO 22
560   FOR J=13 TO 65 STEP 13
570   LOCATE I,J
580   PRINT"!"
Ok


LIST 590-790
590   NEXT J,I
600 FOR I=1 TO 21 STEP 5
610 FOR J=1 TO 66 STEP 13
620 LOCATE I,J
630 X=X+1:PRINT X
640 NEXT J,I
650 RETURN
660 LOCATE 3,2:PRINT CLUE$(X):RETURN
670 LOCATE 3,15:PRINT CLUE$(X):RETURN
680 LOCATE 3,28:PRINT CLUE$(X):RETURN
690 LOCATE 3,41:PRINT CLUE$(X):RETURN
700 LOCATE 3,54:PRINT CLUE$(X):RETURN
710 LOCATE 3,67:PRINT CLUE$(X):RETURN
720 LOCATE 8,2:PRINT CLUE$(X):RETURN
730 LOCATE 8,15:PRINT CLUE$(X):RETURN
740 LOCATE 8,28:PRINT CLUE$(X):RETURN
750 LOCATE 8,41:PRINT CLUE$(X):RETURN
760 LOCATE 8,54:PRINT CLUE$(X):RETURN
770 LOCATE 8,67:PRINT CLUE$(X):RETURN
780 LOCATE 13,2:PRINT CLUE$(X):RETURN
790 LOCATE 13,15:PRINT CLUE$(X):RETURN
Ok


LIST 800-1000
800 LOCATE 13,28:PRINT CLUE$(X):RETURN
810 LOCATE 13,41:PRINT CLUE$(X):RETURN
820 LOCATE 13,54:PRINT CLUE$(X):RETURN
830 LOCATE 13,67:PRINT CLUE$(X):RETURN
840 LOCATE 18,2:PRINT CLUE$(X):RETURN
850 LOCATE 18,15:PRINT CLUE$(X):RETURN
860 LOCATE 18,28:PRINT CLUE$(X):RETURN
870 LOCATE 18,41:PRINT CLUE$(X):RETURN
880 LOCATE 18,54:PRINT CLUE$(X):RETURN
890 LOCATE 18,67:PRINT CLUE$(X):RETURN
900 LOCATE 22,2:PRINT CLUE$(X):RETURN
910 LOCATE 22,15:PRINT CLUE$(X):RETURN
920 LOCATE 22,28:PRINT CLUE$(X):RETURN
930 LOCATE 22,41:PRINT CLUE$(X):RETURN
940 LOCATE 22,54:PRINT CLUE$(X):RETURN
950 LOCATE 22,67:PRINT CLUE$(X):RETURN
960 'DATA
970 DATA "1         ","2         ","3         ","4         ","5         "
980 DATA "BLUE      ","GREEN     ","IVORY     ","RED       ","YELLOW    "
990 DATA "BEARD     ","GOATEE    ","LONG-HAIR","MUSTACHE ","SIDEBURNS"
1000 DATA "BOMB      ","KNIFE     ","PISTOL    ","RIFLE     ","SHOTGUN   "
Ok


Ok
LIST 1010-1200
1010 DATA "BOMBER    ","COMPUTER ","FRIGATE   ","MISSILE   ","RADAR     "
1020 DATA "BULGARIAN","CZECH     ","HUNGARIAN","POLE      ","RUSSIAN   "
```

FIGURE 2–24 (continued)

```
1030 DATA "
1040 '
1050 DATA "1. THERE ARE FIVE HOUSES."
1060 DATA "2. THE HUNGARIAN LIVES IN THE RED HOUSE."
1070 DATA "3. THE SPY IN THE THIRD HOUSE WEARS A GOATEE."
1080 DATA "4. THE POLE IS TRYING TO STEAL PLANS FOR A FRIGATE."
1090 DATA "5. THE CZECH IS ARMED WITH A RIFLE."
1100 DATA "6. THE RUSSIAN LIVES IN THE FIRST HOUSE."
1110 DATA "7. THE SPY WITH THE BOMB IS TRYING TO STEAL PLANS FOR A MISSILE."
1120 DATA "8. THE SPY WEARING THE BEARD IS ARMED WITH A SHOTGUN."
1130 DATA "9. THE SPY IN THE YELLOW HOUSE HAS A KNIFE."
1140 DATA "10. THE SPY WEARING SIDEBURNS LIVES IN THE YELLOW HOUSE."
1150 DATA "11. THE RUSSIAN LIVES NEXT DOOR TO THE BLUE HOUSE."
1160 DATA "12. THE BULGARIAN HAS A MUSTACHE."
1170 DATA "13. THE GREEN HOUSE IS IMMEDIATELY LEFT OF THE IVORY HOUSE."
1180 DATA "14. A KNIFE IS HIDDEN IN THE HOUSE NEXT TO THE SPY WHO IS"
1190 DATA "    TRYING TO STEAL PLANS FOR A RADAR."
1200 DATA "15. THE SPY TRYING TO STEAL PLANS FOR A BOMBER LIVES NEXT"
Ok


Ok
LIST 1210-
1210 DATA "    DOOR TO THE HOUSE WHERE A PISTOL IS HIDDEN."
1220 DATA "16. THE SPY TRYING TO STEAL PLANS FOR A BOMBER LIVES NEXT DOOR"
1230 DATA "    TO THE SPY TRYING TO STEAL PLANS FOR A RADAR."
1240 DATA "17. THE RED HOUSE IS ON THE BLUE HOUSE'S RIGHT."
1250 DATA "18. THE SPY TRYING TO STEAL A BOMBER LIVES IN THE GREEN HOUSE."
1260 DATA " --> WHICH SPY HAS LONG-HAIR?"
1270 DATA " --> WHO IS TRYING TO STEAL PLANS FOR A COMPUTER?"
1280 'THIS MODULE FRAMES A SCREEN
1290 CLS: FOR I=1 TO 80: PRINT"*";: NEXT I
1300 FOR I=2 TO 18: PRINT"*": NEXT I
1310 FOR I=1 TO 80: PRINT"*";: NEXT I
1320 FOR I=2 TO 18: LOCATE I,80: NEXT I
1330 RETURN
1340 'THIS MODULE ADVANCES THE PROGRAM
1350 LOCATE 21,20: INPUT">>TYPE <RETURN> OR <ENTER> TO CONTINUE "; X
1360 RETURN
Ok
```

FIGURE 2-24 (continued)

generator. The third and fourth were the gambling games Roulette and Wheel-of-Fortune. The fifth was a computer version of the board game Clue. The last was called Spy-catcher, and was included purely for your amusement. Incidentally, it was adapted from an Operation Research problem that used to be used at New York University to help cull Ph.D. candidates.

CHAPTER THREE

Random Numbers

We have seen that a sequence of random numbers is a necessary component of any probabilistic simulation. We have said that randomness implies that any number in the range of interest has an equal chance of appearing each time, and that the appearance of any number in no way affects the chance of that number or any other number's appearing. Technically, we say that random numbers must be uniformly distributed, and must not be serially correlated. When numbers follow some distribution other than a uniform one, such as the Poisson distribution, for example, they are properly spoken of as random variates, not random numbers.

TRUE RANDOM NUMBERS

Truly random numbers are the product of mechanical or electrical processes. Even then the producing system may favor some numbers more than others. Technically we say that the generator may be biased. This bias is the result of physical imperfections in the generator. For example, if we were to record the results of plays of a roulette wheel, we could produce a random sequence of the numbers from 00 to 36 provided the wheel were perfectly balanced; otherwise we would observe a bias in the sequence such that one or more numbers would tend to appear more often than others.

There are a lot of other fun ways to generate random-number sequences. Rolling a fair die will generate numbers in the range 1 to 6. A classical way to generate random-number sequences is the top-hat method. You take, say, 100 poker chips and mark each with a unique number from 0 to 99. Then shake them well in a tall silk hat or any convenient receptable and pull one out. Record the number, replace the chip, shake the hat, and draw again. It is slow going, but that is the way researchers laid the bases of the science of statistics in the eighteenth and nineteenth centuries.

In principle, you can generate a random-number sequence by randomly interrupting any uniform process; this is what happens when the ball falls into a slot as a roulette wheel begins to slow down. This exemplifies one of the modern methods for generating random numbers: You can use pulses from the decay of a radioactive isotope to open and close an electronic gate between an oscillator and a counter, then record the number of pulses that reach the counter while the gate is open.

PROGRAM TO GENERATE TRUE RANDOM NUMBERS

The following BASIC program lets you simulate a random-number generator on your personal computer:

```
10 CLS
20 FOR I = 1 TO 100
30 A$ = INKEY$: IF A$ = " " THEN 50
40 PRINT I
50 NEXT I
60 GOTO 20
```

Statements 20 and 50 generate the numbers from 1 to 100 at the rate of a million operations or more every second; statement 60 makes the counting repetitive. In statement 30, the program scans the keyboard (INKEY$), and stores the character currently being transmitted in storage location A$. If no character is being sent (that is, A$ = " " or null)), program control is transferred to the NEXT statement of the FOR-NEXT loop and counting continues. We can therefore regard the counting loop as a continuous process.

This process is interrupted whenever location A$ is found to contain any character. In this case, control is transferred to statement 40 and the program prints the current value of index I; that is, the value of the count when the counting process was interrupted. The act of striking a character on the keyboard can be regarded as a random process because of the great disparity in speed between manual typing and execution of the count loop. Figure 3–1 shows a screen full of random numbers generated this way.

Theoretically it is impossible to generate random numbers by any purely arithmetic process (algorithm) except one that calculates the value of an irrational

```
36  91  51   2  54   6  58   6  58   2  54   1  48  97  43  22  83  25  79  95  42
87  73  17   2  42  95  38  79  29  65   9  55  97  39  83  31  77  17  62   3
49  90  31  73  17  58   1  51  92  33  78  21  66   9  54   1  49  90  35  84
26  74  22  62  10  90  36  83  32  75  31  94  34  87  40   7  58   5  56   2
58  77  71  10  73  23  57   3  36  89  22  68   2  44 100  27  72  81  26  85
44  86   7  61  72  18  71  23  77  88  40  74  22  73  84  29  30  66  18  19
52  61  96  97  46  47  87  90  67   6  13  86  32  72   5  51  87  18  99  93
68  39  40  99  63  16  64  65  23  10  40  10  65  10  55  74  87 100  17
38  62  92  47  79  95   5  15  30  45  59  80  93  14  31  40  48  49  53  54
57  66  77  18  33  42  49  56  63  69  76   1  18  27  34  40  47  54  63  96
23  38  47  54  63  74  75  80  95   9  72  89   4  15  25  32  41  52  61  74
83   2  12  21  27  34  39  44  45  47  49  58  96  97   1  13  18  26  27  28
32  33  36  70  85  96  99   5  13  22  31  48  49  63  74  81  88  93   1   6
14  90  11  18  25  31  36  43  22  60  67  74  81  90  95  82  94   2  10  17
22  27  33  36  91  92  24  29  34  41  49  54  15  28  41  50  58  63  70  77
37  55  64  69  76  81  87  61  74  85  92  99   5  15  76  81  12  19  20  22
31  40   5  32  39  40  44  45  47  48  52  53  55  64  46  77  82  91 100   7
19   1  26  29  31  32  34  37  38  44  80  57  79  88  95   1   6  14  96  11
24  31  39  44  49  54  69  74  34  62  69  75  78  79  80  85  70  81  93  99
 3   8  13  87  20  28  29  34  40  22  41  48  55  61  66  71  46  65  79  84
88  92  63  86  93 100   4  10  15  18  26  82   6  13  26  32  39  46  13  28
35  42  48  53  58  65  31  32  53  62  71  78  85  64  75  83  92  99  80   1
26  27  31  40  32  45  56  65  72  76  96   2   4  10  19  26  35  44  52  65
76  23  72  23  82   7  41  10  42  71  99  43  77  56  75  90   1  17  30  64
```

```
Ok
LIST
10 ' PROGRAM TO GENERATE TRUE RANDOM NUMBERS
20 ' IN THE RANGE 1 TO 100
30 CLS: KEY OFF
40 FOR I = 1 TO 100
50 A$ = INKEY$: IF A$ = "" THEN 70
60 PRINT I;
70 NEXT I
80 GOTO 40
Ok
```

FIGURE 3–1 Program for generating true random numbers and a screen full of its product.

number, such as PI or the square root of two, to, say, a million or more decimal places.

Most arithmetic processes for generating random numbers are recursive in nature; the numbers in a so-called random sequence are generated by performing a predetermined set of operations on the last one selected. For this reason, it cannot be asserted that the numbers are truly independently chosen. Therefore, they are called pseudo- or false random numbers. However, everybody uses them as though they were truly random, and, as we shall see, many sequences of pseudorandom numbers pass the standard statistical tests for randomness.

Let's examine the random properties of the built-in BASIC function RND. RUN this program:

```
10 CLS: KEY OFF
20 RANDOMIZE TIME
30 FOR I = 1 TO 100
40 LOCATE INT(RND*25)+1, INT(RND*80)+1: PRINT "*";
```

```
50 NEXT I
60 IF X = 0 THEN 60
```

The first statement clears the screen and turns off the function-key menu in line 25 so the whole screen is available for display. Statement 20 seeds the random-number generator from the real-time clock. Statements 30 and 50 are a FOR-NEXT loop that will generate 100 random points.

Statement 40 selects the coordinates of a point on the 25-by-80-character matrix of the screen by generating two pseudorandom integers. Then it prints an asterisk at that point. Statement 60 is an infinite loop; it prevents the program from ending and therefore stops the BASIC interpreter from printing "OK" and spoiling the appearance of the display. To stop the program, simultaneously depress the keys SHIFT and BREAK/PAUSE.

There are 2,000 possible points in the character matrix. RUN the program with the limit of the FOR-NEXT loop set to 1,000 and observe how the matrix fills up. Figure 3–2 is a distribution of 100 random points. Figure 3–3 is a distribution of 1,000 points.

You can generate a denser matrix using your personal computer's graph-

FIGURE 3–2 Program for generating random dot patterns and a pattern containing 100 dots.

```
Ok
LIST
10 ' PROGRAM TO GENERATE 100 RANDOM DOTS
20 CLS: KEY OFF
30 RANDOMIZE TIME
40 FOR I = 1 TO 100
50 LOCATE INT(RND * 25) + 1, INT(RND * 80) + 1: PRINT "*";
60 NEXT I
70 IF X = 0 THEN 70
Ok
```

```
** ** ** *** ** ** * **     ***  *  ** * * * ** * ***
*** * ** * * * *** ** **  *  * ***  *  ** ** * *** ** * *
* ** *** * * * *** * ** **   ***  * *** * * **
** ** * * * * * * *** ** *** * * ** ** *
** * * * ** * * * ** ** ***** * * *** * ** * *
* ** ** * * * *** * * * * ** * *** * * **** *** *
** ** * * ** * ** * * ** *** * **** ** * ** *** * * ***
***** * * ** * * ** * ***** * ******* ** ** * ** *
****** *** ** ** ** * * * * * * ** ****  *
** *** * * ** ** * * * * *** * * * *** *** ** ** ***
** * ** ** * ** * * * ** * * ** * * * * * ** ***
* *** * **** * ** * *** ***** *** *** ** * * *
** * ** * * * ** * * **** ** * * * * * *** *
** **** * ** * * * ** * *** * * * * ** * *
* * *** * * * * * ** ** * * *** *** * **** * * **
*** ** * ** ** * * ***** * * * * * ** ** * ** * * * ** **
* ** ** *** * * ** *** ** * * ** * * ** **
* ** ** **** * ** ** **** * * *** ** * *
* * *** * * * ***** * * ** * * * * **** *** **** *  *
*** ** ** ** ** ** * *** * * *** * ** * *** * ** * *
*** ** * ** * * * ** * * *** * * * ** * * * *** *
*** *** * * * ** * ** ** ** * ** ** **** ** * **
* * * * ** ** ** * ***** * * * * * ** *
* * * * * * **** ** * * * * * ** * **** * *
* ** ** * ** * * * **** * *** * * *** * ** * * * ** *
```

```
Ok
LIST
10 ' PROGRAM TO GENERATE 1000 RANDOM DOTS
20 CLS: KEY OFF
30 RANDOMIZE TIME
40 FOR I = 1 TO 1000
50 LOCATE INT(RND * 25) + 1, INT(RND * 80) + 1: PRINT "*";
60 NEXT I
70 IF X = 0 THEN 70
Ok
```

FIGURE 3–3   Program for generating random dot patterns and a pattern containing 1,000
            dots.

ical capability. Unlike the 25-by-80–character matrix, the graphics matrix of the
TI/PC measures 300 by 720. RUN this program for 100, 1,000, and 10,000
points:

```
10 CLS: KEY OFF
20 RANDOMIZE TIME
30 INPUT "ENTER NUMBER OF POINTS: ", NUMBER
40 WHILE COUNT < NUMBER
50 COUNT = COUNT + 1: LOCATE 1,1
60 X = INT (RND*720) + 1: Y = INT (RND*300) + 1
70 PSET (X,Y)
80 WEND
100 PRINT NUMBER; "POINTS"
110 IF COUNT = NUMBER THEN 110
```

Statement 30 invites you to enter the number of points you want to display. Statements 40 and 80 are a WHILE-WEND loop that helps computer scientists avoid using the "infamous" GOTO. Graphic coordinates X and Y are selected at random, and statement 70 prints a small dot at the location selected.

Random pattern showing 100 dots created using the POINT X,Y command.

Random pattern showing 1,000 dots. The display matrix is 720 by 300.

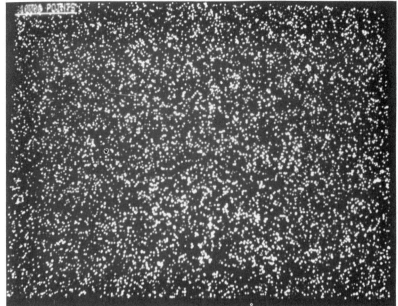

Random pattern showing 10,000 dots. The random coloring is achieved using the statement: COLOR INT (8*RND) + 1).

Pattern consisting of 100 randomly selected and colored graphics characters.

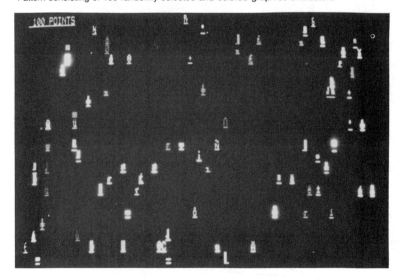

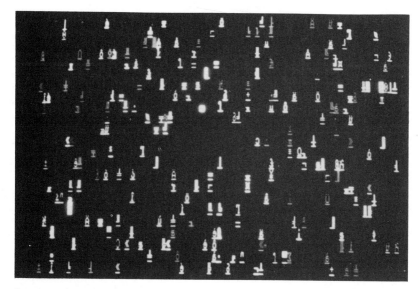

Pattern consisting of 300 random graphics characters. Character selection is made using the statement: PRINT CHR$(127 + INT(128*RND) + 1).

Pattern consisting of 1,000 random graphics characters. The display matrix is 80 by 25.

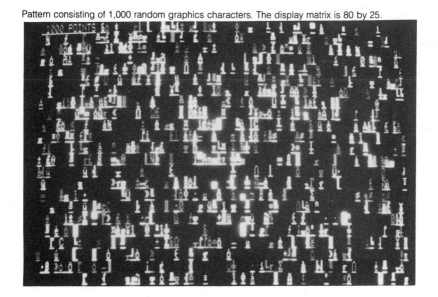

MID-SQUARE RANDOM-NUMBER GENERATOR

The first algorithm for generating pseudorandom numbers was the mid-square method. It was used in the mid-1950s, when the principal use of simulation was in designing thermonuclear weapons. It works this way: Take, say, a four-digit integer; multiply it by itself; chop off the two low-order digits and the two (at most) high-order digits. Report the resulting four-digit number as the first random number in the sequence, and use it to generate the next one.

This program implements the mid-square algorithm:

```
10 CLS: INPUT "ENTER 4-DIGIT SEED NUMBER"; S#
20 FOR I = 1 TO 100
30 X# = S# * S#
40 X# = INT(X# / 100)
50 X# = X# - INT(X# / 10000) * 10000: PRINT X#;
60 S# = X#
70 NEXT I
```

Statement 10 clears the screen and invites the user to type in a four-digit number as a "seed" to start the process. Statement 20 sets up a FOR-NEXT loop to generate 100 pseudorandom numbers. Statement 30 squares the seed; note that we are using double-precision arithmetic. If the seed were 2061, X# would now be equal to 4247721.

In statement 40 we remove the low-order digits, 21, by dividing by 100 and retaining the integer quotient. Statement 50 is a modulo or division-re-maindering operation employed to get rid of the high-order digit, 4. If there were two high-order digits in an eight-digit square (instead of one high-order digit in this seven-digit square), this operation would get rid of both of them. We divide 42477 by 10000, retaining the integer quotient of 4; multiply by 10000; and subtract 40000 from 42477, leaving the mid-square of 2477. This value is reported as the first random number in the sequence, and in statement 60 is set equal to S# in order to generate the second member of the sequence.

The problem with this pseudorandom-number generator (PNG) is that the sequence is very short—only 34 numbers, and then the mid-square degenerates to 0. With very few exceptions, mid-square sequences either degenerate to 0, converge on a constant (the seed 2500 never departs from that value), or cycle forever through a short loop (the seed 7777 ends up in the cycle 2100, 4100, 8100, 6100, . . .). Sequences that are usable—say, on the order of 100,000 or more numbers—can be created using longer seed numbers.

Figure 3–4 shows three degenerate mid-square sequences. The first degenerates to zero; the second degenerates to 7600; and the last degenerates to a repeating short cycle: 2100, 4100, 8100, and 6100.

```
ENTER A FOUR-DIGIT SEED NUMBER ? 2061
2477  1355  8360  8896  1388  9265  8402  5936  2360  5696  4444  7491  1150
3225  4006  480   2304  3084  5110  1121  2566  5843  1406  9768  4138  1230
5129  3066  4003  240   576   3317  24    5     0     0     0     0     0     0     0     0     0     0     0     0     0
0     0     0     0     0     0     0     0     0     0     0     0     0     0     0     0     0     0     0     0
0     0     0     0     0     0     0     0     0     0     0     0     0     0     0     0     0     0     0     0
0
Ok
```

```
ENTER A FOUR-DIGIT SEED NUMBER ? 1357
8414  7953  2502  2600  7600  7600  7600  7600  7600  7600  7600  7600  7600
7600  7600  7600  7600  7600  7600  7600  7600  7600  7600  7600  7600  7600
7600  7600  7600  7600  7600  7600  7600  7600  7600  7600  7600  7600  7600
7600  7600  7600  7600  7600  7600  7600  7600  7600  7600  7600  7600  7600
7600  7600  7600  7600  7600  7600  7600  7600  7600  7600  7600  7600  7600
7600  7600  7600  7600  7600  7600  7600  7600  7600  7600  7600  7600  7600
7600  7600  7600  7600  7600  7600  7600  7600  7600  7600  7600  7600  7600
7600  7600  7600  7600  7600  7600  7600  7600  7600
Ok
```

```
ENTER A FOUR-DIGIT SEED NUMBER ? 1379
9016  2882  3059  3574  7734  8147  3736  9576  6997  9580  7764  2796  8176
8469  7239  4031  2489  1951  8064  280   784   6146  7733  7992  8720  384
1474  1726  9790  8441  2504  2700  2900  4100  8100  6100  2100  4100  8100
6100  2100  4100  8100  6100  2100  4100  8100  6100  2100  4100  8100  6100
2100  4100  8100  6100  2100  4100  8100  6100  2100  4100  8100  6100  2100
4100  8100  6100  2100  4100  8100  6100  2100  4100  8100  6100  2100  4100
8100  6100  2100  4100  8100  6100  2100  4100  8100  6100  2100  4100  8100
6100  2100  4100  8100  6100  2100  4100  8100  6100
Ok
```

```
Ok
LIST
10 ' MID-SQUARE PSEUDO-RANDOM NUMBER GENERATOR
20 CLS: KEY OFF
30 INPUT " ENTER A FOUR-DIGIT SEED NUMBER "; S#
40 FOR I = 1 TO 100
50 X# = S# * S#
60 X# = INT(X# / 100)
70 X# = X# - INT(X# / 10000) * 10000
80 PRINT X#;
90 S# = X#
100 NEXT I
Ok
```

FIGURE 3–4 Mid-square generator program and examples of its output degenerating to
0, to 7600, and to a repeating short sub-set.

An acceptable mid-square generator for 35-bit mainframe computers is:

$$X(1) = (9653042877)^2 \pmod{67108864}/512$$

MULTIPLICATIVE CONGRUENTIAL (MC) GENERATORS

Today most pseudorandom-number generators use the multiplicative congruential algorithm, also called the method of power residues. You start with a prime
number to use as the modulus M (the divisor in a division-remaindering oper-

ation); a multiplier A that must be relatively prime to the modulus, and any seed X(0).

$$X(1) = A * X(0) \bmod M$$

By multiplying the seed by the multiplier and taking the remainder when divided by the modulus, you produce the first member of the pseudorandom sequence X(1), which is also the replacement for the seed in generating the next member.

To illustrate how this algorithm works, take 13 as the modulus, 2 as the multiplier, and 1 as the seed:

$$1 * 2 = 2 \bmod 13 = 2$$
$$2 * 2 = 4 \bmod 13 = 4$$
$$4 * 2 = 8 \bmod 13 = 8$$
$$8 * 2 = 16 \bmod 13 = 3$$
$$3 * 2 = 6 \bmod 13 = 6$$
$$6 * 2 = 12 \bmod 13 = 12$$
$$12 * 2 = 24 \bmod 13 = 11$$
$$11 * 2 = 22 \bmod 13 = 9$$
$$9 * 2 = 18 \bmod 13 = 5$$
$$5 * 2 = 10 \bmod 13 = 10$$
$$10 * 2 = 20 \bmod 13 = 7$$
$$7 * 2 = 14 \bmod 13 = 1$$

The cycle continues forever. What you have done is to shuffle the numbers from 1 to 12. You can never generate 0, nor can you generate 13. In this problem, the number 12 has a special name; it is called the Euler function. It is one less than the modulus. Of course, this sequence is very short; it is no better than the mid-square sequence. However, if the number chosen as the modulus is very large, the pseudorandom-number sequence acquires the properties of a true random-number sequence.

FULL-PERIOD MC GENERATORS

To get a full cycle of M-1 pseudorandom numbers, the multiplier A must be a primitive (prime) root of the modulus. Primitive roots of large numbers are not that easy to find. The definition of a primitive root is circular: A primitive root is a number that, when used as a multiplier in a pseudorandom-number generator, produces a sequence of length M-1 without repetition.

The important parameters are the multiplier A and the modulus M. The seed X(0) is not important, because the sequence can begin at any point. One of the earliest generators used A = 23 and M = 2^35 + 1 (34,359,738,369). The problem with this generator is that it has high first-order serial autocorrelation, as do all MC generators with low values of A; the value should be on the order of the square root of M.

With 36-bit mainframe computers such as the DEC System 10, the values are: A = 3125 and M = 2^35 − 31 (34,359,738,337). The modulus is the largest prime number less than the value of a full-length register filled with ones.

With 32-bit mainframe computers such as the IBM System 370/30XX models, the values are A = 16807 and M = 2^31 − 1 (2,147,483,647).

Other values that have been used are: A = 7^11 (366,714,004) and M = 2^29 + 1 (536,790,913); and A = 13^13 (455,470,314) and M = 2^31 − 1 (2,147,483,647).

PARTIAL-PERIOD MC GENERATORS

If you can't find a suitable primitive root, you can use a multiplicative congruential generator with the following specifications:

M = 2^L where L is the full length of a computer register in bits
A = 8*K + or − 3 where L is any integer, and
A is approximately equal to the square root of M.

Unfortunately, this is not a full-period generator. If you start with an even seed, you will produce no odd numbers and your cycle length will only be M/8. If you start with an odd seed, you will produce no even numbers and your cycle length will be M/4.

MIXED MULTIPLICATIVE CONGRUENTIAL (MMC) GENERATORS

You can improve things by using a mixed multiplicative generator:

X(1) = X(0)*A + C (mod M)

where C is any prime less than or equal to A (usually 1); and

A = 4*K + 1 and 2^T + 1

where K is any integer and T is any integer >= 2.

The MMC generator produces a sequence of length M. Its first-order (Pearson product-moment) serial autocorrelation for pairs can be found from:

$$rho = (1/A) - (6*C)/(A*M) * (1 - (C/M) + or - (A/M)$$

so keep C small and A on the order of the square root of M. For both these generators, serial autocorrelation for triples is bad.

ARITHMETIC CONGRUENTIAL GENERATOR

Another kind of PNG is the arithmetic congruential generator. Here:

$$X(L+1) = X(L-1) + X(L) (mod M)$$

Just start with two random integers, add them to get the third number, add the third number to the second to get the fourth, and so on. The cycle length (also called "period") is $K*2^{(L-1)}$ where K is some integer. The serial autocorrelation can be quite high for high-order lags (see page 115).

SHIFT REGISTER GENERATORS

A digital circuit known as a maximal-length linear-shift register (MLLSR) can be used as a PNG. However, I have found that it tends to produce sequences with extremely high first-order serial autocorrelation.

A 34-stage MLLSR employs feedback that XORs stages 1, 8, 33, and 34. It generates a sequence of 17,179,869,183 pseudorandom numbers.

SUMMARY OF PN GENERATORS

In summary, the best PNG is a multiplicative one that uses a primitive root of the modulus as a multiplier. Preferably, the multiplier should be on the order of the square root of the modulus (to minimize first-order serial autocorrelation). Most built-in pseudorandom-number-generating functions use at least two generators: one fills a matrix (two-way table) with random numbers; the other (maybe two) makes random selections from the table. Some computers have hardware generators. They operate on the principle of random pulses gating a high-frequency oscillator into a pulse counter. Some don't use radioactive isotopes as the source of the random pulses because these substances may be expensive and dangerous. They may use fluorescent tubes or heating elements.

This program uses the 3125/34359738337 multiplier/modulus combination, which is used on some 36-bit-word mainframes, such as the Digital Equipment Corporation's System 10:

```
10 CLS: INPUT "ENTER SEED"; SEED#
20 M# = 34359738337
30 A# = 3125#
40 FOR I = 1 TO 100
50 R# = SEED# * A# - INT(SEED# * A# / M#) * M#
60 N = R# / (M# - 1): PRINT USING " .######;"; N;
70 SEED# = R#
80 NEXT I
```

Statement 10 clears the screen and invites the user to enter a seed number. The seed determines the starting place in the pseudorandom-number sequence; any number will do.

Statements 20 and 30 insert the modulus and multiplier as double precision constants. Statements 40 and 80 set up a FOR-NEXT loop to generate 100 random numbers. In statement 50, the seed is multiplied by the multiplier. The operation of division-remaindering is performed as was done in the mid-square algorithm, and in statement 70 the seed is set to the value of the first number generated in order to generate the next number. Statement 60 differs from our presentation of the mid-square algorithm. The 100 random numbers are printed out, ten to a line, in conventional format: as six-place decimals normalized by dividing each member of the sequence by the Euler function (Modulus − 1). Figure 3–5 shows the results of using a multiplicative congruential pseudorandom-number generator.

TESTING GENERATORS FOR RANDOMNESS

We are going to use two classical tests for randomness to compare the 3125/34359738337 multiplicative congruential algorithm with the RND function built into the MS/BASIC subsystem. The first test is to determine whether or not the numbers of a sequence are uniformly distributed; that is, whether every number has an equal chance of being chosen.

The second test is for serial autocorrelation between adjacent pairs of numbers; it tells whether or not the appearance of one number affects the chance of another one's appearing next. There are many other tests for randomness. Sometimes the serial autocorrelation test is set up so that instead of just comparing adjacent pairs of numbers, it will compare numbers separated by 1, 2, 3, . . . up to as many as 19 or more intervening numbers. I have found these two tests to be sufficient for most practical purposes.

```
ENTER SEED ? 123456
 .011228 .088306 .955081 .629462 .068434 .857208 .776229 .715801 .877917 .490802
 .754903 .071632 .850283 .135462 .320145 .454036 .863225 .577546 .831027 .959469
 .339908 .212226 .205684 .762764 .636415 .796255 .296088 .274326 .268745 .828392
 .725263 .448245 .765677 .740735 .795419 .685180 .186833 .853124 .012863 .197943
 .572156 .986003 .258166 .767215 .546305 .202271 .096487 .521574 .919491 .410011
 .283204 .012213 .164945 .452377 .679077 .116470 .968026 .080498 .555942 .317285
 .514288 .150914 .605853 .291953 .351931 .784508 .586355 .358842 .381479 .121532
 .787007 .396028 .587635 .360379 .185580 .937993 .228644 .513522 .757292 .537442
 .506254 .043098 .680897 .801541 .816710 .217307 .083165 .889571 .909959 .622918
 .617811 .658809 .776566 .769411 .409323 .134698 .931324 .388593 .351809 .403120
Ok
```

```
Ok
LIST
10 ' MULTIPLICATIVE CONGRUENTIAL PSEUDO-RANDOM NUMBER GENERATOR
20 CLS: KEY OFF
30 INPUT "ENTER SEED "; SEED#
40 '
50 ' BUILT-IN GENERATOR
60 M#=34359738337#
70 A#=3125#
80 '
90 FOR I = 1 TO 100
100 R# = SEED# * A# - INT(SEED# * A# / M#) * M#
110 N = R# / (M# - 1): PRINT USING " .######"; N;
120 SEED# = R#
130 NEXT I
Ok
```

FIGURE 3-5 Multiplicative congruential generator and an example of its output.

Uniformity Test

The test for uniformity generates 500 numbers in the range from zero to one. (If you are wondering how a multiplicative congruential generator can possibly produce the value zero, it would be a very low number that rounds off to zero in the sixth decimal place.) It classifies the numbers as to whether they are less than or equal to 1/10, less than or equal to 1/5, 3/10, 2/5, 1/2, 3/5, 7/10, 4/5, 9/10, or 1. Then it plots a bar chart, or histogram, by printing an asterisk for each number in each class. If the 500 numbers generated were distributed among these 10 classes with perfect uniformity, there would be 50 asterisks in each of the 10 bars.

Test Evaluation by Chi-Squared

When comparing two generators, it is convenient to use a single number that captures the essence of the histogram. One such number is the statistic called chi-square. This is computed by subtracting the number of asterisks in each bar from the number we expect will be there (that is, 50), squaring the difference, adding the results from each of the ten bars, and dividing the sum of squares by the expectation (50). There are tables of chi-square that will tell us how good our results are. The acceptable value of chi-square for a given test depends upon the number of classes (expressed as "degrees of freedom") and the confidence we wish to place in our results. A test like this has 9 (10 classes minus 1) degrees of freedom; and at the 95 percent level of confidence (that means there will be 1 chance in 20 that our results are wrong) the acceptable value of chi-square is 16.9.

In our program, statement 10 sets up a ten-component array to hold the count of numbers in each class. Statement 20 obtains a seed from the computer's real-time clock. Statements 30 and 140 establish a FOR-NEXT loop that generates 500 random numbers. Statement 40 branches to a subroutine that generates a random number. Statements 60 to 80 constitute a FOR-NEXT loop that classifies each random number into one of the ten groups. Statements 100 to 160 display the results. Statements 120 to 140 are a FOR-NEXT loop that prints the asterisks of each bar. Statement 150 is a FOR-NEXT loop that calculates the value of chi-square.

Figure 3–6 shows the frequency distribution of pseudorandom numbers produced by a multiplicative congruential generator and a listing of the 28 statements of the analysis program.

When we compared the RND and MC generators, we found that both generators produced a relatively flat or uniform distribution; from a statistical point of view, anything better would be suspect. The value of chi-square is 4.12 for the algorithm and 3.76 for the built-in generator; both are well below the criterion value of 16.9. One could jump to the conclusion that the built-in generator is better than the algorithm. Figure 3–7 displays the results of this test.

In fact, we don't yet have enough evidence for such a conclusion in this test alone. However, I have run a large number of tests and the built-in generator always produces the lower value of chi-squared. However, the test for uniformity is only a necessary test for randomness, not a sufficient one. The sequence .1, .2, .3, .4, .5, .6, .7, .8, .9, 1, . . . would produce a perfectly flat distribution whose value of chi-square would be 0. It could hardly be regarded as a sequence of random numbers.

Maximum Test

Here's an interesting point: If you divide the sequence into groups of two numbers, three numbers, . . . or N numbers, select the largest number in each group, and multiply it by itself as many times as there are numbers in the group, the resulting sequence of numbers should be uniformly distributed. This test works not just for numbers but for their individual digits as well if the underlying sequence is truly random.

```
                    ***** DISTRIBUTION OF RANDOM NUMBERS *****

R<+ .1 ************************************************

R<+ .2 *********************************************************

R<+ .3 ********************************-*-************************

R<+ .4 **********************************************************

R<+ .5 ************************************

R<+ .6 **************************************************

R<+ .7 **********************************

R<+ .8 **********************************************************

R<+ .9 *****************************************************

R<+ 1 ***************************************
CHI SQUARED= 12.96
Ok

Ok
LIST -190
10 DIM C(10)
20 SEED#=TIME
30 FOR J=1 TO 500
40 GOSUB 180
50 X=N
60 FOR I=1 TO 10
70 IF X<=(I/10) THEN C(I)=C(I)+1:GOTO 90
80 NEXT I
90 NEXT J
100 CLS
110 LOCATE 1,19: PRINT "***** DISTRIBUTION OF RANDOM NUMBERS *****"
120 FOR I=1 TO 10
130 LOCATE 1+I*2,1: PRINT "R<+"I/10;: FOR J=1 TO C(I): PRINT "*";: NEXT J
140 NEXT I
150 FOR I=1 TO 10: CHI.SQ=CHI.SQ+(C(I)-50)*(C(I)-50)/50: NEXT I
160 LOCATE 22,1: PRINT "CHI SQUARED="CHI.SQ
170 END
180 M#=34359738337#
190 A#=3125#
Ok

Ok
LIST 200-
200 ' ***********************************************************
210 ' TRY THESE A:M PAIRS:
220 ' 23:34359738369  3125:34359738337  16807:2147483647
230 ' 366714004:536790913  455470314:2147483647
240 ' ***********************************************************
250 R#=SEED#*A#-INT(SEED#*A#/M#)*M#
260 N=R#/(M#-1)
270 SEED#=R#
280 RETURN
Ok
```

FIGURE 3-6 Program for plotting the frequency distribution of pseudo-random numbers and calculating chi-squared for its goodness-of-fit to a uniform distribution; with an example of its output.

```
          ***** DISTRIBUTION OF RANDOM NUMBERS *****
R<+ .1 **********************************************************************
R<+ .2 *****************************************************
R<+ .3 *********************************************
R<+ .4 ***************************************************
R<+ .5 **********************************************
R<+ .6 ************************************************
R<+ .7 ***********************************************
R<+ .8 ****************************************************
R<+ .9 **********************************************
R<+ 1 **************************************************
CHI SQUARED= 4.12
Ok


          ***** DISTRIBUTION OF RANDOM NUMBERS *****
R<+ .1 ***************************************************
R<+ .2 *****************************************
R<+ .3 *************************************************
R<+ .4 *********************************************************
R<+ .5 ***************************************************
R<+ .6 ************************************************
R<+ .7 **************************************************
R<+ .8 **********************************************
R<+ .9 ******************************************************
R<+ 1 *************************************************
CHI SQUARED= 3.76
Ok
```

FIGURE 3–7 Comparative results of tests for uniformity on a multiplicative congruential generator, and the built-in BASIC random-number function.

TESTING GENERATORS FOR AUTOCORRELATION

If we were to generate the sequence of numbers 1, 2, 3, 4, 5, 6, 7, 8, 9, 0, 1, 2, . . . , it would easily pass the test for uniformity even though the numbers are far from random. The reason they are not random is that they are not independent. The appearance of one number—say, 1—means that the next number will be 2, and so on. We call this defect "serial autocorrelation" of adjacent pairs of numbers.

The test for serial autocorrelation is a more rigorous one than the test for uniformity. In its classical form the test makes use of a 10 by 10 matrix (checkerboard). The rows and columns both represent the classifications 1/10,

1/5, ... 9/10, 1, as used in the uniformity test. However, the rows will contain the counts of the first member of each overlapping pair of random numbers; the columns will contain the counts of the second member of each pair. For example, if the first number of a pair is .42 and the second number is .68, the count stored in the cell found at the intersection of the fifth row and the seventh column would be increased by one. Displaying the results as a histogram would demand 100 bars, one for each square of the checkerboard.

Since we can't display 100 bars on a 25-by-80 screen, we have made some simplifications in this test. We use only three classifications: less than or equal to 1/3, less than or equal to 2/3, and less than or equal to 1. Thus we can get by with only 9 bars instead of 100. We shall generate 396 numbers, providing for an expectation of 44 asterisks in each bar. (We want a short bar because the legend is long, since it has to express both the row and column limits.)

Figure 3–8 lists the analysis program for serial autocorrelation and shows the results of a test on an MC generator.

In the program, statement 10 obtains the seed of the random number generator from the real-time clock; lines 320 to 420 are the random-number generator; statements 110–120 and 120–130 call it to get a pair of random numbers. Statements 20–50 and 290–310 set up and label the histogram display.

Statements 50 and 250 set up a FOR-NEXT loop that will generate, classify, and print histograms of 396 pairs of random numbers. Statements 80–100 are a FOR-NEXT loop that classifies the first member of each random-number pair into one of three equal classes. Statements 130–140 do the same for the second member of the pair. Statements 90, 140, and 160 map the three-by-three checkerboard into a linear histogram of nine bars in which R1 cycles through all three classes while R2 advances in value 1/3 for each cycle of R1. Statements 170–190 are a FOR-NEXT loop that counts the pairs in the nine

FIGURE 3–8 Program for plotting the results of the checkerboard test for serial autocorrelation and calculating chi-squared; with an example of its output.

```
LIST -210
10 SEED#=TIME
20 FOR I=1 TO 9: READ K$(I): NEXT I
30 FOR I=1 TO 9: READ L$(I): NEXT I
40 FOR I=1 TO 3: READ M(I): NEXT I
50 FOR I=1 TO 396
60 GOSUB 300
70 X=N
80 FOR J=1 TO 3
90 IF X<=J/3 THEN C1=J: GOTO 110
100 NEXT J
110 GOSUB 300
120 X=N
130 FOR J=1 TO 3
140 IF X<=J/3 THEN C2=M(J): GOTO 160
150 NEXT J
160 IX=C1+C2-1
170 FOR K=1 TO 9
180 IF K=IX THEN C(K)=C(K)+1
190 NEXT K
200 NEXT I
210 CLS: LOCATE 2,16: PRINT "***** RANDOM NUMBER SERIAL AUTOCORRELATION *****"
Ok
```

```
LIST 220-
220 FOR I=1 TO 9
230 LOCATE 2+I*2,1: PRINT "R1<="K$(I)" AND R2 <="L$(I)" ";
240 FOR J=1 TO C(I): PRINT "*";:NEXT J
250 NEXT I
260 FOR I=1 TO 9: CHI.SQ=CHI.SQ+(C(I)-44)*(C(I)-44)/44: NEXT I
270 PRINT: PRINT "CHI SQUARED="CHI.SQ
280 END
290 DATA ".33",".67","1.0",".33",".67","1.0",".33",".67","1.0"
300 DATA ".33",".33",".33",".67",".67",".67","1.0","1.0","1.0"
310 DATA 1,4,7
320 M#=34359738337#
330 A#=3125#
340 ' ****************************************************************
350 ' TRY THESE A:M PAIRS:
360 ' 23:34359738369  3125:34359738337  16807:2147483647
370 ' 366714004:536790913  455470314:2147483647
380 ' ****************************************************************
390 R#=SEED#*A#-INT(SEED#*A#/M#)*M#
400 N=R#/(M#-1)
410 SEED#=R#
420 RETURN
Ok
```

```
              ***** RANDOM NUMBER SERIAL AUTOCORRELATION *****

R1<=.33 AND R2 <=.33 *****************************************

R1<=.67 AND R2 <=.33 ****************************************

R1<=1.0 AND R2 <=.33 *****************************************

R1<=.33 AND R2 <=.67 ******************************************

R1<=.67 AND R2 <=.67 *****************************

R1<=1.0 AND R2 <=.67 ************************************************

R1<=.33 AND R2 <=1.0 *****************************************

R1<=.67 AND R2 <=1.0 ********************************************************

R1<=1.0 AND R2 <=1.0 ***************************************
CHI SQUARED= 10.18182
Ok
```

FIGURE 3–8 (continued)

classes, while statements 230 and 240 print the bars. Statements 260 and 270 calculate and display the value of chi-squared.

In this example there are nine minus two, or seven, degrees of freedom (because there are two variables, R1 and R2, instead of just R, as in the last test). The criterion value of chi-squared for seven degrees of freedom and 95 percent confidence is 14.1. The value for the sequence produced by the algorithm is 5.23, while the value for the built-in generator is 9.68; both are comfortably within acceptable limits. Usually I find the built-in generator does better than the algorithm, but this is a statistical test, and some variation is to be expected. Figure 3–9 displays the results of this test.

In some cases you may want to test for serial autocorrelation of pairs of numbers separated by one or more intervening numbers, which are called "lags."

```
         ***** RANDOM NUMBER SERIAL AUTOCORRELATION *****

R1 <=.33 AND R2 <=.33 ******************************************

R1 <=.67 AND R2 <=.33 *****************************************

R1 <=1.0 AND R2 <=.33 ***********************************

R1 <=.33 AND R2 <=.67 **************************************************

R1 <=.67 AND R2 <=.67 **************************************

R1 <=1.0 AND R2 <=.67 *********************************************

R1 <=.33 AND R2 <=1.0 ****************************************

R1 <=.67 AND R2 <=1.0 ****************************************

R1 <=1.0 AND R2 <=1.0 **********************************************
CHI SQUARED= 5.227273
Ok



         ***** RANDOM NUMBER SERIAL AUTOCORRELATION *****

R1 <=.33 AND R2 <=.33 *****************************************

R1 <=.67 AND R2 <=.33 **********************************

R1 <=1.0 AND R2 <=.33 *************************************************

R1 <=.33 AND R2 <=.67 ****************************

R1 <=.67 AND R2 <=.67 ****************************************

R1 <=1.0 AND R2 <=.67 **************************************************

R1 <=.33 AND R2 <=1.0 **********************************************

R1 <=.67 AND R2 <=1.0 ************************************

R1 <=1.0 AND R2 <=1.0 **********************************************
CHI SQUARED= 9.681818
Ok
```

FIGURE 3-9 Comparative results of tests for serial autocorrelation on a multiplicative congruential generator and the built-in BASIC random-number function.

The sequence: 1, 5, 2, 8, 3, 7, 4, 1, 5, 7, 6, 0, 7, 5, 8, 4, 9, 2, 0, . . . illustrates serial-autocorrelation lag one. Tests can be made of serial autocorrelation of overlapping pairs lag 0, 1, 2, . . . 19, 20, and even more. Moreover, tests can also be made for serial autocorrelation of overlapping triples; here we would require a matrix with $10 \times 10 \times 10$, or 1,000, cells.

RUNS TESTING

Another family of tests looks at runs of numbers in a random sequence. A run is a sequence of one or more numbers that does something specific. There are two kinds of runs of interest in testing numbers for randomness: runs up or down, and runs above and below the median. The sequence: 7, 2, 5, 8, 3 contains a run-up of three numbers. The sequence: 2, 6, 8, 7, 4 contains a run above the median (that is, 5) of three numbers. The science of combinatorics tells us how many runs of each kind we may expect to find in a sequence of numbers that are truly random.

The expected number of runs of length K in a sequence of length N is given by:

$$EX = [2/(K+3)] * [N*(K\hat{}2 + 3*K+1) - (K\hat{}3 + 3*K\hat{}2 - K - 4)]$$

as long as K is $<=$ N $-$ 2. The expected number of runs of length N $-$ 1 is 2/N!

In a sequence of 1,000 random numbers we may expect to find:

417 runs of 1
183 runs of 2
 53 runs of 3
 11 runs of 4
  2 runs of 5
  1 run of 6 or more

We should expect that half of each group would be runs above the median, and half would be runs below the median. Similarly, we should expect half to be runs-up, and half to be runs-down. A run of length 1 is regarded as a run-up when it terminates a run-down; and as a run-down when it terminates a run-up.

POKER TEST

Not only can we test the numbers of the sequence; we can also test the digits comprising these numbers. One of these tests involves regarding every sequence of five digits as a poker hand: 77059 would be a pair; 44881 would be two pair; 33327 would be three-of-a-kind; 55533 would be a full house; and 99992 would be four-of-a-kind. Unlike real poker, five-of-a-kind is an acceptable, albeit rare, hand (and not a fight). The order of the "cards" within a "hand" is unimportant; we disregard straights, and there are no flushes or royals. Combinatorists can predict how many hands of each kind should occur in a perfectly random sequence. Of course, gamblers were able to do this long before combinatorists even knew they were combinatorists.

In 10,000 random and independent (not overlapping groups of five digits each) poker hands, you may expect to find:

3,024 with five different digits
5,040 pairs
1,080 two-pairs
  720 three-of-a-kinds

90 full houses
45 four-of-a-kinds
1 five-of-a-kind

GAP TEST

Another test for the randomness of the digits making up our numbers is the gap test. We take each of the ten digit types 0 to 9 at a time and go through a sample of our supposedly random sequence (say, 1,000 numbers) and count the digits that intervene between each appearance of the digit we are testing; in other words, we count the gaps between zeros, ones, twos, . . . nines. For example, when looking at nines: 99 is a gap of 0; 92472159 is a gap of 6. Combinatorists can tell us how many gaps of each length we can expect to find in a given-sized sample of numbers if the digits are in fact random.

In 1,000 gaps, we should expect to find:

271 gaps of 0, 1, or 2
198 gaps of 3, 4, or 5
144 gaps of 6, 7, or 8
105 gaps of 9, 10, or 11
86 gaps of 12, 13, or 14
56 gaps of 15, 16, or 17
41 gaps of 18, 19, or 20
29 gaps of 21, 22, or 23
22 gaps of 24, 25, or 26
16 gaps of 27, 28, or 29
11 gaps of 30, 31, or 32
9 gaps of 33, 34, or 35
6 gaps of 36, 37, or 38
4 gaps of 39, 40, or 41
3 gaps of 42, 43, or 44
3 gaps of 45, 46, or 47
1 gap of 48, 49, or 50

Of course the expected frequencies of the lengths of gap are the same for all digits.

YULE TEST

Another test for the randomness of the digits of a number is the Yule test (which has nothing to do with Christmas holidays). Add up the four least significant digits of 5,000 numbers. The sums will range in value from 0 to 36. The expected occurrence frequencies of the possible sums (for chi-squared testing) are:

Sum	Occurrences	Sum	Occurrences
0	1	19	330
1	2	20	316
2	5	21	296
3	10	22	270
4	17	23	240
5	28	24	207
6	42	25	174
7	60	26	141
8	83	27	110
9	110	28	83
10	141	29	60
11	174	30	42
12	208	31	28
13	240	32	17
14	270	33	10
15	296	34	5
16	316	35	2
17	330	36	1
18	335		

BIT-WISE TESTING

Tests for uniformity, correlation, and digit randomness can be combined by regarding a sample of a random-number sequence as a bit matrix measuring 32-by-10,000. There are four tests: (1) longitudinal count of ones, (2) longitudinal count of overlapping pairs of ones and zeros, (3) lateral count of pairs of ones and zeros in adjacent columns, and (4) lateral count of ones and zeros in columns separated by a column. These tests are used in Europe on one-time-tape cryptographic aids.

We shall illustrate with a sequence of ten numbers in the range 0 to 31.

NUMBER	16	8	4	2	1
27	1	1	0	1	1
12	0	1	1	0	0
28	1	1	1	0	0
3	0	0	0	1	1
23	1	0	1	1	1
31	1	1	1	1	1
20	1	0	1	0	0
9	0	1	0	0	1
26	1	1	0	1	0
1	0	0	0	0	1

1. The longitudinal counts of ones are: $16 = 6$, $8 = 6$, $4 = 5$, $2 = 5$, and $1 = 6$. For the complete test the counts should lie between 4,950 and 5,050.

2. The longitudinal counts of $1-1$ and $0-0$ pairs are: $16=2$, $8=4$, $4=5$, $2=4$, and $1=3$. For the complete test the counts should lie between 4,900 and 5,100.

3. The lateral counts of $1-1$ and $0-0$ pairs in adjacent columns are: $1-2=7$, $2-4=4$, $4-8=5$, $8-16=6$, and $16-1=4$. For the complete test all lateral counts should lie between 4,800 and 5,200.

4. The lateral counts of $1-1$ and $0-0$ pairs in columns lagged 1 are: $1-4=3$, $2-8=5$, $4-16=7$, and $16-2=7$.

SUMMARY

In this chapter we have discussed the concept of randomness and described some ways true random numbers can be produced. One of these, randomly interrupting a counting loop by signals from the computer keyboard, was presented as a computer program.

We explained the difference between true random numbers and pseudorandom numbers produced by algorithms. We presented a program implementing the mid-square algorithm, which was the first technique used, and pointed out the deficiencies of this method.

Finally, we presented a program for generating random numbers by the multiplicative congruential algorithm and a table of acceptable multipliers and moduli. We showed two tests for randomness: one for goodness of fit to a uniform distribution and the other for absence of serial autocorrelation. These tests present their results graphically, in the form of histograms, and by calculating the chi-square statistic. We used these tests to compare a popular algorithm with the built-in MS/BASIC RND function. The results strongly suggest that it is not worthwhile to program your own pseudorandom-number generator. The built-in function does as well if not better.

We also presented without examples some of the more esoteric tests for randomness, including tests not just for the randomness of numbers in a sequence but also for the randomness of the digits making up the individual numbers.

CHAPTER FOUR

Time-Oriented Simulation

An important use of computer simulation programs is in studying the dynamics of waiting-line queues. (The application is the *waiting line*: the *queue* is a specific data structure.) Waiting-line queues are often observed in real life. One example would be a line of people waiting to buy airline tickets; another, a line of cars stopped for a red traffic light; or a line of television sets in a repair shop waiting for attention from the technicians.

There are many other applications for simulation; a sampling of these is presented in Chapter Ten. However, applications of simulation to queuing systems are useful from a tutorial point of view for three reasons: (1) Many complex systems contain queues as subsystems. (2) A queue is a simple system, in which the dynamics of simulation are clearly evident. (3) Some queuing systems have analytic solutions, so the accuracy of a simulation can be assessed.

The components of a waiting-line queue are:

1. A population from which customers are drawn
2. The waiting-line queue itself
3. The service facility
4. A population into which customers return

Two attributes determine the properties of a waiting-line queue: arrival rate and service rate. The arrival rate is the average number of customers who join the waiting line per second, minute, hour, or whatever unit of time is convenient. The service rate is the average number of customers who are served per unit time in the service facility. Another way to express these attributes is by their reciprocals: the average time between customer arrivals, and the average service time.

One reason for studying a waiting-line queue is to determine the loading on the service facility. If the service facility is idle too much of the time, the facility is uneconomical and may be redundant where alternative facilities are available.

Back in 1920, an engineer named Erlang studied waiting-line queues of telephone calls in Copenhagen, Denmark. He found that the ideal loading on the telephone-switching facility was to be busy 70 percent of the time; it's a compromise between customer disaffection caused by too much waiting and unwarranted spending for additional facilities. In the telephone-switching model at 70 percent loading, customers are seldom unable to get a dial tone when they want to use the phone.

Installation of resources to bring loading lower—say, to zero—would not benefit the customer. The cost of these resources would eventually be passed on to the customer, who would derive little or no benefit from them.

Another reason for studying waiting lines is to determine the average length of the queue. A knowledge of the average, or maximum, length of a queue is necessary to provide adequate waiting rooms for travelers and medical patients, large enough toll plazas in front of tunnels and bridges for waiting lines of cars, and sufficient storage space for equipment awaiting repair.

The length of waiting lines is important to business. Too long a waiting line may discourage prospective customers. The absence of a waiting line may suggest that the service offered is not worth waiting for.

The time a customer has to wait in line is another matter of concern. If the waiting time is excessive, the service facility may lose business to facilities that can offer service more promptly. Even if the waiting line is composed of employees rather than customers, such as the lines that form at tool cribs or copying machines, the lines are undesirable because the time the employees spend waiting is unproductive. It may be desirable in a study to separate the waiting time spent in line from that spent in the service facility, since the service time may be unavoidable even if service facilities were to be duplicated to such an extent that nobody had to queue up at all.

To make a study complete, you will have to account for all of the arrivals: those who have been served, the one(s) left in the service facility at the end of the study, and those still waiting in line at the end of the study.

There are two kinds of waiting-line simulation programs: time-oriented and event-oriented. The time-oriented simulation examines the system during sequential equal slices of time. The event-oriented simulation examines only major events, especially arrivals, and jumps over the time between them. This chapter will deal with time-oriented simulations.

The programming logic behind time-oriented simulations is easier to understand than the logic of event-oriented simulations. However, the slice of time must be sufficiently short that the events occurring within it can be regarded as happening simultaneously. This means that the program may have to cycle unproductively most of the time, especially if customers tend to arrive in bunches.

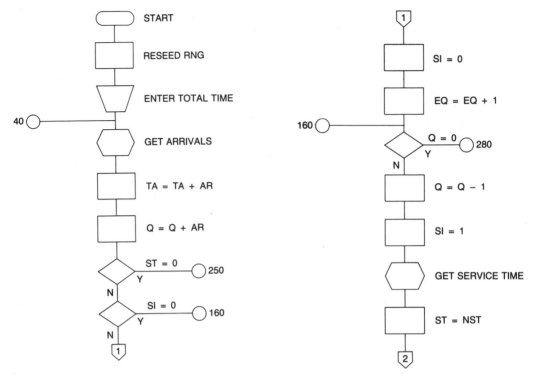

FIGURE 4–1 Logic flow chart of a time-oriented simulation.

PROGRAM LOGIC

Figure 4–1 is the logic flow chart of a time-oriented simulation program. Figure 4–2 is a listing of the 39 statements of the program.

After reseeding the random-number generator, the program asks the user to enter the total number of time units to be simulated. It then establishes an all-encompassing FOR-NEXT loop that will execute as many iterations as the user selected, one for each unit of time.

Now the program calls the arrival generator to see how many customers arrive during the current time unit ("Get Arrivals"). We shall discuss the problems associated with arrival and service-time generators in Chapter Six. The number of arrivals is returned from the arrival generator in a field called AR-RIVALS and is added to a field called TOTAL.ARRIVALS.

The ARRIVALS are then figuratively placed on the waiting-line queue by adding them to a field called QUEUE ("Put Arrivals on Work Queue").

We test to see whether a customer is currently receiving service ("Test for Service Complete"). The service time to be received by the current customer is stored in a field called SERVICE.TIME, which is decremented one unit each

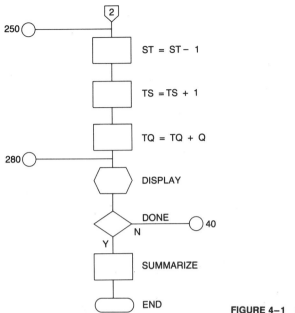

FIGURE 4–1 (continued)

time the program executes an iteration until it is equal to zero. If SERV-ICE.TIME is greater than zero, it means that a customer is currently receiving service.

If SERVICE.TIME is determined to be greater than zero, control is transferred to statement 250, SERVICE-TIME is decremented one time unit, and TOTAL.SERVICE.TIME is incremented by one time unit. All customers in the QUEUE remain there; and QUEUE is added to TOTAL.QUEUE, which is the total number of time units spent in the waiting line by all customers who had to wait. Then the program branches to the "Display Results" subroutine, which depicts what transpired during the iteration, which then terminates.

If SERVICE.TIME is equal to zero, a test is performed to see whether a customer who has been served is still in the service facility ("Test for Service Just Completed"). This test involves seeing if the SERVICE.INDICATOR is equal to one or zero. If it is equal to one, meaning a customer has just completed service and is still in the service facility, two things are done: The SERV-ICE.INDICATOR is reset to zero, and the EXIT.QUEUE is incremented by one, effectively removing the customer from the service facility. If the SERV-ICE.INDICATOR is equal to zero, the program skips around the two previous statements and goes directly to statement 160 ("Fill the Service Facility").

Before filling the service facility, it is necessary to see whether or not there is anybody waiting ("Test for No Queue"). If QUEUE is equal to zero, it is a "do nothing" iteration, and the program branches directly to statement 280,

```
Ok
LIST -200
10 ' TIME ORIENTED SIMULATION
20 RANDOMIZE TIME
30 CLS: INPUT "ENTER TOTAL TIME TO BE SIMULATED ";TOTAL.TIME
40 FOR I=1 TO TOTAL.TIME
50 ' GET ARRIVALS
60 GOSUB 440 ' ARRIVAL GENERATOR
70 TOTAL.ARRIVALS=TOTAL.ARRIVALS+ARRIVALS
80 ' PUT ARRIVALS ON WORK QUEUE
90 QUEUE=QUEUE+ARRIVALS
100 ' TEST FOR SERVICE COMPLETE
110 IF SERVICE.TIME>0 THEN 250
120 ' TEST FOR SERVICE JUST COMPLETED
130 IF SERVICE.INDICATOR=0 THEN 160
140 SERVICE.INDICATOR=0
150 EXIT.QUEUE=EXIT.QUEUE+1
160 ' FILL THE SERVICE FACILITY
170 ' TEST FOR NO QUEUE
180 IF QUEUE=0 THEN 280
190 QUEUE=QUEUE-1
200 '
Ok


LIST 210-390
210 SERVICE.INDICATOR=1
220 ' GET SERVICE TIME
230 GOSUB 500 ' SERVICE TIME GENERATOR
240 SERVICE.TIME=NEW.SERVICE.TIME
250 SERVICE.TIME=SERVICE.TIME-1
260 TOTAL.SERVICE.TIME=TOTAL.SERVICE.TIME+1
270 TOTAL.QUEUE=TOTAL.QUEUE+QUEUE
280 'GOSUB 320
290 NEXT I
300 GOSUB 580
310 END
320 ' DISPLAY RESULTS
330 CLS: LOCATE 1,16: PRINT "***** RESULTS OF TIME-ORIENTED SIMULATION *****"
340 LOCATE 3,1: PRINT "TIME PERIOD #"I" OF"TOTAL.TIME
350 LOCATE 5,5: PRINT "WORK QUEUE        ";:
    FOR J=1 TO QUEUE: PRINT "*";: NEXT J
360 LOCATE 5,75: PRINT QUEUE
370 IF SERVICE.INDICATOR=1 THEN FLAG$="*" ELSE FLAG$=""
380 LOCATE 10,5: PRINT "SERVICE FACILITY ";:
    PRINT FLAG$
390 LOCATE 10,75: PRINT SERVICE.INDICATOR
Ok


400 LOCATE 15,5: PRINT "EXIT QUEUE        ";:
       FOR J=1 TO EXIT.QUEUE: PRINT "*";: NEXT J
410 LOCATE 15,75: PRINT EXIT.QUEUE
420 LOCATE 20,5: INPUT "TYPE <RETURN> OR <ENTER> TO CONTINUE ";X
430 RETURN
440 ' ARRIVAL GENERATOR
450 X=RND
460 IF X<=.4 THEN ARRIVALS=1 ELSE ARRIVALS=0
470 'IF X<=.9 THEN ARRIVALS=1: GOTO 490
480 'ARRIVALS=2
490 'RETURN
500 ' SERVICE-TIME GENERATOR
510 X=RND
520 IF X<=.5 THEN NEW.SERVICE.TIME=1 ELSE NEW.SERVICE.TIME=2
530 'IF X<=.7 THEN NEW.SERVICE.TIME=2: GOTO 570
540 'IF X<=.8 THEN NEW.SERVICE.TIME=3: GOTO 570
```

FIGURE 4-2 Program listing of a time-oriented simulation.

```
550 'IF X<=.9 THEN NEW.SERVICE.TIME=4: GOTO 570
560 'NEW.SERVICE.TIME=5
570 RETURN
580 ' SUMMARIZE RESULTS
590 CLS
600 LOCATE 1,25: PRINT "***** SUMMARY OF RESULTS *****"
Ok


Ok
LIST 610-
610 LOCATE 4,1: PRINT "ARRIVAL RATE="TOTAL.ARRIVALS/TOTAL.TIME
620 LOCATE 4,40: PRINT "SERVICE RATE="EXIT.QUEUE/TOTAL.SERVICE.TIME
630 LOCATE 7,1: PRINT "ARRIVAL TIME="TOTAL.TIME/TOTAL.ARRIVALS
640 LOCATE 7,40: PRINT "SERVICE TIME="TOTAL.SERVICE.TIME/EXIT.QUEUE
650 LOCATE 10,1: PRINT "TOTAL QUEUE="TOTAL.QUEUE
660 LOCATE 10,40: PRINT "AVERAGE QUEUE="TOTAL.QUEUE/TOTAL.TIME
670 LOCATE 13,1: PRINT "AVERAGE WAIT="TOTAL.QUEUE/TOTAL.ARRIVALS
680 LOCATE 13,40:PRINT"FACILITY LOADING="TOTAL.SERVICE.TIME/TOTAL.TIME
690 LOCATE 16,1: PRINT "BUSY TIME="TOTAL.SERVICE.TIME
700 LOCATE 16,40: PRINT "IDLE TIME="TOTAL.TIME-TOTAL.SERVICE.TIME
710 LOCATE 19,1: PRINT "TOTAL ARRIVALS="TOTAL.ARRIVALS
720 LOCATE 19,40: PRINT "TOTAL SERVICES="EXIT.QUEUE
730 LOCATE 22,1: PRINT "LEFT IN QUEUE="QUEUE
740 LOCATE 22,40: PRINT "LEFT IN SERVICE="SERVICE.INDICATOR
750 RETURN
Ok
```

FIGURE 4–2 (continued)

which calls a subroutine to display the results of the iteration and hence to statement 290, the NEXT I statement, to terminate it.

If QUEUE is greater than zero, QUEUE is decremented by one, effectively putting a customer into the service facility. Then we set the SERVICE.INDICATOR equal to one to indicate that the service facility is occupied. We call the service time subroutine and obtain a value of NEW.SERVICE.TIME that we set equal to the SERVICE.TIME for the customer. SERVICE.TIME is decremented by one to take into account the service received during the first time unit in the service facility, TOTAL.SERVICE.TIME is incremented by one, and the customers waiting in the QUEUE are added to TOTAL.QUEUE. The program branches to display results and then the iteration terminates.

After all the predetermined time units have simulated, the program branches to a subroutine called "Summarize Results" and then ends.

This is a demonstration program, so after every iteration—that is, time interval—the "Display Results" subroutine runs to show the current condition of the waiting-line system. The subrouting shows the results of each iteration of the time-oriented simulation. It is labeled with the iteration number and the total number of iterations to be performed; for example, "Time Period #1 of 20" (see Figure 4–3).

The waiting line (called "Work Queue") is shown as a series of asterisks, one for each customer who had to wait for this time period. The display would show one asterisk for each customer waiting when the period began, plus one for each new arrival, minus the one who goes into the service facility, if anyone

```
ENTER TOTAL TIME TO BE SIMULATED ? 20


              ***** RESULTS OF TIME-ORIENTED SIMULATION *****
TIME PERIOD # 8   OF 20
     WORK QUEUE          *                                           1



     SERVICE FACILITY *                                              1



     EXIT QUEUE          **                                          2



     TYPE <RETURN> OR <ENTER> TO CONTINUE ?
                    ***** SUMMARY OF RESULTS *****

ARRIVAL RATE= .4                    SERVICE RATE= .5

ARRIVAL TIME= 2.5                   SERVICE TIME= 2

TOTAL QUEUE= 3                      AVERAGE QUEUE= .15

AVERAGE WAIT= .375                  FACILITY LOADING= .7

BUSY TIME= 14                       IDLE TIME= 6

TOTAL ARRIVALS= 8                   TOTAL SERVICES= 7

LEFT IN QUEUE= 0                    LEFT IN SERVICE= 1
Ok
```

FIGURE 4–3 Steps in running a time-oriented simulation; establishing the total time of the simulation; reporting the results of each iteration; and summarizing the results of the simulation run.

does. The number of customers in the waiting line is shown at the right of the row of asterisks.

The next line of the display depicts the current condition of the service facility. If the facility is engaged, a single asterisk is displayed with the number 1 on the right. If the service facility is empty, no asterisk is shown and a 0 is displayed on the right.

The last line shows the exit queue. A row of asterisks symbolically represents those customers who have already received service, and the number is displayed on the right. The sum of the three lines—length of waiting line, customer currently receiving service, and the exit queue—add up to the total number of arrivals up to and including the time period shown.

The "Summarize Results" subroutine runs after the last iteration and tells what happened during the run (Figure 4–3). In a simulation experiment there are usually several runs. The following quantities are displayed:

ARRIVAL RATE   This, you recall, is one of the two main parameters of a waiting-line simulation. It is what we call an exogenous variable; that is, a quantity that is fed in by the user. All the same, we calculate it by dividing TOTAL.TIME (another exogenous variable) into TOTAL.ARRIVALS. We do this to check on the program and give the user confidence that the random-number generator is truly simulating what the user wants it to simulate. Actually, if the calculated arrival rate is different than that which the user programmed into the arrivals generator, it nearly always means that the simulation run was not long enough for the law of averages to work out. Speaking technically, we would say that the waiting-line system had not yet reached a "steady state." This would be taken as an indication that the simulation run was not long enough.

SERVICE RATE   This is another exogenous variable. We recalculate it as a check on our work and the work of the program, and especially to see whether the simulation run is long enough for the system to attain a steady state. We divide EXIT.QUEUE (all those who have completed service) by TOTAL. SERVICE.TIME. This neglects the customer still in service, but over the length of a typical simulation run, the error introduced is negligible.

ARRIVAL TIME   This is simply the reciprocal of ARRIVAL RATE, and is included for the benefit of users who prefer to think of time rather than rate. Actually, in time-oriented simulations, it is most common to speak of arrival rate rather than arrival time.

SERVICE TIME   This is simply the reciprocal of SERVICE RATE. In time-oriented simulations, it is most common to speak of service time rather than service rate.

TOTAL QUEUE   This is the total number of customer periods spent waiting in line, or the total time wasted. Sometimes we program in an additional probe and report the maximum queue; that is, the longest queue observed during any single time period. This latter figure would be important in establishing the number of seats required in a waiting room, for example. TOTAL.QUEUE is known as an endogenous variable because its value is determined solely by events that occur within the waiting-line system.

AVERAGE QUEUE   This is the number of customers we may expect to see waiting during any time period. It is found by dividing TOTAL.TIME into TOTAL.QUEUE. This quantity is a measure of how busy the service facility appears to be.

AVERAGE WAIT This tells how long each customer may expect to wait for service. It is the best measure of customer dissatisfaction arising from the inability of the service facility to process customers fast enough to fulfill their expectations. It is found by dividing TOTAL.QUEUE by TOTAL.ARRIVALS.

BUSY TIME This measures the productive time of the service facility. It is simply TOTAL.SERVICE.TIME. Sometimes users find it convenient to divide BUSY TIME by TOTAL.TIME and express it as a percentage. A result between 70 and 80 percent busy usually denotes an efficient system.

IDLE TIME This is the unproductive time of the system, when the service facility is doing nothing, waiting for customers to arrive. It is just the difference between BUSY TIME and TOTAL.TIME. Sometimes idle time represents an opportunity for improvement. The service facility might be eliminated if it is idle too much of the time, or it could be assigned to perform other duties while waiting for customers. An example is assigning tape librarians in a computer center to clean tapes while waiting for operators to make withdrawals or returns of magnetic media.

The next four quantities audit the performance of the simulation run and strengthen the confidence of the user in the results:

TOTAL ARRIVALS The total number of simulated customers entering the system.

TOTAL SERVICES The total number of customers completing service during the simulation run; final contents of the EXIT.QUEUE.

LEFT IN QUEUE The number of customers left in the waiting line (that is, quantity QUEUE) when the simulated time expires.

LEFT IN SERVICE The number of customers left in the service facility when the simulated time expires (in this case, 1 or 0, the final condition of the service indicator).

RESULTS

To obtain some results from this simulation, we have to assign some values to arrival rate and service time. We shall set the arrival rate initially at .4 arrival per time period. The following subroutine will do this:

```
X = RND
IF X<= .4 THEN ARRIVALS = 1 ELSE ARRIVALS = 0
RETURN
```

We shall set the service time equal to 1.5 time units; which is the same as saying the service rate is equal to .67. Since the service rate significantly exceeds the arrival rate, we would expect there to be little waiting. (When the arrival rate exceeds the service rate, the length of the queue tends to infinity.) We shall use the following subroutine:

```
X = RND
IF X<= .5 THEN NEW.SERVICE.TIME = 1
         ELSE NEW.SERVICE.TIME = 2
RETURN
```

The fundamental relationships between waiting line variables state that:

QUEUE = ARRIVAL.RATE∗AVERAGE.WAIT
SYSTEM.WAITING.TIME = AVERAGE.WAIT + SERVICE.TIME
QUEUE + SERVICE.INDICATOR =
            ARRIVAL.RATE∗SYSTEM.WAITING.TIME

If we run the simulation for 1,000 time periods, we find:

```
ARRIVAL.RATE = .429    (Should be .4)
ARRIVAL.TIME = 2.33    (Should be 2.5)
SERVICE.RATE = .67     (Should be .67)
SERVICE.TIME = 1.50    (Should be 1.50)
TOTAL.QUEUE = 250
AVERAGE.QUEUE = .25
AVERAGE.WAIT = 58
BUSY.TIME = 642        IDLE.TIME = 358
FACILITY.LOADING = .64
TOTAL.ARRIVALS = 429   TOTAL.SERVICES = 429
LEFT.IN.QUEUE = 0      LEFT.IN.SERVICE = 0
```

The calculated length of queue is:

QUEUE = .43∗.58 = .25

The total time in the system is:

SYSTEM.WAITING.TIME = .58 + 1.50 = 2.1

The total number of customers in the system is:

```
QUEUE+SERVICE.INDICATOR = .43*2.1 = .9
```

Figuring this another way:

```
QUEUE+SERVICE.INDICATOR = QUEUE +
          SERVICE.INDICATOR * FACILITY.LOADING =
          .25 + 1*.64= .89
```

because the service indicator is set to one only 64 percent of the time. So our simulation produces results in agreement with those expected.

Note that the results are not in complete agreement. For example, the arrival rate was input at .4 per unit time and the average arrival rate came out to be .43. This is characteristic of a random process. You would expect that after the simulation program runs for a large number of iterations, the average results would converge to a value and we would find that the system was in a steady state. In the case of this example, this is not true. Let's see what happens as the simulation program starts up.

We shall run the program for 5, 10, . . . 45, 50 iterations and tabulate the calculated arrival and service rates, average length of queue, and facility loading:

ITERATION	ARRIVAL.RATE	SERVICE.RATE	AVERAGE.QUEUE	LOADING
5	.80	.50	.20	.80
10	.50	.57	.10	.70
15	.40	.56	.00	.60
20	.45	.53	.15	.75
25	.32	.67	.04	.48
30	.47	.55	.06	.73
35	.43	.70	.06	.57
40	.45	.59	.33	.68
45	.47	.67	.11	.67
50	.46	.65	.22	.64

All we can really say is that the system approaches the expected value and then oscillates around it, achieving a kind of dynamic equilibrium. The condition of dynamic equilibrium becomes clearer if we look at simulations varying in length from 100 to 500 time units:

ITERATION	ARRIVAL.RATE	SERVICE.RATE	AVERAGE.QUEUE	LOADING
100	.42	.70	.20	.60
200	.39	.68	.18	.56
300	.42	.68	.29	.62
400	.42	.68	.17	.61
500	.37	.68	.17	.55

Since we are randomly reseeding the random-number generator, it is highly unlikely that you could ever reproduce these results. The "best" answer would be found by taking, say, 500 iterations as the run length, repeating the experiment several times, and averaging the results. The number of times you should repeat it can be found by statistics; it depends upon the spread you observe in the values in which you are interested and the confidence you wish to place in the results.

Now let's see what happens when we run a series of 500-iteration simulations holding the service rate at a nominal .67 and increasing the arrival rate in steps of .05. We would expect that an increasingly long queue would form as the service facility becomes increasingly unable to handle the influx of customers:

ARRIVAL.RATE	A.R. (CALC)	S.R. (CALC)	AVERAGE.QUEUE
.40	.37	.68	.17
.45	.46	.71	.22
.50	.47	.67	.49
.55	.51	.69	.34
.60	.56	.66	1.20
.65	.66	.67	3.91
.70	.70	.71	3.55
.75	.76	.68	17.10

When the arrival rate exceeds the service rate, the waiting-line system is said to be unstable. The queue will just grow and grow, and many customers will never get served at all.

EXAMPLE

A certain factory has a large number of bench-welding machines. On 70 percent of the work days none of the bench welders fail. On 20 percent of the days, one welder fails. On 10 percent of the days, two fail.

Inoperable machines are taken to a repair shop. On average, 30 percent of them are fixed in one day, 40 percent are fixed in two days, 10 percent are fixed in three days, 10 percent are fixed in four days, and 10 percent are fixed in five days.

Determine the average number of machines out of service at a time. How much space must be provided for storage of broken machines outside of the repair shop? What is the average loading on the repair shop? Run the simulation for five years of simulated time.

First we calculate the average arrival and service rates to see whether the problem has a solution (i.e., is not unstable).

$$ARRIVAL.RATE = 0*.7 + 1*.2 + 2*.1 = .40$$

$$SERVICE.RATE = 1/(1*.3 + 2*.4 + 3*.1 + 4*.1 + 5*.1) = .43$$

Since the service rate is greater than the arrival rate, the problem has a solution; that is, a finite queue.

We write the arrival and service generators by using a cumulative distribution function of the given empirical distribution:

```
X = RND
IF X<= .7 THEN ARRIVALS = 0: RETURN
IF X<= .9 THEN ARRIVALS = 1: RETURN
ARRIVALS = 2
RETURN

X = RND
IF X<= .3 THEN NEW.SERVICE.TIME = 1: RETURN
IF X<= .7 THEN NEW.SERVICE.TIME = 2: RETURN
IF X<= .8 THEN NEW.SERVICE.TIME = 3: RETURN
IF X<= .9 THEN NEW.SERVICE.TIME = 4: RETURN
NEW.SERVICE.TIME = 5
RETURN
```

To keep track of the maximum value of QUEUE, we insert this statement into the program right after the one that accumulates TOTAL.QUEUE:

```
TOTAL.QUEUE = TOTAL.QUEUE + QUEUE
IF QUEUE>BIG.QUEUE THEN BIG.QUEUE = QUEUE
```

We add the value of BIG.QUEUE to the "Summarize Results" subroutine and, since there is room at the end of the line, we document TOTAL.TIME:

```
LOCATE 24,1: PRINT "MAXIMUM QUEUE = "BIG,QUEUE
LOCATE 24,40: PRINT "LENGTH OF RUN = "TOTAL.TIME
```

We find that the average number of machines out of service at a time would be:

```
MACHINES.IN.REPAIR.SYSTEM = ARRIVAL.RATE*
    (AVERAGE.WAIT + SERVICE.TIME) =
    .41*(9.7 + 2.28) = 4.9 or 5
```

Space would have to be left to accommodate 14 machines awaiting repair. The average loading on the service facility is .92.

SUMMARY

In this chapter we have concentrated upon the logical design and operational characteristics of the time-oriented or time-slice simulation. This is the easiest kind of simulated queuing system program to understand, although it can be expensive in terms of running time.

For example, in simulating a traffic light, the time increment might be seconds and the time of interest might be four hours. Each run would therefore require 14,400 iterations. In a tool-crib simulation, the time increment might be five seconds and the time of interest might be seven hours; each run would require 5,040 iterations. These experiments would typically require 20 runs to converge on a credible answer.

We introduced the major components of a waiting-line system and explained how the behavior of the system is determined by the interaction between the arrival rate and the service rate.

We listed some of the characteristics of waiting-line systems that may be determined by simulation: service-facility loading, average length of queue, and average waiting time, and discussed why they are important to system developers and users.

After differentiating between time-oriented and event-oriented simulations, we discussed in detail the programming logic of the time-oriented simulation.

The arrival- and service-time generators of the program were configured to produce simple uniform distributions. Then the program was used to present a step-by-step picture of the operation of the waiting-line system and to validate the fundamental relationships of waiting lines.

We showed how the system converged fairly rapidly on average values of variables after start-up but how it tends to oscillate about the mean values in a kind of dynamic equilibrium. We also demonstrated the meaning of an unstable system by observing how the system behaved when the arrival rate exceeded the service rate.

Finally, we used the program to solve a problem in planning industrial repair facilities.

CHAPTER FIVE

Event-Oriented Simulation

Unlike the time-oriented simulation in which the program looks sequentially at very small increments of time, the event-oriented simulation fixates upon arrivals of customers. It processes the customer as far as it is able until it encounters a previous customer still in the system; then the customer must wait until the desired service facility is free.

However, when there are long waits between customers, the program skips over the times during which there are no arrivals. In many situations, customers tend to arrive in bunches; in those instances, the event-oriented simulation can depict system behavior much more efficiently than can time-oriented simulation. Some examples of situations in which customers arrive in bunches are: employees lining up at tool cribs when jobs tend to be dispatched at the start of shifts, at office copying machines when deadlines coincide, or at office canteens during coffee breaks; warplanes returning to an airfield or aircraft carrier after a mission; customer arrivals at banks during rush hours; cars arriving at a traffic light after having been bunched by a previous traffic light; and transport trucks arriving at a truck stop or weigh station (they tend to travel in "convoys," as CB listeners know).

We are going to examine a program that produces a simple event-oriented simulation. As in the case of our time-oriented program, this one will have a single service facility and all customers will arrive from the same population. Moreover, all customers will be served on a first-come, first-served basis; and the service they receive will be the same except for variation in the time it takes to render it.

Since the event-oriented simulation is conceptually more difficult than the time-oriented simulation, we will use a logic-flow diagram to explain the workings of the program. Figure 5–1 is the logic-flow diagram.

PROGRAM LOGIC

There are five paths in this program that accommodate the possible states of the system:

PATH #1 A customer arrives, finds the service facility empty, and goes directly into service with no waiting.

PATH #2 Service is completed for a customer. The customer leaves the service facility and joins the exit queue or pool of serviced customers, but there is no customer waiting. Path #2 sets the stage for Path #1.

PATH #3 A customer arrives to find the service facility occupied. The customer must join the waiting-line queue.

PATH #4 A customer completes service, leaves the service facility, and joins the pool of serviced customers. However, unlike Path #2, other customers are waiting, and one of them goes into the service facility.

PATH #5 The total elapsed simulated time equals or exceeds the predetermined time of the simulation run. The program displays the results of the run and terminates.

As in the case of the time-oriented simulation, there are three exogenous, or input, variables:

1. ARRIVAL.TIME, which is generated by a subroutine that utilizes the RND function
2. SERVICE.TIME, which is also generated by a random number subroutine
3. TOTAL.TIME, which is typed in by the user

There are four variables that are used to switch control of the program among the five paths:

1. ARRIVAL.ALARM is the simulated time remaining until the arrival of the next customer.
2. SERVICE.ALARM is the simulated time remaining for the customer currently receiving service.
3. SERVICE.INDICATOR is a binary variable that tells whether the service facility is currently occupied (1) or vacant (0).
4. QUEUE is the number of customers currently making up the waiting line.

The values of ARRIVAL.ALARM and SERVICE.ALARM are compared to tell whether the service facility is currently busy or idle. If SERVICE.ALARM is less than ARRIVAL.ALARM, the service facility is idle. If SERVICE.ALARM is greater than ARRIVAL.ALARM, the service facility is busy. If the service facility is idle, then a customer will enter from the queue provided QUEUE is greater than zero (Path #4); or program control will be switched to Path #2 if there is no queue. This, in turn, sets the system up so the next customer arriving can go directly into service (Path #1). During a traverse of Path #2,

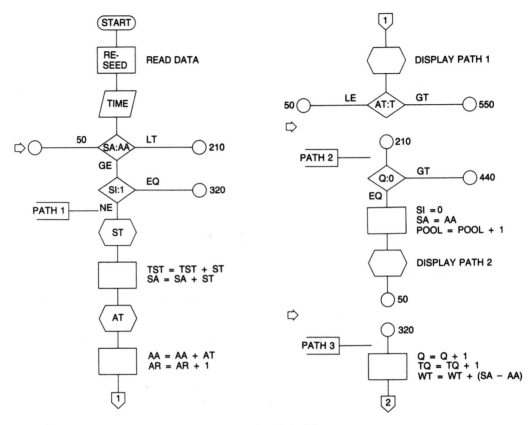

FIGURE 5–1 Logic flow diagram of an event-oriented simulation.

SERVICE.ALARM is arbitrarily set equal to ARRIVAL.ALARM in order to switch program control to Path #1.

If the service facility is busy, which is indicated by SERVICE. ALARM greater than or equal to ARRIVAL.ALARM and SERV-ICE.INDICATOR equal to 1, then newly arriving customers must join the wait-ing-line queue (Path #3). However, if SERVICE.ALARM has been arbitrarily set equal to ARRIVAL.ALARM, then SERVICE.INDICATOR will be equal to 0, control will be switched to Path #1, and a newly arriving customer will go directly into the service facility (Path #1).

The service-time generator is called when a customer enters the service facility either directly (Path #1) or from the waiting-line queue (Path #4). In both cases, the SERVICE.ALARM is incremented by the amount of SERV-ICE.TIME returned from the service-time generator; and the TOTAL. SERVICE.TIME is also incremented by the new value of SERVICE.TIME.

Although we can use the ARRIVAL.ALARM to keep track of total elapsed time, we cannot use SERVICE.ALARM to keep track of total elapsed service

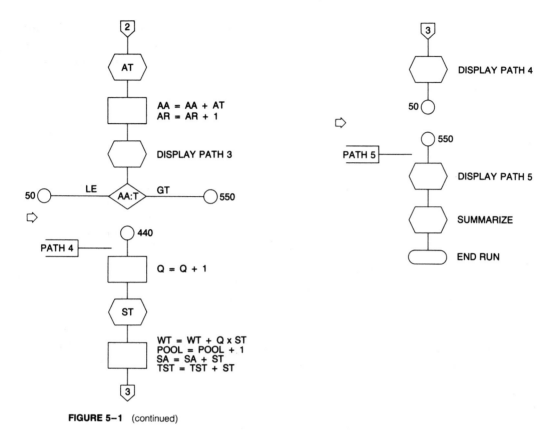

FIGURE 5–1 (continued)

time, because we arbitrarily equate it to ARRIVAL.ALARM in Path #2; that's the reason for storing total elapsed service time in TOTAL.SERVICE.TIME.

The arrival-time generator is called whenever the current arrival is disposed of by either being admitted directly into the service facility (Path # 1), or being placed on the waiting-line queue (Path #3). The new value of ARRIVAL.TIME returned from the generator is added to ARRIVAL.ALARM, and the count ARRIVALS is incremented by one.

Whenever comparison of SERVICE.ALARM with ARRIVAL.ALARM indicates that a service has been completed (Paths #2 and #4), the customer that has received it is symbolically kicked out of the service facility by incrementing the variable POOL by one.

When a customer joins the queue (Path #3), the total number of customers who had to wait (TOTAL.QUEUE) is incremented by one. Each time a customer leaves the waiting line to enter the service facility (Path #4), the total time customers spend waiting in line (WAITING.TIME) is increased by adding to it the product of the SERVICE.TIME of the customer just entering the service facility and the number of customers who have to wait for that customer (QUEUE).

Not so obvious is the fact that this computation does not include part of the waiting time of a new arrival who joins the waiting-line queue during the time a customer is being serviced. This discrepancy is taken care of in Path #3 by adding to WAITING.TIME the difference between SERVICE.ALARM and ARRIVAL.ALARM.

PATH DISPLAYS

Since this is a teaching program, it has been configured to show the condition of the waiting-line system after the traversal of each program path. The display subroutine labels which path has been followed. It displays an asterisk for each customer who has arrived up to the time depicted, one for each customer currently in the waiting line, a single asterisk if the service facility is currently occupied, and one for each customer for whom service is complete (POOL or Exit Queue). The display also shows the current value of the ARRIVAL.ALARM (total elapsed time) and the TOTAL.TIME, so the user can tell how long the simulation run has to go. Figure 5–2 shows the state of the system after a traversal of path #1. Figure 5–3 shows system state after traversing Path #2. Figure 5–4 shows the system after Path #3, and Figure 5–5 after Path #4.

The results of the simulation run are displayed after the display for Path #5 (see Figure 5–6). The calculated values of ARRIVAL.RATE and AR-RIVAL.TIME and of SERVICE.RATE and SERVICE.TIME are shown to indicate how closely the simulation is approaching a steady state (that is, how closely the calculated values approach the input parameters of the random generators).

The results display also accounts for all customer arrivals: TO-

FIGURE 5–2 Demonstration program showing the state of the system after following Path #1.

```
***** RESULTS OF EVENT-ORIENTED SIMULATION *****

FOLLOWING PATH #1 - ENTRY TO SERVICE FACILITY

ARRIVALS          *******                                    7

WORK QUEUE                                                   0

SERVICE INDICATOR *                                          1

FACILITY OUTPUT  ******                                      6

ARRIVAL ALARM= 17.22116  X  20   TOTAL TIME

TYPE <RETURN> OR <ENTER> TO ADVANCE PROGRAM ?
```

```
      ***** RESULTS OF EVENT-ORIENTED SIMULATION *****

FOLLOWING PATH #2 - LEAVE SERVICE FACILITY EMPTY

ARRIVALS           *******                                          7

WORK QUEUE                                                          0

SERVICE INDICATOR                                                   0

FACILITY OUTPUT  *******                                           7

ARRIVAL ALARM= 17.22116  X  20   TOTAL TIME

TYPE <RETURN> OR <ENTER> TO ADVANCE PROGRAM ?
```

FIGURE 5-3 State of an event-oriented simulation system after following Path #2.

TAL.ARRIVALS, TOTAL.SERVICES, LEFT.IN.QUEUE, and LEFT.IN.SERVICE. This is principally an auditing function.

We report TOTAL.QUEUE. This is the number of customers who had to wait. Unlike the time-oriented simulation, this program does not dump every arrival on the queue, so it is easy to differentiate between those customers who had to wait and those who went directly into the service facility. We also report AVERAGE.QUEUE, which is equal to WAITING.TIME divided by AR-RIVAL.ALARM.

We report AVERAGE.WAIT, which is equal to WAITING.TIME divided by ARRIVALS (this effectively includes those customers who went directly into service and sets their waiting times to zero). We also report

FIGURE 5-4 State of an event-oriented simulation system after following Path #3.

```
      ***** RESULTS OF EVENT-ORIENTED SIMULATION *****

FOLLOWING PATH #3 - JOIN WORK QUEUE

ARRIVALS           ******                                          6

WORK QUEUE         *                                               1

SERVICE INDICATOR *                                                1

FACILITY OUTPUT  ****                                             4

ARRIVAL ALARM= 15.37126  X  20   TOTAL TIME

TYPE <RETURN> OR <ENTER> TO ADVANCE PROGRAM ?
```

```
      ***** RESULTS OF EVENT-ORIENTED SIMULATION *****

FOLLOWING PATH #4 - ENTER SERVICE FACILITY FROM QUEUE

ARRIVALS          ******                                        6

WORK QUEUE                                                      0

SERVICE INDICATOR *                                            1

FACILITY OUTPUT   *****                                        5

ARRIVAL ALARM= 15.37126   X   20   TOTAL TIME

TYPE <RETURN> OR <ENTER> TO ADVANCE PROGRAM ?
```

FIGURE 5-5 State of an event-oriented simulation system after following Path #4.

MEAN.TIME.IN.QUEUE, which is equal to WAITING.TIME divided by TOTAL.QUEUE.

Finally, we determine the loading on the service facility. We report BUSY.TIME, which is the same thing as TOTAL.SERVICE.TIME; and IDLE.TIME, which is the difference between TOTAL.TIME and TOTAL.SERVICE.TIME. FACILITY.LOADING is, of course, BUSY.TIME divided by TOTAL.TIME. Figure 5–7 lists all 110 statements of the program.

FIGURE 5-6 Summary of the results of a simulation run.

```
        ***** RESULTS OF SIMULATION *****

ARRIVAL RATE= .4              SERVICE RATE= .5147903

ARRIVAL TIME= 2.5            SERVICE TIME= 1.942539

TOTAL QUEUE= 4              AVERAGE QUEUE= .1577324

AVERAGE WAIT= .4169846      MEAN TIME IN QUEUE= .8339693

BUSY TIME= 13.59777         IDLE TIME= 6.40223
FACILITY LOADING= .6798886

TOTAL ARRIVALS= 8           TOTAL SERVICES= 7

LEFT IN QUEUE= 0            LEFT IN SERVICE= 1
Ok
```

```
Ok
LIST -200
10 ' EVENT-ORIENTED SIMULATION
20 FOR I=1 TO 5: READ PATH.NAME$(I): NEXT I
30 RANDOMIZE TIME
40 CLS: INPUT "ENTER LENGTH OF SIMULATION "; TOTAL.TIME
50 IF SERVICE.ALARM < ARRIVAL.ALARM THEN 210
60 IF SERVICE.INDICATOR=1 THEN 320
70 '
80 ' DIRECT ENTRY OF AN ARRIVAL INTO AN EMPTY SERVICE FACILITY
90 SERVICE.INDICATOR=1
100 GOSUB 610 ' GET SERVICE TIME FOR THIS ARRIVAL
110 TOTAL.SERVICE.TIME=TOTAL.SERVICE.TIME+SERVICE.TIME
120 SERVICE.ALARM=SERVICE.ALARM+SERVICE.TIME
130 GOSUB 650 ' GET TIME UNTIL NEXT ARRIVAL
140 ARRIVAL.ALARM=ARRIVAL.ALARM+ARRIVAL.TIME
150 ARRIVALS=ARRIVALS+1
160 CLS: LOCATE 4,5: PRINT "FOLLOWING PATH #"PATH.NAME$(1)
170 GOSUB 690 ' DISPLAY RESULTS
180 IF ARRIVAL.ALARM>TOTAL.TIME THEN 550
190 GOTO 50
200 '
Ok


Ok
LIST 210-400
210 ' TEST QUEUE
220 IF QUEUE>0 THEN 440
230 '
240 'EMPTYING THE SERVICE FACILITY WITH NOBODY WAITING
250 SERVICE.INDICATOR=0
260 SERVICE.ALARM=ARRIVAL.ALARM
270 POOL=POOL+1 ' EXIT FROM SERVICE FACILITY
280 CLS: LOCATE 4,5: PRINT "FOLLOWING PATH #"PATH.NAME$(2)
290 GOSUB 690 ' DISPLAY RESULTS
300 GOTO 50 ' SYSTEM IS SET UP FOR A DIRECT ENTRY
310 '
320 ' SERVICE FACILITY ENGAGED, ARRIVAL JOINS WORK QUEUE
330 QUEUE=QUEUE+1
340 TOTAL.QUEUE=TOTAL.QUEUE+1
350 WAITING.TIME=WAITING.TIME+(SERVICE.ALARM-ARRIVAL.ALARM)
360 GOSUB 650 ' GET TIME TO NEXT ARRIVAL
370 ARRIVAL.ALARM=ARRIVAL.ALARM+ARRIVAL.TIME
380 ARRIVALS=ARRIVALS+1
390 CLS: LOCATE 4,5: PRINT "FOLLOWING PATH #"PATH.NAME$(3)
400 GOSUB 690 ' DISPLAY RESULTS
Ok


Ok
LIST 410-600
410 IF ARRIVAL.ALARM>TOTAL.TIME THEN 550
420 GOTO 50
430 '
440 ' EMPTYING THE SERVICE FACILITY, ARRIVAL ENTERS FROM QUEUE
450 QUEUE=QUEUE-1
460 GOSUB 610 ' GET SERVICE TIME
470 TOTAL.SERVICE.TIME=TOTAL.SERVICE.TIME+SERVICE.TIME
480 SERVICE.ALARM=SERVICE.ALARM+SERVICE.TIME
490 WAITING.TIME=WAITING.TIME+QUEUE*SERVICE.TIME
500 POOL=POOL+1
510 CLS: LOCATE 4,5: PRINT "FOLLOWING PATH #"PATH.NAME$(4)
```

FIGURE 5-7 Program listing for an event-oriented simulation.

```
520 GOSUB 690 ' DISPLAY RESULTS
530 GOTO 50
540 '
550 ' FINISH UP
560 CLS: LOCATE 4,5: PRINT "FOLLOWING PATH #"PATH.NAME$(5)
570 GOSUB 690 ' DISPLAY RESULTS
580 GOSUB 920 ' SUMMARIZE RESULTS
590 END
600 '
Ok


Ok
LIST 610-800
610 ' SERVICE TIME SUBROUTINE
620 SERVICE.TIME=RND*3
630 RETURN
640 '
650 ' ARRIVAL TIME SUBROUTINE
660 ARRIVAL.TIME=RND*5
670 RETURN
680 '
690 ' DISPLAY SUBROUTINE
700 IF SERVICE.INDICATOR=1 THEN FLAG$="*" ELSE FLAG$=""
710 LOCATE 1,16: PRINT "***** RESULTS OF EVENT-ORIENTED SIMULATION *****"
720 LOCATE 7,5: PRINT "ARRIVALS        ";
730 FOR I=1 TO ARRIVALS: PRINT "*";: NEXT I
740 LOCATE 7,75: PRINT ARRIVALS
750 LOCATE 10,5: PRINT "WORK QUEUE        ";
760 FOR I=1 TO QUEUE: PRINT "*";: NEXT I
770 LOCATE 10,75: PRINT QUEUE
780 LOCATE 13,5: PRINT "SERVICE INDICATOR ";: PRINT FLAG$
790 LOCATE 13,75: PRINT SERVICE.INDICATOR
800 LOCATE 16,5: PRINT "FACILITY OUTPUT   ":
Ok


Ok
LIST 810-1000
810 FOR I=1 TO POOL: PRINT "*";: NEXT I
820 LOCATE 16,75: PRINT POOL
830 LOCATE 19,5: PRINT "ARRIVAL ALARM="ARRIVAL.ALARM" X "TOTAL.TIME" TOTAL TIME"
840 LOCATE 22,5: INPUT "TYPE <RETURN> OR <ENTER> TO ADVANCE PROGRAM ";X
850 RETURN
860 DATA "1 - ENTRY TO SERVICE FACILITY         "
870 DATA "2 - LEAVE SERVICE FACILITY EMPTY      "
880 DATA "3 - JOIN WORK QUEUE                   "
890 DATA "4 - ENTER SERVICE FACILITY FROM QUEUE"
900 DATA "5 - END OF SIMULATION RUN            "
910 '
920 ' RESULTS SUBROUTINE
930 CLS
940 LOCATE 1,23: PRINT "***** RESULTS OF SIMULATION *****"
950 LOCATE 4,1: PRINT "ARRIVAL RATE="ARRIVALS/TOTAL.TIME
960 LOCATE 4,40: PRINT "SERVICE RATE="POOL/TOTAL.SERVICE.TIME
970 LOCATE 7,1: PRINT "ARRIVAL TIME="TOTAL.TIME/ARRIVALS
980 LOCATE 7,40: PRINT "SERVICE TIME="TOTAL.SERVICE.TIME/POOL
990 LOCATE 10,1: PRINT "TOTAL QUEUE="TOTAL.QUEUE
1000 LOCATE 10,40: PRINT "AVERAGE QUEUE="WAITING.TIME/ARRIVAL.ALARM
Ok
```

FIGURE 5–7 (continued)

```
Ok
LIST 1010-
1010 LOCATE 13,1: PRINT "AVERAGE WAIT="WAITING.TIME/ARRIVALS
1020 LOCATE 13,40: PRINT "MEAN TIME IN QUEUE="WAITING.TIME/TOTAL.QUEUE
1030 LOCATE 16,1: PRINT "BUSY TIME="TOTAL.SERVICE.TIME
1040 LOCATE 16,40: PRINT "IDLE TIME="TOTAL.TIME-TOTAL.SERVICE.TIME
1050 LOCATE 17,1: PRINT "FACILITY LOADING="TOTAL.SERVICE.TIME/TOTAL.TIME
1060 LOCATE 19,1: PRINT "TOTAL ARRIVALS="ARRIVALS
1070 LOCATE 19,40: PRINT "TOTAL SERVICES="POOL
1080 LOCATE 22,1: PRINT "LEFT IN QUEUE="QUEUE
1090 LOCATE 22,40: PRINT "LEFT IN SERVICE="SERVICE.INDICATOR
1100 RETURN
Ok
```

FIGURE 5–7 (continued)

COMPARISON OF RESULTS

We ran the event-oriented simulation program with inputs comparable to those of the time-oriented simulation program. You may recall that the arrival rate for the time-oriented simulation was .4 arrivals per unit time. In the event-oriented simulation, we used this arrival generator:

```
' ARRIVAL TIME SUBROUTINE
ARRIVAL.TIME=RND*5
RETURN
```

This subroutine generates a decimal value of time between arrivals that can range from 0 to 5. Statistically the expected value will be 2.5, which would produce an average arrival rate of .4. This procedure involves randomly sampling from a uniform distribution.

We use this subroutine to generate a service rate of .67:

```
' SERVICE TIME GENERATOR
SERVICE.TIME=RND*3
RETURN
```

This subroutine generates a decimal value of service time that can range from 0 to 3. The expected value is 1.5; which produces an average service rate of .67.

We ran the event-oriented simulation for 1,000 units of simulated time. (Note that when you want to make a long run with a teaching program, you can save a lot of time and trouble by "commenting out" the path-by-path results;

just use the BASIC screen-editing capability to insert apostrophes after the line number of the statements that call or label the path-results display.)

Comparison of Results of Time- and Event-Oriented Simulations

QUANTITY	TIME-ORIENTED	EVENT-ORIENTED
ARRIVAL.RATE	.43	.41
ARRIVAL.TIME	2.33	2.47
SERVICE.RATE	.67	.68
SERVICE.TIME	1.50	1.48
TOTAL.ARRIVALS	429	405
TOTAL.SERVICES	429	404
LEFT.IN.QUEUE	0	0
LEFT.IN.SERVICE	0	1
TOTAL.QUEUE	250	169
AVERAGE.QUEUE	.25	.24
AVERAGE.WAIT	.58	.59
BUSY.TIME	642	597.84
IDLE.TIME	358	402.16
FACILITY.LOADING	.64	.60

These results are all within the range of expected statistical variation in random processes; they indicate that results are independent of whether time-oriented or event-oriented simulation programs are used. The choice is usually dictated by considerations of efficiency. Frequency of arrivals is usually not a consideration, because the time slice can be chosen to accommodate as much or as little time between arrivals as may be required. Rather, the event-oriented simulation is clearly superior from the standpoint of efficiency when customers tend to arrive in tight bunches with long periods in between.

EXAMPLES

FORTUNE TELLER The first example concerns simulating the waiting line outside a fortune teller's tent at a county fair. The average time between customer arrivals is 25 minutes plus or minus 7 minutes. The fortune teller takes 25 minutes plus or minus 15 minutes to predict the customer's future. Simulate the flow of 50 customers through the fortune teller's tent.

We simulate the customer arrival time with a uniform distribution. The 25 plus or minus 7 minutes corresponds to a uniform distribution between 18 and 32 minutes. We can simulate this distribution by making a random choice between 0 and 14 and adding 18 to it:

```
ARRIVAL.TIME=RND*14+18
```

We simulate the service-time distribution by making random choices between 0 and 30 and adding 10.

```
SERVICE.TIME=RND*30+10
```

To simulate 50 customers when customers arrive 25 minutes apart, we shall require 50 × 25, or 1,250 minutes.

The principal results from running this simulation are:

```
AVERAGE QUEUE     = 1.75 CUSTOMERS
AVERAGE WAIT      = 42.22 MINUTES
FACILITY LOADING = .99
```

As a check on our work, we find that the average time between customer arrivals was 24.1 minutes, the average service time was 25.8 minutes, and there were 54 arrivals.

We observe that the fortune teller was busy almost all the time, but people would have to really believe in prognostication to wait on average three quarters of an hour to have their fortunes told.

BLOOD BANK Donors arrive at a blood clinic every 600 seconds plus or minus 600 seconds. There is a single bed, and it takes between 150 and 450 seconds to give blood. Simulate the flow of 1,000 donors through the clinic.

We generate arrivals with the statement:

```
ARRIVAL.TIME=RND*1200
```

We generate services (that is, giving blood) with the subroutine:

```
SERVICE.TIME=RND*300+150
```

With an average interarrival time of 600 seconds to generate 1,000 arrivals will require 600,000 seconds; this establishes the value of TOTAL.TIME.

The results are:

```
AVERAGE.QUEUE      =   0.1
AVERAGE.WAIT       = 59.5
FACILITY.LOADING =    .48
```

As a check on our work, we find that the average time between arrivals is 619 seconds, the average service time is 299 seconds, and 970 donors arrived at the clinic.

Here facility loading is less than 50 percent and donors wait less than a minute.

CATALOG ORDER COUNTER Customers arrive at a catalog service counter with a mean time between arrivals of 1,000 seconds plus or minus 1,000 seconds. The clerk serves the customers with an average service time of 700 seconds plus or minus 700 seconds. Simulate the activity at this counter for 200 customers.

We simulate the arrival of customers with the subroutine:

```
ARRIVAL.TIME = RND*2000
```

We simulate customer service with the subroutine:

```
SERVICE.TIME = RND*1400
```

The simulation of 200 customers will require simulating 1,000 × 200 = 200,000 seconds.

The results are:

```
AVERAGE.QUEUE            =    .54
AVERAGE.WAIT             = 544
FACILITY.LOADING         =    .71
```

Checking our work, we find that the mean interarrival time is 1,005 seconds, average service time is 720, and there were 199 arrivals. (Interarrival time is a short way of saying time between arrivals; even if it is less meaningful, it is more commonly used in simulation literature.)

Here we have a moderately loaded facility. Waiting lines were short but waiting time was significant, because customer service took a long time even though there was a considerable time between arrivals.

TICKET COUNTER Customers arrive at a ticket counter with a mean interarrival time of 125 seconds plus or minus 125 seconds. It takes an average of 50 seconds to serve a customer, and the spread of service time is 25 seconds. Simulate the servicing of 1,000 customers.

We simulate customer arrivals with the subroutine:

```
ARRIVAL.TIME=RND;*250
```

We simulate customer service time with the subroutine:

```
SERVICE.TIME=RND*50+25
```

We require a simulation run of 125 × 1,000, or 125,000 seconds to generate 1,000 arrivals.

The results are:

```
AVERAGE.QUEUE     = 0.06
AVERAGE.WAIT      = 7.17
FACILITY.LOADING =  .39
```

Checking on our work: Average interarrival time is 128 seconds, average service time is 49.7 seconds, and there were 974 customer arrivals.

We observe a lightly loaded facility with short waiting lines and short waiting time.

SUMMARY

This chapter has dealt with event-oriented simulations that move in time from arrival to arrival and simulate the processing of each arrival, rather than simulating all the activity in each of a large number of small, sequential time slices. The event-oriented approach is efficient when simulating systems in which customers tend to arrive in bunches.

We discussed the logic of an event-oriented computer simulation program, and reran a problem we had solved using the time-oriented computer simulation program to demonstrate that one can achieve comparable results using either approach.

We then solved four elementary waiting-line problems using the event-oriented simulation program: a fortune teller, blood-donor clinic, catalog sales counter, and a ticket counter.

CHAPTER SIX

Distribution Functions

We have seen that the factors that determine how a queuing system behaves are the times between customer arrivals and the service times, or the reciprocals of these quantities: the arrivals per unit time and the services per unit time. Their values for any particular customer are governed by chance, or, to put it in technical language, are stochastically determined.

BERNOULLI PROBABILITY

A stochastic determination is made according to a probability law. So far, we have considered three probability laws. The first was the Bernoulli case. Here the probability that an event will occur—for example, that a customer will arrive during the next time slice—remains constant.

With a probability of .4, we can predict that, on average, a customer will arrive during four out of ten time slices. We found it was easy to simulate the Bernoulli case: We just drew a random number, and if it was less than or equal to .4, we said a customer would arrive during the next time slice; if the random number was greater than .4, we said no customer would arrive during the next time slice. Obviously, the Bernoulli law works best when choosing arrivals per unit time in a time-oriented simulation.

UNIFORM PROBABILITY

The uniform-probability law states that all values in a given range are equally likely to occur. Suppose we say that service times are uniformly distributed between 40 and 100 seconds. This means we will not see a service completed in less than 40 seconds or one that takes longer than 100 seconds. On the average, a service will take 70 seconds. This is the median value. It is found by adding the low value to the high value and dividing the sum by 2.

We simulate a uniform-probability law by scaling our random numbers from the standard range of 0 to 1 up or down to whatever range we want to simulate. Say that range is 100 minus 40, or 60. We multiply our random number by the range (60) and add the offset from 0, which, in this case, is 40. The uniform distribution can be used to select service times in a time-oriented simulation or to select either service times or times between arrivals in an event-oriented simulation. When we invoke the uniform-probability law we are assuming that all events designated by numbers ranging from A on the low side to B on the high side are equally likely. It models the condition of ignorance; as we learn more about a system, we shall be able to model it using a distribution that better describes its behavior. You can use Figure 6–1 to generate and display a uniform distribution. You will be asked to enter parameters A and B and the range over which you wish to display the resulting histogram.

EMPIRICAL DISTRIBUTION

When we construct a probability law based upon experimental observation, we construct an empirical distribution. This is the best possible simulation of our experiment. However, how well it represents the general case depends entirely upon the generality of the experimental situation. In our example of the bench-welder repair shop, experimental evidence showed that during the time period when observations were conducted, no welders failed on 70 percent of working days. Whether this can be taken as a general rule for the factory in question, for similar factories, or for factories in general depends upon many factors. For example: Are the welders old or new? Heavily used or not? Well maintained or poorly maintained? Are the operators experienced or inexperienced?

Recall that we simulated the distributions per unit time by adding the probabilities from the left and solving in terms of our random-number draws. We chose a random number and asked if it was less than or equal to .70, .80, .90, or 1.0 (the last decision was made implicitly). Depending upon the outcome of these decisions, we asserted that there were to be 0, 1, 2, or 3 arrivals during the next time period.

We used the same approach to select service times. We added the probabilities .30, .40, .10, .10, and .10, obtaining the cumulative values .30, .70, .80, .90, and 1.0. Then we made a random draw and identified the lowest cumulative value greater than that draw. This enabled us to assert whether the repair time for the next welder was 1, 2, 3, 4, or 5 days.

The general approach to working with an empirical distribution is called the integral inverse, which is how one would describe mathematically the approach we have been using. The procedure of adding values from the left is

```
10 ' UNIFORM DISTRIBUTION
20 '
30 CLS: KEY OFF
40 INPUT "ENTER PARAMETER A"; A
50 INPUT "ENTER PARAMETER B"; B
60 EX=(A+B)/2
70 STDX=(B-A)/SQR(12)
80 LOCATE 1,30: PRINT "EX="EX
90 LOCATE 2,30: PRINT "STND DEV="STDX
100 DIM S(20), D(20)
110 TIME=VAL(RIGHT$(TIME$,2))+VAL(MID$(TIME$,4,2))
120 TIME=TIME+VAL(LEFT$(TIME$,2))
130 RANDOMIZE TIME
140 LOCATE 1,55: INPUT "ENTER RANGE "; RANGE
150 FOR I=1 TO 20
160 S(I)=RANGE*I/20
170 NEXT I
180 FOR I=1 TO 100
190 GOSUB 320
200 FOR J=1 TO 20
210 IF R<=S(J) THEN D(J)=D(J)+1: GOTO 230
220 NEXT J
230 NEXT I
240 LOCATE 3,1
250 FOR I=1 TO 20
260 PRINT USING "###.## ";S(I);
270 FOR J=1 TO D(I)
280 PRINT"*";
290 NEXT J: PRINT
300 NEXT I
310 END
320 ' SUBROUTINE UNIFORM
330 R=A+(B-A)*RND
340 RETURN
```

FIGURE 6-1   Program to generate and plot a uniform distribution.

called integration in calculus. Statistically speaking, we form a cumulative distribution function. When we solve the probability law in terms of our random-number draw, we algebraically take the inverse of the law.

You can simulate any theoretical distribution this way. If you have the explicit cumulative distribution function, just solve for F(X) at incremental values of X covering the range of interest and connect the X, F(X) points with straight lines. Draw a random number, which will of course be in the range of F(X), and use the corresponding value of X as your random variate.

NORMAL DISTRIBUTION

There are two probability laws that describe most of the behavior that can be observed in real-life situations. There are many other laws derived from them. These other laws are used where finer precision is needed in a simulation. The basic laws are those of normal probability and exponential probability.

The normal distribution has many names. It is called the Gaussian distribution, after the mathematician who first described it; it is also known as the bell curve, because of its shape. The normal distribution is used to depict the distribution of such things as heights of male or female adults; numerical results of academic tests; dimensions of parts made on a machine; lifetimes of things subject to wearing out, such as light bulbs, automobiles, or people; slaughter weights of cattle or pigs; acre yields of grain; or, in two dimensions, the spread of bullets around a target bull's eye. (This is more properly called a Rayleigh distribution.)

The easiest way to describe the normal distribution is to call it the distribution of the sums of uniformly distributed random numbers. In the antediluvian days before computers, teachers used to illustrate this fact by assigning students the task of adding up every group of four of the last four digits of telephone numbers on two pages taken at random from a city telephone directory and plotting the sums as a histogram. We are fortunate; we can let our personal computer do it for us:

```
10 CLS: RANDOMIZE TIME
20 ' THIS PROGRAM PLOTS A HISTOGRAM
30 ' OF THE NORMAL DISTRIBUTION
40 INPUT "INPUT NUMBER OF UNIFORM DISTRIBUTIONS TO
ADD "; RANGE
50 CLS: DIM BAR(10)
60 FOR I = 1 to 1000
70 GOSUB 170 ' GET AN OCCURRENCE IN THE RANGE 0-1
80 X = INT(X*10 + 1)
90 BAR(X) = BAR(X) = BAR(X) + 1
100 NEXT I
110 FOR I = 1 TO 10
120 LOCATE I*2,1: PRINT BAR(I)
130 LOCATE I*2,10: FOR J = 1 TO INT(BAR(I)/10) + 1: PRINT
"*";: NEXT J
140 NEXT I
150 LOCATE 23,15: PRINT"DISTRIBUTION OF THE SUM OF "
RANGE " UNIFORM DISTRIBUTIONS"
160 END
170 ' SUBROUTINE UNIFORM
180 X = 0
190 FOR K = 1 TO RANGE
200 X = X + RND
210 NEXT K
220 X = X/RANGE
230 RETURN
```

```
 96      *********
109      **********
 95      *********
 88      ********
101      **********
102      **********
 94      *********
108      **********
117      ***********
 90      *********
```

            DISTRIBUTION OF THE SUM OF 1 UNIFORM DISTRIBUTIONS
Ok

FIGURE 6–2 Histogram of a uniform frequency distribution.

The program adds a selected number of values from a uniform distribution and plots a histogram of the sums. In statement 30 we choose the number of samples to add, and call that number RANGE. The program produces 1,000 sums. The sums are generated in a subroutine beginning with statement 160. We scale the sum back into the range 0 to 1 by dividing it by RANGE. Then we scale it into the range 1 to 10, integerize it, and assign it to one of the ten bars of a histogram; we make a count of the number of sums assigned to each bar and plot the histogram by printing one asterisk for every ten occurrences.

If we run the program and set RANGE equal to 1, we generate the same kind of distribution we encountered in Chapter Three when we were experimenting with the uniform distribution (see Figure 6–2).

However, if we set RANGE equal to 2, we generate a triangular distribution (Figure 6–3). When we set RANGE equal to 4, the histogram is a trapezoid, but it is beginning to assume the characteristic shape of the bell curve (Figure 6–4). With RANGE equal to 12, the distribution becomes a true normal distribution with a mean equal to 5 (because of our scaling rules) and a standard deviation equal to 1 (see Figure 6–5).

We can use this approach, called convolution, to generate random draws from any normal distribution we desire; we only need to know the mean and the standard deviation of the particular normal distribution we want to simulate. The routine is:

```
' NORMAL DISTRIBUTION
SUM = 0
FOR I = 1 TO 12
SUM = SUM + RND
```

```
21      ***

58      ******

92      **********

155     *****************

160     *****************

204     ********************

150     ****************

79      ********

59      ******

22      ***
```

```
                DISTRIBUTION OF THE SUM OF  2  UNIFORM DISTRIBUTIONS
Ok
```

FIGURE 6–3 Histogram of two uniform frequency distributions added together, observation by observations (i.e., convolved), to make a triangular distribution.

```
NEXT I
NORMAL = ( SUM − 6 ) * STD . DEV + MEAN
RETURN
```

When we add 12 random numbers in the range 0 to 1, the result can range from 0 to 12. We want to scale this into a standard normal distribution; this distribution has, by definition, a mean equal to 0 and a standard deviation equal to 1. We make the mean equal 0 by subtracting 6 from each sum. The

FIGURE 6–4 Four uniform frequency distributions added together to produce a trapezoidal distribution that is approximately normal.

```
1       *

10      **

54      ******

175     ******************

242     ************************

252     *************************

178     ******************

76      ********

12      **

0       *
```

```
                DISTRIBUTION OF THE SUM OF  4  UNIFORM DISTRIBUTIONS
Ok
```

```
 0       *

 0       *

 11      **

 114     ***********

 358     **********************************

 415     *******************************************

 95      *********

 7       *

 0       *

 0       *

              DISTRIBUTION OF THE SUM OF  12  UNIFORM DISTRIBUTIONS
Ok
```

FIGURE 6–5 Twelve uniform frequency distributions added together to produce a truly normal distribution.

fact that we used 12 random draws takes care of making the standard deviation equal to 1.

The mean of a uniform distribution is given by:

MEAN = (B + A) / 2

In the case of our random numbers, B = 1 and A = 0, so the mean equals .5. Since we are adding 12 distributions, the mean of the resulting distribution is equal to 12 × .5, or 6.

The variance of a uniform distribution is given by:

VARIANCE = (B − A)^2 / 12

In the case of our random numbers, the variance equals $\frac{1}{12}$. Since we are adding 12 distributions, the variance of the resulting distribution is equal to 1. The standard deviation is defined as the square root of the variance and is also equal to 1.

We then fatten (or narrow) the spread of our distribution by multiplying each observation by STD.DEV, the standard deviation of the distribution we desire to simulate. We then translate our simulated distribution along the X-axis by adding MEAN to every observation, where MEAN is the mean of the distribution we want to simulate. NORMAL, the result returned by the subroutine, is one observation from the distribution we want.

We can do many things with this distribution, depending upon the system we want to simulate. We can squeeze it, stretch it, translate it left or right along the horizontal axis; and we can truncate it or chop off regions in the tail that

```
10 ' NORMAL DISTRIBUTION
20 '
30 CLS: KEY OFF
40 INPUT "ENTER EX"; EX
50 INPUT "ENTER STDX"; STDX
60 DIM S(20), D(20)
70 TIME=VAL(RIGHT$(TIME$,2))+VAL(MID$(TIME$,4,2))
80 TIME=TIME+VAL(LEFT$(TIME$,2))
90 RANDOMIZE TIME
100 LOCATE 1,40: INPUT "ENTER RANGE "; RANGE
110 FOR I=1 TO 20
120 S(I)=RANGE*I/20
130 NEXT I
140 FOR I=1 TO 100
150 GOSUB 280
160 FOR J=1 TO 20
170 IF R<=S(J) THEN D(J)=D(J)+1: GOTO 190
180 NEXT J
190 NEXT I
200 LOCATE 3,1
210 FOR I=1 TO 20
220 PRINT USING"###.## ";S(I);
230 FOR J=1 TO D(I)
240 PRINT"*";
250 NEXT J: PRINT
260 NEXT I
270 END
280 ' SUBROUTINE NORMAL
290 SUM=0
300 FOR II=1 TO 12
310 SUM=SUM+RND
320 NEXT II
330 R=STDX*(SUM-6)+EX
340 RETURN
```

FIGURE 6–6 Program to generate and plot a normal distribution by using the principle of the central limit theorem (i.e., the tendency of sample means or sums to approach normality).

make no sense in our simulation, such as negative numbers if we are simulating the time to accomplish a task.

There are at least three ways to generate a normal distribution. We have just described a method, one that makes use of the central-limit theorem. Figure 6–6 will generate and display a normal distribution using this technique. You must enter the mean (EX for expectation), standard deviation (STDX), and range of display. Figure 6–7 shows a normal distribution with a mean of 10 and a standard deviation of 3 plotted over a range of 20.

The direct method of generating a normal distribution makes use of sines, cosines, and logarithms. The program in Figure 6–8 implements this method, and the result is plotted in Figure 6–9. It can be faster than the central-limit technique, because two observations are produced in each call to the generating routine. However, in the program shown, one of these is discarded.

If you are interested in modeling normally distributed events that occur rarely, such as a high water level in a river that exceeds the height of the protecting levee, you will want to make sure that the tails of your distribution are faithfully reproduced. Teichroew's approximation, implemented by the program in Figure 6–10, makes use of a polynomial to correct the shape of the tails. A distribution produced by it is shown in Figure 6–11. Note how all three methods produce similar results, as shown by Figures 6–7, 6–9, and 6–11.

```
ENTER EX? 10                          ENTER RANGE ? 20
ENTER STDX? 3
  1.00 *
  2.00
  3.00 **
  4.00 **
  5.00 **
  6.00 ******
  7.00 ********
  8.00 ******
  9.00 *********
 10.00 *********
 11.00 ***********
 12.00 ***************
 13.00 ********
 14.00 ****
 15.00 ********
 16.00 ****
 17.00 **
 18.00 *
 19.00
 20.00
Ok
```

FIGURE 6–7   Normal distribution produced by the central-limit technique.

FIGURE 6–8   Program to generate and plot a normal distribution using the direct method, which involves using logarithms, sines, and cosines.

```
10 ' NORMAL DISTRIBUTION -- DIRECT APPROACH
20 '
30 TWOPI=6.2832
40 CLS: KEY OFF
50 INPUT "ENTER EX"; EX
60 INPUT "ENTER STDX"; STDX
70 DIM S(20), D(20)
80 TIME=VAL(RIGHT$(TIME$,2))+VAL(MID$(TIME$,4,2))
90 TIME=TIME+VAL(LEFT$(TIME$,2))
100 RANDOMIZE TIME
110 LOCATE 1,40: INPUT "ENTER RANGE "; RANGE
120 FOR I=1 TO 20
130 S(I)=RANGE*I/20
140 NEXT I
150 FOR I=1 TO 100
160 GOSUB 290
170 FOR J=1 TO 20
180 IF R<=S(J) THEN D(J)=D(J)+1: GOTO 200
190 NEXT J
200 NEXT I
210 LOCATE 3,1
220 FOR I=1 TO 20
230 PRINT USING"###.## ";S(I);
240 FOR J=1 TO D(I)
250 PRINT"*";
260 NEXT J: PRINT
270 NEXT I
280 END
290 ' SUBROUTINE NORMAL
300 IF RND >=.5 THEN 320
310 R=STDX*SQR(-2*LOG(RND))*COS(TWOPI*RND)+EX: GOTO 330
320 R=STDX*SQR(-2*LOG(RND))*SIN(TWOPI*RND)+EX
330 RETURN
```

```
ENTER EX? 10                              ENTER RANGE ? 20
ENTER STDX? 3
   1.00
   2.00
   3.00 *
   4.00 *
   5.00
   6.00 *****
   7.00 ****
   8.00 *********
   9.00 **********
  10.00 **************
  11.00 *************
  12.00 ***********
  13.00 *******
  14.00 **********
  15.00 ***
  16.00 *****
  17.00 ***
  18.00 **
  19.00
  20.00
Ok
```

FIGURE 6–9   Normal distribution produced by the direct method.

FIGURE 6–10   Program to generate and plot a normal distribution using Teichroew's approximation.

```
10 ' TEICHROEW'S APPROXIMATION TO THE NORMAL DISTRIBUTION
20 '
30 CLS: KEY OFF
40 INPUT "ENTER EX"; EX
50 INPUT "ENTER STDX"; STDX
60 DIM S(20), D(20)
70 TIME=VAL(RIGHT$(TIME$,2))+VAL(MID$(TIME$,4,2))
80 TIME=TIME+VAL(LEFT$(TIME$,2))
90 RANDOMIZE TIME
100 LOCATE 1,40: INPUT "ENTER RANGE "; RANGE
110 FOR I=1 TO 20
120 S(I)=RANGE*I/20
130 NEXT I
140 FOR I=1 TO 100
150 GOSUB 280
160 FOR J=1 TO 20
170 IF R<=S(J) THEN D(J)=D(J)+1: GOTO 190
180 NEXT J
190 NEXT I
200 LOCATE 3,1
210 FOR I=1 TO 20
220 PRINT USING"###.## ";S(I);
230 FOR J=1 TO D(I)
240 PRINT"*";
250 NEXT J: PRINT
260 NEXT I
270 END
280 ' SUBROUTINE TEICHROEW
290 SUM=0
300 FOR II=1 TO 12
310 SUM=SUM+RND
320 NEXT II
330 Y=(SUM-6)/4
340 Z=Y*(3.949846138#+Y*Y(.252408784#+Y*Y(.076542912#
    +Y*Y(8.355968E-03+Y*Y(.029899776#)))))
350 R=STDX*Z+EX
360 RETURN
```

```
ENTER EX? 10                          ENTER RANGE ? 20
ENTER STDX? 3
  1.00
  2.00
  3.00
  4.00 **
  5.00
  6.00 ****
  7.00 *****
  8.00 ************
  9.00 **********
 10.00 ****************
 11.00 **************
 12.00 *********
 13.00 *********
 14.00 ******
 15.00 *****
 16.00 ******
 17.00
 18.00
 19.00
 20.00
Ok
```

FIGURE 6–11 Normal distribution produced using Teichroew's approximation.

LOGNORMAL DISTRIBUTION

The normal distribution can be regarded as the result of the additive interaction of several independent uniform distributions. If these distributions interact multiplicatively, then the proper model is the lognormal distribution. A program for generating and displaying a lognormal distribution is given in Figure 6–12, and a histogram generated by it is shown in Figure 6–13.

Notice that in this distribution there is no negative region and the values tend to bunch up on the left and tail off to the right. This distribution has been used to model the distribution of particles by size, companies by capitalization, and the frequency of appearance of words in texts. It fits the same general class of models as does the exponential distribution (which will be discussed in the next section), but in some cases gives a better fit to empirical data.

Accurately representing system behavior by appropriate statistical distributions is the essence of simulation modeling. The best way to gain skill in doing this is to experiment on your own with the generating programs in this chapter.

Because the normal distribution is a continuous function, its use in waiting-line simulations is restricted to simulations of intervals of time; simulating events per unit time requires use of a discrete distribution. Actually, arrival times are usually simulated best by one of the family of exponential distributions.

EXPONENTIAL DISTRIBUTION

The exponential distribution is useful when you want to simulate a system in which the vast majority of events take place in a relatively short time, while there

```
10 ' LOGNORMAL DISTRIBUTION
20 CLS: KEY OFF
30 INPUT "ENTER EX"; EX
40 INPUT "ENTER STDX"; STDX
50 STDY=SQR(LOG(((STDX*STDX)/(EX*EX))+1))
60 EY=LOG(EX)-.5*LOG(((STDX*STDX)/(EX*EX))+1)
70 LOCATE 1,30: PRINT "EY="EY
80 LOCATE 2,30: PRINT "STND DEV="STDY
90 DIM S(20), D(20)
100 TIME=VAL(RIGHT$(TIME$,2))+VAL(MID$(TIME$,4,2))+VAL(LEFT$(TIME$,2))
110 RANDOMIZE TIME
120 LOCATE 1,55: INPUT "ENTER RANGE "; RANGE
130 FOR I=1 TO 20
140 S(I)=RANGE*I/20
150 NEXT I
160 FOR I=1 TO 100
170 GOSUB 270
180 FOR J=1 TO 20
190 IF R<=S(J) THEN D(J)=D(J)+1: GOTO 210
200 NEXT J
210 NEXT I
220 LOCATE 3,1
230 FOR I=1 TO 20
240 PRINT USING"###.## ";S(I);: FOR J=1 TO D(I): PRINT"*";: NEXT J: PRINT
250 NEXT I
260 END
270 ' SUBROUTINE LOGNORMAL
280 SUM=0
290 FOR II=1 TO 12
300 SUM=SUM+RND
310 R=EXP(EY+STDY*(SUM-6))
320 NEXT II
330 RETURN
```

FIGURE 6–12 Program to generate and plot a lognormal distribution.

are a few that can take a very long time indeed. Typical examples are: the lifetimes of some electronic parts, the times between the arrivals of vehicles on a highway, and the times to serve customers on the teller line in a bank (most people are served quickly, but the little old lady ahead of you is depositing the day's receipts from a penny-candy store—and she didn't even roll her pennies!).

FIGURE 6–13 Lognormal distribution illustrating its positive skew.

```
ENTER EX? 5                    EY= 1.535228           ENTER RANGE ? 20
ENTER STDX? 2                  STND DEV= .3852531
  1.00
  2.00 *
  3.00 ********
  4.00 **************************
  5.00 *********************
  6.00 ********************
  7.00 **********
  8.00 *****
  9.00 ***
 10.00 *
 11.00 **
 12.00
 13.00 **
 14.00
 15.00
 16.00
 17.00
 18.00
 19.00
 20.00
Ok
```

We can plot histograms of exponential distributions using the same program as we used to plot normal distributions with a couple of changes:

. . .

```
30 ' OF AN EXPONENTIAL DISTRIBUTION
40 INPUT " ENTER MEAN "; MEAN
```
. . .

```
150 LOCATE 23,15:PRINT"NEGATIVE EXPONENTIAL
DISTRIBUTION WITH MEAN = "MEAN
```
. . .

```
170 ' SUBROUTINE EXPONENTIAL
180 X = -LOG(RND)*MEAN
190 IF X > 1 THEN 170
200 RETURN
```

In this program, statement 190 constrains values to the range 0 to 1 because the subroutine can generate values outside of this range. Figures 6–14, 6–15, 6–16, and 6–17 show exponential distributions (or portions of them) having means equal to .1, .5, 1.0, and 5.0.

FIGURE 6–14   Histogram of a negative exponential frequency distribution having a mean of 0.1.

```
634     ******************************************************************
236     ***********************
90      *********
20      ***
15      **
3       *
1       *
1       *
0       *
0       *

          NEGATIVE EXPONENTIAL DISTRIBUTION WITH MEAN =  .1
Ok
```

```
196      ********************
175      *****************
152      ***************
101      ***********
101      ***********
 84      *********
 62      *******
 59      ******
 37      ****
 33      ****
```

```
              NEGATIVE EXPONENTIAL DISTRIBUTION WITH MEAN =  .5
Ok
```

FIGURE 6-15   Negative exponential frequency distribution having a mean of 0.5.

The derivation of the formula for generating exponentially distributed random variates is a good example of the integer-inverse process.

The frequency function of the negative exponential distribution is given by:

$$f(x) = A*e\char94(-A*X) \text{ where } A = 1/M \text{ and } e = 2.7183$$

Integrating this expression from 0 and X, we obtain:

$$CUM.PROB = 1 - e\char94(A*X)$$

FIGURE 6-16   Negative exponential distribution having a mean of 1.0.

```
148      **************
153      ***************
125      *************
 98      **********
104      **********
 83      *********
 78      ********
 88      *********
 55      ******
 68      *******
```

```
              NEGATIVE EXPONENTIAL DISTRIBUTION WITH MEAN =  1
Ok
```

```
128      *************
94       *********
99       *********
103      **********
101      **********
106      **********
86       *********
97       *********
84       *********
102      **********
```

          NEGATIVE EXPONENTIAL DISTRIBUTION WITH MEAN =   5
Ok

FIGURE 6–17 Exponential distribution (truncated) having a mean of 5.0.

We can regard $1 - CUM.PROB$ as a random number, so we have:

$$e\hat{\ } - (A*X) = RND$$

We take the inverse by taking the natural logarithm of each side and solving for X:

$$LOG (e\hat{\ } - (A*X)) = LOG(RND)$$

$$-X/M = LOG(RND)$$

$$X = -M*LOG(RND)$$

If you run the program several times, varying MEAN from .1 to 5, you will observe that the shape of the curve changes from being sharply concave upward to being slightly concave downward. For high values of MEAN, the general shape looks something like that of the normal distribution except that it is bunched up at the left and stretched out on the right. It is, in fact, a plot of the function:

$$Y = e\hat{\ }(-M*X)$$

which is where the name negative exponential comes from.

Figure 6–18 is a program that generates and plots exponential distributions.

```
10 ' EXPONENTIAL DISTRIBUTION
20 '
30 CLS: KEY OFF
40 INPUT "ENTER MEAN"; EX
50 DIM S(20), D(20)
60 TIME=VAL(RIGHT$(TIME$,2))+VAL(MID$(TIME$,4,2))
70 TIME=TIME+VAL(LEFT$(TIME$,2))
80 RANDOMIZE TIME
90 LOCATE 1,30: PRINT "STND DEV="EX
100 LOCATE 1,55: INPUT "ENTER RANGE "; RANGE
110 FOR I=1 TO 20
120 S(I)=RANGE*I/20
130 NEXT I
140 FOR I=1 TO 100
150 GOSUB 290
160 FOR J=1 TO 20
170 IF R<=S(J) THEN D(J)=D(J)+1: GOTO 190
180 NEXT J
190 NEXT I
200 LOCATE 3,1
210 FOR I=1 TO 20
220 PRINT USING "###.## ";S(I);
230 FOR J=1 TO D(I)
240 PRINT"*";
250 NEXT J: PRINT
260 NEXT I
270 END
280 ' SUBROUTINE EXPONENTIAL
290 R=-EX*LOG(RND)
300 RETURN
```

FIGURE 6–18 Program to generate and plot a negative exponential distribution.

ELEMENTARY QUEUING THEORY

There exists in a branch of mathematics called Queuing Theory an analytic solution for a waiting-line system in which both the times between customer arrivals and the service times can be represented by exponential distributions. If we call the arrival rate L and call the service rate U, the average length of the waiting line, Q, is given by:

$$Q = L\char94 2 / U*(U - L)$$

Notice that if the arrival rate equals or exceeds the service rate (that is, if customers arrive faster than they can be served), the length of the waiting line becomes either infinite or negative; this means that the system is unstable and there is no analytic answer.

You can check out the analytic solution using the event-oriented simulation program. If we say that the mean time between arrivals (1/L) is 120 seconds and the mean service time (1/U) is 90 seconds, queuing theory tells us that the average length of the waiting line should be 2.25.

If we run the simulation program for 200,000 seconds, we find that there are 1,633 arrivals, the mean time between arrivals is 122.5 seconds, the mean service time is 92.2 seconds, and the average queue length is 2.11. If we run it for 500,000 seconds (almost 6 days in real time), we have 4,227 arrivals, arrival time is 118.3 seconds, service time is 90.6 seconds, and queue length is 2.29. This suggests that the value returned by the simulation program will eventually converge upon the analytic solution.

POLLACZEK-KHINTCHINE EQUATION

Queuing theory also provides a solution to the case in which the service times are distributed according to some probability law other than the exponential distribution. In this formula we make use of a quantity R, which is equal to L/U; and the standard deviation S of the service time distribution:

$$Q = (L\char94 2 * S\char94 2 + R\char94 2) / 2 * (1 - R\char94 2)$$

We shall check out this solution with our event-oriented simulation program using the NORMAL SUBROUTINE to obtain the service times. We shall let the MEAN equal 90 seconds and the STANDARD DEVIATION equal 10 seconds. The formula tells us that the average length of queue should be 1.14 customers.

```
10 ' GAMMA FUNCTION
20 '
30 DIM FX(22), FFX(22)
40 CLS: KEY OFF
50 LOCATE 1, 1
60 INPUT "ENTER SHAPING PARAMETER 'A' (A > -1) "; A
70 LOCATE 2, 1
80 INPUT "ENTER SHAPING PARAMETER 'B' (B > 0) "; B
90 GOSUB 210 ' GAMMA FUNCTION SUBROUTINE
100 FOR I=1 TO 22
110 FX(I) = (((B^(A+1))*FA)^(-1))*(I^A)
    *(2.718282^(-I/B))
120 FFX=FFX+FX(I): FFX(I)=FFX
130 NEXT I
140 FOR I = 1 TO 22
150 IF FX(I)<.00005 THEN 200
160 LOCATE I+2, 1
170 PRINT USING "## ";I;
180 PRINT USING " #.####"; FX(I); FFX(I)
190 NEXT I
200 END
210 ' GAMMA(A+1) = A!
220 FA = 1
230 IF A = 0 THEN 280
240 IF A = 1 THEN 280
250 FOR II = 1 TO A
260 FA = FA*II
270 NEXT II
280 RETURN
```

An alternative way to generate the grammar distribution function in Figure 6-19.

Running the event-oriented simulation program for 200,000 seconds, we obtain 1,660 arrivals, a mean interarrival time of 120.5 seconds, a mean service time of 90.4 seconds, and an average queue length of 1.07. If we run it for 500,000 seconds, service time is 90.4 seconds, and queue length is 1.23. The simulated value appears to be converging on the analytic value but not nearly as fast as in the purely exponential case.

There is a whole family of probability distributions related to the exponential that are used in special applications. These include the hyper-exponential—that is, one with two means; the Weibul distribution, which is used in Reliability Theory; and the Erlang distribution, which is actually the sum of several exponential distributions. The exponential distribution is used in deriving the beta distribution, which is used to model a Bernoulli case in which the probability varies.

These experiments should convince you that, just as it is usually easier to find areas and volumes by geometry or calculus rather than by simulation, you should resort to simulation to solve waiting-line problems only if:

1. You are dealing with an oddball problem for which there is no analytic solution.
2. Your problem is extremely complex.
3. You don't know enough about queuing theory to solve it.

The ideal approach is to select the best of both worlds. Simplify your problem, or, as we say, "skeletonize" it, until you can get an approximate solution using queuing theory; then simulate using the analytic solution as a guide to how many iterations of the simulation program it will take to converge on an acceptably precise answer.

GAMMA (CHI-SQUARED) DISTRIBUTION

The gamma distribution may be fitted to many skewed distributions of empirical data. It has the following distribution function:

$$f(X) = (A\char94 K*x\char94(K-1)*exp(-A*X))/ (K-1)!$$

where A and K are shaping parameters. The mean is given by:

$$EX = K/A$$

The standard deviation is given by:

$$STDX = SQR(K)/A$$

When K is an integer, the gamma distribution is called an Erlang distribution. This distribution is derived from the exponential distribution in a way similar to that by which the normal distribution was derived from the uniform distribution: by adding up a certain number of observations.

The two shaping parameters of this gamma distribution are A, the reciprocal of the mean of the exponential distributions from which it is made; and K, the number of observations from exponential distributions going to make up one observation from the gamma distribution.

If the times between arrivals of vehicles on a lightly traveled highway are exponentially distributed with a mean of two minutes and every fifth vehicle is determined to be a truck, then the times between arrivals of trucks would be modeled by a gamma distribution with A equal to .5 and K equal to 5.

However, the gamma distribution is more commonly used to fit normally appearing distributions that are skewed or flattened. These include distributions of times to accomplish tasks. They exist only in the positive domain and are often skewed to the right, because some people will take a very long time to do a job if you let them.

Figure 6–19 generates and plots an Erlang gamma distribution. It does not add the exponential observations; instead it takes the logarithm of their product, which is an equivalent procedure. Figure 6–20 is a gamma distribution with A equal to .5 and K equal to 3.

Another way to generate gamma distributions is to add up the squares of random observations from a standard normal distribution. The result is called the chi-squared distribution. Its mean is equal to M, the number of squared

```
10 ' GAMMA DISTRIBUTION
20 '
30 CLS: KEY OFF
40 INPUT "ENTER PARAMETER A"; A
50 INPUT "ENTER PARAMETER K"; K
60 EX=K/A: STDX=SQR(K/(A*A))
70 LOCATE 1,30: PRINT "EX="EX
80 LOCATE 2,30: PRINT "STND DEV="STDX
90 DIM S(20), D(20)
100 TIME=VAL(RIGHT$(TIME$,2))
        +VAL(MID$(TIME$,4,2))+VAL(LEFT$(TIME$,2))
110 RANDOMIZE TIME
120 LOCATE 1,55: INPUT "ENTER RANGE "; RANGE
130 FOR I=1 TO 20
140 S(I)=RANGE*I/20
150 NEXT I
160 FOR I=1 TO 100
170 GOSUB 280
180 FOR J=1 TO 20
190 IF R<=S(J) THEN D(J)=D(J)+1: GOTO 210
200 NEXT J
210 NEXT I
220 LOCATE 3,1
230 FOR I=1 TO 20
240 PRINT USING"###.## ";S(I);
250 FOR J=1 TO D(I): PRINT"*";: NEXT J: PRINT
260 NEXT I
270 END
280 ' SUBROUTINE GAMMA
290 TR=1
300 FOR II=1 TO K
310 TR=TR*RND
320 R=-LOG(TR)/A
330 NEXT II
340 RETURN
```

FIGURE 6–19 Program to generate and plot a gamma (Erlang) distribution.

```
ENTER PARAMETER A? .5        EX= 6                  ENTER RANGE ? 10
ENTER PARAMETER K? 3         STND DEV= 3.464102
   0.50
   1.00 **
   1.50 ****
   2.00 **
   2.50 **
   3.00 ******
   3.50 *******
   4.00 ****
   4.50 *
   5.00 ********
   5.50 ***
   6.00 *********
   6.50 ****
   7.00 ********
   7.50 ***
   8.00 *****
   8.50 *
   9.00 **
   9.50 *
  10.00 **
Ok
```

FIGURE 6–20   Histogram of a gamma distribution.

normal deviates going into one chi-squared observation; its standard deviation is SQR(2*M). Actually the chi-squared distribution is a special case of the gamma distribution in which A is equal to .5 and K is equal to M/2.

Figure 6–21 is a program that generates and plots a chi-squared distribution. Figure 6–22 is a chi-squared distribution equivalent to the gamma distribution shown in Figure 6–20.

BETA DISTRIBUTION

The beta distribution is also exponentially derived. It exists only between the limits of zero and one. It is often used to model a variable rate, such as the proportion of defective parts coming off an assembly line. The proportion is often very high on Monday, when assembly workers are recovering from a weekend. It may also be high on Friday, when the workers have their minds on holidays rather than business. The lowest percent defective occurs on Wednesday. It is said that members of the Ford family always order "Wednesday" cars as their personal vehicles.

The beta distribution follows the probability law:

$$f(X) = ((A + B - 1)! *^{(A - 1)} * (1 - X)^{(B - 1)})/(A - 1)! * (B - 1)!$$

where the mean is given by:

$$EX = A/(A + B)$$

```
10 ' CHI-SQUARED DISTRIBUTION
20 '
30 CLS: KEY OFF
40 INPUT "ENTER PARAMETER M ";M
50 EX=M: STDX=SQR(2*M)
60 LOCATE 1,35: PRINT "EX="EX
70 LOCATE 2,35: PRINT "STND DEV="STDX
80 DIM S(20), D(20)
90 TIME=VAL(RIGHT$(TIME$,2))+VAL(MID$(TIME$,4,2))
100 TIME=TIME+VAL(LEFT$(TIME$,2))
110 RANDOMIZE TIME
120 LOCATE 1,55: INPUT "ENTER RANGE "; RANGE
130 FOR I=1 TO 20
140 S(I)=RANGE*I/20
150 NEXT I
160 FOR I=1 TO 100
170 GOSUB 300
180 FOR J=1 TO 20
190 IF R<=S(J) THEN D(J)=D(J)+1: GOTO 210
200 NEXT J
210 NEXT I
220 LOCATE 3,1
230 FOR I=1 TO 20
240 PRINT USING"###.## ";S(I);
250 FOR J=1 TO D(I)
260 PRINT"*";
270 NEXT J: PRINT
280 NEXT I
290 END
300 ' SUBROUTINE CHI-SQUARED
310 R=0
320 FOR JJ=1 TO M
330 SUM=0
340 FOR II=1 TO 12
350 SUM=SUM+RND
360 NEXT II
370 R=R+(SUM-6)*(SUM-6)
380 NEXT JJ
390 RETURN
```

FIGURE 6-21 Program to generate and plot a chi-squared distribution.

FIGURE 6-22 Histogram of a chi-squared distribution that is equivalent to the gamma distribution shown in Figure 6-20.

```
ENTER PARAMETER M ? 6              EX= 6              ENTER RANGE ? 10
                                  STND DEV= 3.464102
    0.50
    1.00 *
    1.50 **
    2.00 ****
    2.50 *****
    3.00 *****
    3.50 *******
    4.00 *
    4.50 *****
    5.00 ******
    5.50 ******
    6.00 ***********
    6.50 ********
    7.00 ******
    7.50 ***
    8.00 ****
    8.50 ****
    9.00 *
    9.50 **
   10.00 ***
Ok
```

and the variance (STNX^2) by:

$$VX = EX*B/(A + B + 1)*(A + B)$$

The beta distribution can be generated as the ratio of two gamma distributions having identical values of A (.1 works well) and parameters K1 and K2 such that K = K1 + K2 is the parameter of (X1 + X2). The beta variable is given by:

$$X = X1/(X1 + X2)$$

Gamma parameters K1 and K2 correspond to beta parameters A and B.

I have used the beta distribution to help expert informants quantify qualitative estimates. The experts were asked to estimate whether a certain effect was "high," "medium," or "low"; to hedge their estimate as being "high," "medium," or "low"; and to state whether their confidence in their estimate was "high," "medium," or "low."

I used these qualitative estimates to select shaping parameters from 27 sets of pairs and to construct beta distributions characteristic of the expert's qualitative estimate. I then sampled from the distribution depicting the expert's qualitative estimate and displayed these beta variates to the expert until the expert chose one that he thought best quantified his estimate.

The following table gives the parameters of the beta distributions used to represent the different qualitative estimates. The codes for the qualitative estimates are: H = high, M = medium, and L = low. They are given in the order: PRIMARY estimate, HEDGE, and CONFIDENCE.

CODE	EX	VX	PARAMETER A	PARAMETER B
HHH	.91	.007	10	1
HHM	.90	.008	9	1
HHL	.89	.009	8	1
HMH	.88	.012	7	1
HMM	.86	.015	6	1
HML	.83	.019	5	1
HLH	.75	.014	9	3
HLM	.75	.021	6	2
HLL	.75	.038	3	1
MHH	.63	.014	10	6
MHM	.64	.017	7	4
MHL	.63	.026	5	3
MMH	.50	.012	10	4
MMM	.50	.014	9	9
MML	.50	.017	7	7
MLH	.375	.014	6	10
MLM	.385	.017	5	8

continued

CODE	EX	VX	PARAMETER A	PARAMETER B
MLL	.375	.026	3	5
LHH	.250	.014	3	9
LHM	.222	.017	2	7
LHL	.250	.038	1	3
LMH	.125	.012	1	7
LMM	.142	.015	1	6
LML	.167	.020	1	5
LLH	.091	.006	1	10
LLM	.100	.008	1	9
LLL	.111	.009	1	8

Figure 6–23 is a program to generate and display beta distributions. You will be asked to enter three estimates each of which may by H, M, or L. Figure 6–24 is an optimistic estimate (H, H, H); note how the points are piled up on the right (bottom). Figure 6–25 is a pessimistic estimate (L, L, H) and points are piled up on the left. Figure 6–26 is a middling estimate (M, M, M) and points are spread out through the midrange of the distribution.

POISSON DISTRIBUTION

If you want to use time-oriented simulation programs and are dealing with a waiting-line system in which the times between customer arrivals are exponentially distributed, it may be useful to use the discrete version of the exponential distribution, which is called the Poisson distribution. The Poisson distribution provides us with the probabilities of observing 0, 1, 2, . . . N events within some selected slice of time. One of its first applications was in representing the probable number of Prussian cavalry troopers killed each year by being kicked in the head by a horse. Like the remainder of distributions to be described, the Poisson distribution is discrete, as contrasted with the continuous ones we have been examining.

The Poisson distribution has been used to model the number of typographical errors on a newspaper page, the number of fatal accidents per year per mile of highway, the number of flaws per square yard of carpet, the number of inclusions per square foot of tin-plated steel, or the number of crimes per hour per census tract.

The probability of X events per unit (unit time or whatever) is given by the formula:

$$p(x) = e^{-X} * L^X / X!$$

where e is the Naperian or natural logarithm base equal to 2.718282 . . . , L is

```
10 ' BETA DISTRIBUTION
20 CLS: KEY OFF
30 DIM S(20), D(20), A(27), B(27)
40 FOR I=1 TO 27: READ A(I): NEXT I
50 FOR I=1 TO 27: READ B(I): NEXT I
60 DATA 9,8,7,6,5,4,8,5,2,9,6,4,9,8,6,5,4,2,0,0,0,0,0,0,2,1,0
70 DATA 0,0,0,0,0,0,2,1,0,5,3,2,9,8,6,9,7,4,9,8,7,6,5,4,8,6,2
80 TIME=VAL(RIGHT$(TIME$,2))+VAL(MID$(TIME$,4,2))+VAL(LEFT$(TIME$,2))
90 RANDOMIZE TIME
100 FOR I=1 TO 20: S(I)=I/20: NEXT I
110 PRINT "ENTER ESTIMATES: PRIMARY; HEDGE; CONFIDENCE: "
120 INPUT "TYPE: H, M, L";A$, B$, C$
130 IF A$="H" THEN A=1
140 IF A$="M" THEN A=10
150 IF A$="L" THEN A=19
160 IF B$="H" THEN B=0
170 IF B$="M" THEN B=3
180 IF B$="L" THEN B=6
190 IF C$="H" THEN C=0
200 IF C$="M" THEN C=1
210 IF C$="L" THEN C=2
220 IK=A+B+C
230 FOR I=1 TO 100
240 GOSUB 340
250 FOR J=1 TO 20
260 IF R<=S(J) THEN D(J)=D(J)+1: GOTO 280
270 NEXT J
280 NEXT I
290 LOCATE 3,1
300 FOR I=1 TO 20
310 PRINT USING"###.## ";S(I);: FOR J=1 TO D(I): PRINT"*";: NEXT J: PRINT
320 NEXT I
330 END
340 ' SUBROUTINE BETA
350 K=A(IK)+1
360 GOSUB 430
370 NU=G
380 K=A(IK)+B(IK)+2
390 GOSUB 430
400 DE=G
410 R=NU/DE
420 RETURN
430 ' SUBROUTINE GAMMA
440 TR=1
450 FOR II=1 TO K
460 TR=TR*RND
470 G=-LOG(TR)/10
480 NEXT II
490 RETURN
```

FIGURE 6–23 Program that generates and plots a beta distribution to help informants quantify qualitative estimates on a zero to one scale.

the mean or expected value of the probability (p) of X events occurring in the selected slice of time or space, and X! stands for "X factorial"; that is:

$$X! = 1 * 2 * \ldots * X$$

When X = 0, X! is defined as being equal to 1. Note that here, with a discrete distribution instead of a continuous one, we are still talking about a probability function p(X) rather than a frequency function f(X).

Actually, the Poisson formula helps us to create an array of probabilities, which we then handle the same way we handled the empirical probabilities in our introduction to time-oriented simulation; that is, we cumulate the probabilities and apply a "less than or equal to" criterion to each random number drawn. The following program allows us to see several different arrays of Poisson probabilities:

```
10 CLS: PRINT "                      POISSON PROBABILITY
LAW": PRINT: PRINT
20 INPUT "ENTER MEAN "; MEAN
30 INPUT "ENTER RANGE "; RANGE
40 DIM COUNT(RANGE), CUMPROB(RANGE)
50 FOR X=0 TO RANGE
60 GOSUB 200 ' FACTORIAL SUBROUTINE
70 PROB=(2.718282)^-MEAN)+(MEAN^X)/FACTORIAL
80 CUMPROB(X)=LASTPROB+PROB
90 LASTPROB=CUMPROB(X)
100 NEXT X
110 FOR K=1 TO 100
120 X=RND
130 FOR J=0 to RANGE
140 IF R <= CUMPROB(J) THEN COUNT(J)=COUNT(J)+1:GOTO
160
150 NEXT J,K
160 FOR I=1 TO RANGE
170 LOCATE I+3,5:PRINT USING "## ";I;:FORJ=1 TO
COUNT(I):PRINT "*";:NEXT J
180 NEXT I
190 END
200 ' FACTORIAL SUBROUTINE
210 FACTORIAL=0
220 IF X=0 THEN RETURN
230 IF X=1 THEN RETURN
240 FOR I=1 TO X
250 FACTORIAL=FACTORIAL*I
260 NEXT I
270 RETURN
```

```
ENTER ESTIMATES: PRIMARY; HEDGE; CONFIDENCE:
TYPE: H, M, L? H,H,H
 0.05
 0.10
 0.15
 0.20
 0.25
 0.30
 0.35 *
 0.40 **
 0.45 ****
 0.50 ***
 0.55 *****
 0.60 ****
 0.65 ******
 0.70 ****
 0.75 *****
 0.80 ******
 0.85 ********
 0.90 *******
 0.95 *****
 1.00 ******
Ok
```

FIGURE 6–24 Histogram of a beta distribution depicting extreme optimism: high primary expectation, skewed high, and held with high confidence.

```
ENTER ESTIMATES: PRIMARY; HEDGE; CONFIDENCE:
TYPE: H, M, L? L,L,H
 0.05 **
 0.10 ***************
 0.15 ***************
 0.20 *********
 0.25 ********
 0.30 ************
 0.35 **********
 0.40 ******
 0.45 ******
 0.50 *
 0.55 **
 0.60 ***
 0.65 ****
 0.70 *
 0.75
 0.80
 0.85 ***
 0.90 *
 0.95
 1.00
Ok
```

FIGURE 6–25 Histogram of a beta distribution depicting extreme pessimism: low primary expectation, skewed low, and held with high confidence.

```
ENTER ESTIMATES: PRIMARY; HEDGE; CONFIDENCE:
TYPE: H, M, L? M,M,M
 0.05
 0.10
 0.15
 0.20 *****
 0.25 **
 0.30 *****
 0.35 *******************
 0.40 *************
 0.45 ******
 0.50 *********
 0.55 *************
 0.60 ***
 0.65 ******
 0.70 ***
 0.75 ******
 0.80 ******
 0.85
 0.90
 0.95 *
 1.00
Ok
```

FIGURE 6–26 Histogram of a beta distribution depicting uncertainty: middling expectation, no skew, and held with medium confidence.

```
                    POISSON DISTRIBUTION

ENTER MEAN ?  1
ENTER RANGE ?  12

        0    ******************************
        1    *********************************************
        2    ***************
        3    ********
        4    **
        5
        6
        7
        8
        9
       10
       11
       12
Ok
```

FIGURE 6–27 Histogram of a Poisson frequency distribution having a mean of 1.

The input quantity **MEAN** is the average probability; **RANGE** is the largest possible number of occurrences in a time slice.

Statements 50 to 100 are a FOR-NEXT loop that gets the cumulative probability of each number of occurrences from none to RANGE. Statement 60 calls the FACTORIAL SUBROUTINE (statements 200 to 270) that recursively computes the value of X!. Statement 70 computes the probability of exactly X arrivals in a time slice. Statements 80 and 90 compute the cumulative probability of X arrivals in a time slice; that is, the probability of X or fewer arrivals.

Statements 110 to 160 draw 100 random numbers and, regarding each of them as a probability, classify them as to whether the draw would denote 0, 1, 2, ... or RANGE arrivals. An appropriate increment is made to one of the components of the COUNT vector. Statements 170 to 190 print and annotate the histogram for each value of X. Figures 6–27, 6–28, 6–29, and 6–30 show Poisson distributions having means of 1, 3, 6, and 9.

You can check out this program by reproducing the cumulated entries from a table of Poisson probabilities, which can be found in any statistics text

```
                    POISSON DISTRIBUTION

ENTER MEAN ?  3
ENTER RANGE ?  12

        0    *
        1    ***************
        2    ****************
        3    **************************
        4    **********************
        5    *******
        6    *******
        7    **
        8    *
        9
       10
       11
       12
Ok
```

FIGURE 6–28 Poisson frequency distribution having a mean of 3.

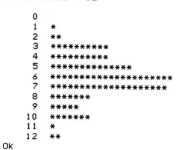

FIGURE 6–29 Poisson distribution having a mean of 6.

```
                    POISSON DISTRIBUTION
ENTER MEAN ? 6
ENTER RANGE ? 12

    0
    1  *
    2  **
    3  **********
    4  **********
    5  *************
    6  *********************
    7  ********************
    8  *******
    9  *****
   10  *******
   11  *
   12  **
Ok
```

or handbook. For example, if MEAN equals 3, RANGE equals 12, and the probabilities are:

ARRIVALS PER UNIT TIME	PROB	CUMULATIVE PROB
0	.0498	.0498
1	.1494	.1992
2	.2240	.4232
3	.2240	.6472
4	.1680	.8152
5	.1008	.9160
6	.0504	.9664
7	.0216	.9880
8	.0081	.9961
9	.0027	.9988
10	.0008	.9996
11	.0002	.9998
12	.0001	.9999

```
                    POISSON DISTRIBUTION
ENTER MEAN ? 9
ENTER RANGE ? 15

    0
    1
    2
    3  *
    4
    5  ********
    6  ********
    7  *********
    8  **************
    9  ******************
   10  ************
   11  ************
   12  ******
   13  **
   14  *******
   15  *
Ok
```

FIGURE 6–30 Poisson distribution with a mean of 9.

```
10 ' POISSON DISTRIBUTION
20 CLS: KEY OFF
30 INPUT "ENTER EX"; EX
40 LOCATE 1,30: PRINT "STND DEV=" SQR(EX)
50 DIM S(20), D(20)
60 TIME=VAL(RIGHT$(TIME$,2))+VAL(MID$(TIME$,4,2))+VAL(LEFT$(TIME$,2))
70 RANDOMIZE TIME
80 LOCATE 1,55: INPUT "ENTER RANGE "; RANGE
90 FOR I=1 TO 20
100 S(I)=RANGE*I/20
110 NEXT I
120 FOR I=1 TO 100
130 GOSUB 230
140 FOR J=1 TO 20
150 IF R<=S(J) THEN D(J)=D(J)+1: GOTO 170
160 NEXT J
170 NEXT I
180 LOCATE 3,1
190 FOR I=1 TO 20
200 PRINT USING"###.## ";S(I);: FOR J=1 TO D(I): PRINT"*";: NEXT J: PRINT
210 NEXT I
220 END
230 ' SUBROUTINE POISSON
240 R=0
250 B=EXP(-EX)
260 TR=1
270 TR=TR*RND
280 IF TR-B <0 THEN 290 ELSE R=R+1: GOTO 270
290 RETURN
```

FIGURE 6–31 Program to generate and plot a Poisson distribution.

If you want to write a Poisson subroutine for a time-oriented simulation, calculate the CUMPROB vector in advance, store the results in your service-time subroutine, and use them just as we used the empirical arrival-rate distribution in Chapter Four. Figure 6–31 will generate and plot a Poisson distribution.

NEGATIVE BINOMIAL DISTRIBUTION

When Bernoulli trials are repeated until K successes occur, the random variate X signifying the number of failures that occur will follow a negative binomial distribution. When K is an integer, this distribution is called a Pascal distribution. When K is equal to one, it is called a geometric distribution.

The next three probability functions make use of the binomial coefficient. In its simplist form it is expressed as "N CHOOSE X." Operationally it corresponds to:

$$N!/X!*(N-X)!$$

The probability function of the negative binomial distribution incorporates the binomial coefficient in the form: $(K+X-1)$ CHOOSE X. The function is given by:

$$p(X) = ((K+X-1)!/X!*(K-1)!)*P\char`\^K*Q\char`\^K$$

where P is the proportion of desired outcomes in the universe under consideration and Q is equal to $1 - P$. The mean is given by:

$$EX = KQ/P$$

and the variance is given by:

$$VX = KQ/P^2$$

Figure 6–32 is a program to generate and plot a Pascal distribution. Figure 6–33 is the plot of a geometric distribution (K = 1) with P equal to .5. The geometric distribution turns out to describe the distribution of queue lengths in the case of exponential times between arrivals and exponential service times. I have also used it to describe the distribution of the occurrence frequencies of some word types and the distribution of sensitive documents among different security classifications. Figure 6–34 shows a Pascal distribution with P equal to .5 and K equal to 3.

```
10 ' PASCAL (GEOMETRIC) DISTRIBUTION
20 '
30 CLS: KEY OFF
40 INPUT "ENTER PARAMETER P";P
50 INPUT "ENTER PARAMETER K";K
60 Q=1-P: EX=(K*Q)/P
70 VX=(K*Q)/(P*P)
80 LOCATE 1,35: PRINT "EX="EX
90 LOCATE 2,35: PRINT "STND DEV="SQR(VX)
100 DIM S(20), D(20)
110 TIME=VAL(RIGHT$(TIME$,2))+VAL(MID$(TIME$,4,2))
120 TIME=TIME+VAL(LEFT$(TIME$,2))
130 RANDOMIZE TIME
140 LOCATE 1,55: INPUT "ENTER RANGE "; RANGE
150 FOR I=1 TO 20
160 S(I)=RANGE*I/20
170 NEXT I
180 FOR I=1 TO 100
190 GOSUB 320
200 FOR J=1 TO 20
210 IF R<=S(J) THEN D(J)=D(J)+1: GOTO 230
220 NEXT J
230 NEXT I
240 LOCATE 3,1
250 FOR I=1 TO 20
260 PRINT USING"###.## ";S(I);
270 FOR J=1 TO D(I)
280 PRINT"*";
290 NEXT J: PRINT
300 NEXT I
310 END
320 ' SUBROUTINE PASCAL
330 TR=1
340 QR=LOG(Q)
350 FOR II=1 TO K
360 TR=TR*RND
370 NEXT II
380 R=LOG(TR)/QR
390 RETURN
```

FIGURE 6–32 Program to generate and plot a negative binomial (Pascal) distribution.

```
ENTER PARAMETER P? .5          EX= 1              ENTER RANGE ? 20
ENTER PARAMETER K? 1           STND DEV= 1.414214
   1.00 *********************************************
   2.00 ************************
   3.00 *****************
   4.00 *******
   5.00 ****
   6.00 **
   7.00
   8.00 *
   9.00
  10.00
  11.00
  12.00
  13.00
  14.00
  15.00
  16.00
  17.00
  18.00
  19.00
  20.00
Ok
```

FIGURE 6–33 Pascal distribution with K = 1. Also known as the geometric distribution.

BINOMIAL DISTRIBUTION

When random samples are taken N at a time from an infinitely large population having a proportion P of desired characteristics (e.g., red balls, as opposed to white ones; or defective parts in a quality-control application), the distribution of the number of successes in each draw X is given by the binomial. In the case

FIGURE 6–34 Pascal distribution that is the sum (convolution) of three geometric distributions.

```
ENTER PARAMETER P? .5          EX= 3              ENTER RANGE ? 20
ENTER PARAMETER K? 3           STND DEV= 2.44949
   1.00 **
   2.00 *********
   3.00 ***************
   4.00 ****************
   5.00 ****************
   6.00 *************
   7.00 ********
   8.00 ********
   9.00 *****
  10.00 **
  11.00 ****
  12.00
  13.00
  14.00
  15.00
  16.00
  17.00
  18.00
  19.00
  20.00
Ok
```

of a finite population, samples should be returned and the population randomly mixed before another draw is made; this is called sampling with replacement.

The probability function is given by:

$$p(X) = (N!/X!*(N-X)!)*P^X*Q^(N-X)$$

where $X = 0, 1, 2, \ldots N$ and $Q = 1 - P$, and the coefficient is N CHOOSE P. The mean is given by:

$$EX = N*P$$

and the variance is given by:

$$VX = N*P*Q$$

Figure 6–35 is a program that generates and plots binomial distributions. Figure 6–36 is one of them with P = .5 and N = 10.

```
10 ' BINOMIAL DISTRIBUTION
20
30 CLS: KEY OFF
40 INPUT "ENTER PARAMETER P";P
50 INPUT "ENTER PARAMETER N";N
60 EX=N*P
70 Q=1-P: VX=N*P*Q
80 LOCATE 1,35: PRINT "EX="EX
90 LOCATE 2,35: PRINT "STND DEV="SQR(VX)
100 DIM S(20), D(20)
110 TIME=VAL(RIGHT$(TIME$,2))
120 TIME=TIME+VAL(MID$(TIME$,4,2))
130 TIME=TIME+VAL(LEFT$(TIME$,2))
140 RANDOMIZE TIME
150 LOCATE 1,55: INPUT "ENTER RANGE "; RANGE
160 FOR I=1 TO 20
170 S(I)=RANGE*I/20
180 NEXT I
190 FOR I=1 TO 100
200 GOSUB 320
210 FOR J=1 TO 20
220 IF R<=S(J) THEN D(J)=D(J)+1: GOTO 240
230 NEXT J
240 NEXT I
250 LOCATE 3,1
260 FOR I=1 TO 20
270 PRINT USING"###.## ";S(I);
280 FOR J=1 TO D(I)
290 PRINT"*";: NEXT J: PRINT
300 NEXT I
310 END
320 ' SUBROUTINE BINOMIAL
330 R=0
340 FOR II=1 TO N
350 IF RND-P <=0 THEN R=R+1
360 NEXT II
370 RETURN
```

FIGURE 6–35 Program to generate and plot the binomial distribution.

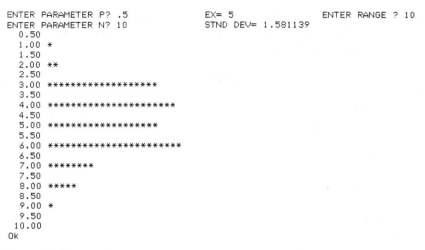

```
ENTER PARAMETER P? .5          EX= 5                    ENTER RANGE ? 10
ENTER PARAMETER N? 10          STND DEV= 1.581139
  0.50
  1.00 *
  1.50
  2.00 **
  2.50
  3.00 ******************
  3.50
  4.00 **********************
  4.50
  5.00 ******************
  5.50
  6.00 ***********************
  6.50
  7.00 ********
  7.50
  8.00 *****
  8.50
  9.00 *
  9.50
 10.00
Ok
```

FIGURE 6–36 Histogram of a binomial distribution.

HYPERGEOMETRIC DISTRIBUTION

If the population with initial proportion P of desired events from which samples of size N are to be taken is of finite size M and samples are taken without replacement, the appropriate probability distribution to describe the distribution of successes X is the hypergeometric distribution.

Its probability function is the product of two binomial coefficients: M*P CHOOSE X and M*Q CHOOSE (N − X); divided by a third, M CHOOSE N. The complete expression is:

$$p(X) = ((M*P!/X!*(M*P - X)!)*(M*Q!/ (N - X)!*(M*Q - N + X)!)/(M!/N!*(M - N)!$$

The mean is given by:

$$EX = N*P$$

and the variance is given by:

$$VX = ((M - N)/(M - 1))*N(P*Q)$$

Figure 6–37 is a program that generates and displays hypergeometric distributions. Figure 6–38 is one such distribution that differs from the one shown in the binomial case in that the population is finite. An error trap has been incorporated in the program to intercept attempts to divide by zero that may occur if the sample size and/or the number of trials is too great for the population size.

```
10 ' HYPERGEOMETRIC DISTRIBUTION
20 '
30 ON ERROR GOTO 450
40 CLS: KEY OFF
50 INPUT "ENTER PARAMETER P";P
60 INPUT "ENTER PARAMETERS M AND N"; M,N
70 EX=N*P
80 Q=1-P: VX=N*P*Q*((M-N)/(M-1))
90 LOCATE 1,35: PRINT "EX="EX
100 LOCATE 2,35: PRINT "STND DEV="SQR(VX)
110 DIM S(20), D(20)
120 TIME=VAL(RIGHT$(TIME$,2))+VAL(MID$(TIME$,4,2))
130 TIME=TIME+VAL(LEFT$(TIME$,2))
140 RANDOMIZE TIME
150 LOCATE 1,55: INPUT "ENTER RANGE "; RANGE
160 LOCATE 2,55: INPUT "ENTER TRIALS "; TRIALS
170 FOR I=1 TO 20
180 S(I)=RANGE*I/20
190 NEXT I
200 FOR I=1 TO TRIALS
210 GOSUB 340
220 FOR J=1 TO 20
230 IF R<=S(J) THEN D(J)=D(J)+1: GOTO 250
240 NEXT J
250 NEXT I
260 LOCATE 3,1
270 FOR I=1 TO 20
280 PRINT USING"###.## ";S(I);
290 FOR J=1 TO D(I)
300 PRINT"*";
310 NEXT J: PRINT
320 NEXT I
330 END
340 ' SUBROUTINE HYPERGEO
350 R=0
360 FOR II=1 TO N
370 IF RND-P >0 THEN 400
380 S=1: R=R+1
390 GOTO 410
400 S=0
410 P=(M*P-S)/(M-1)
420 M=M-1
430 NEXT II
440 RETURN
450 PRINT "TOO MANY TRIALS!"
```

FIGURE 6-37 Program to generate and plot a hypergeometric distribution.

SUMMARY

We have introduced the three most important probability distributions used in simulation modeling: the normal, exponential, and Poisson. We have presented programs that will display the appearance of them and can be used in simulation programs to generate random observations from them.

We presented and compared three different ways to generate the normal distribution: the central limit technique, the direct method, and Teichreow's approximation.

Then we introduced two exponentially derived distributions: the gamma and the beta. We discussed the chi-squared distribution and demonstrated that it can be equivalent to the gamma. We explained that the gamma we generated was actually a special case known as the Erlang distribution.

```
ENTER PARAMETER P? .5                 EX= 5           ENTER RANGE ? 10
ENTER PARAMETERS M AND N? 1100,10 STND DEV= 1.574651  ENTER TRIALS ? 100
   0.50
   1.00 *
   1.50
   2.00 ***
   2.50
   3.00 ************
   3.50
   4.00 *********************
   4.50
   5.00 **************************
   5.50
   6.00 *****************
   6.50
   7.00 *************
   7.50
   8.00 ***
   8.50
   9.00 **
   9.50
  10.00
Ok
```

FIGURE 6–38 Hypergeometric distribution equivalent to the binomial distribution in Figure 6–36 with sampling without replacement from a finite population.

We discussed three discrete distributions in addition to the Poisson: the negative binomial, binomial, and hypergeometric. We explained that the negative binomial we were generating was actually a special case called the Pascal distribution, and introduced the geometric distribution as a special case of the Pascal.

As a final word of advice about selection of probability distributions for simulation modeling: when you set out to model a process, first generate empirical probability laws governing the important parts of the process such as the arrival times and service times. Then compare these distributions with at least the three most common theoretical distributions. You can use the chi-squared test for goodness-of-fit, as we did when testing random-number generators for uniformity, and thereby confirm your guess as to whether your empirical distribution really conforms to a theoretical one.

If your empirical distribution does appear to fit a theoretical distribution and the circumstances of the case suggest that it may, in fact, describe the underlying process, then you will improve the generality of the results of a simulation experiment, and consequently the range of applicability of your work, by using a theoretical distribution in your simulation programs rather than the empirical one.

CHAPTER SEVEN:

Complex Waiting Lines

Thus far we have been simulating the simplest problem relating to waiting-line queues: Customers arrive from an infinitely large, homogeneous, and stable population; they queue up in a single waiting line; are served on a first-come, first-served basis; receive service from a single server whose operational characteristics are stable; and leave the system permanently. If the times between arrivals are exponentially distributed in the event-oriented case, or if the arrivals per unit time are Poisson distributed in the time-oriented case, it is not necessary to simulate at all. A simple analytic solution exists, as we saw in the last chapter.

However, nothing in real life is that simple. A number of complications can and do arise. Some can be handled analytically, but the solutions are not simple and sometimes involve making assumptions that may not be realistic in all cases.

FINITE POPULATIONS

Even the bench-welder example we used in Chapter Four is oversimplified. We assumed an infinite population, which is not realistic. There are just so many welders in a factory. We assumed that once a welder was fixed, it did not return to the repair queue again. Anybody who owns an automobile, a TV set, or a home computer knows that things that break and are fixed seldom stay fixed. Moreover, the failure rate is different the second, third, and so forth time around. The service time varies as well. It may become shorter as the repair person becomes familiar with the idiosyncrasies of a particular unit, or the repair time may become longer as the repair person runs out of "quick fixes" and has to undertake major rebuilding steps.

We may have to construct a data base to store the history of every item in the shop. Instead of just calling an arrival-rate subroutine to find out how many units failed on a particular day, we may have to interrogate the record of every one of, say, 500 units.

For each unit, we might consult the data base to obtain the number of prior failures, the time since the last repair, and how long that repair took. We might use these facts to obtain a probability of failure for that particular machine, and then draw a random number to determine which machines did in fact malfunction on the day being simulated.

We would obtain, for each failed unit, a probability of the number of days to repair using the same historical data and draw a second random number to determine how long the repair in question actually takes. In this kind of simulation, every machine in the repair queue will be tagged with a service time before it enters the repair facility.

FINITE QUEUES

The waiting line may be finite; that is, have an upper limit imposed upon it. Consider a barbershop that has only five places for waiting customers to sit. The queue can be regarded as having a maximum length of five because people seldom queue up outside a barbershop; they leave and come back some other time when they anticipate the place will not be so busy. When a waiting-line system has a finite queue, we must check the length of the queue before a customer is allowed to join it. we must also write logical functions to take care of customers who are not allowed to join it: Do they join another queue, for example, outside the shop? Go away and never return? Return after some stochastically determined time interval?

An important case of a finite queue is the buffer. A buffer is used to decouple two queing systems in series when the output of one system is not perfectly matched to the input of the next; this is the usual case. Many times the objective of a simulation experiment is to determine the optimal size of a buffer, which is, in fact, the waiting line before the second of two sequential service facilities.

One example is in a brewery, where the operation of capping bottles is followed by the operation of packaging them into six-packs, twelves, or twenty-fours. If the buffer, which in this case is a long metal table with guardrails, is too large, then valuable manufacturing space is wasted. If the buffer is too small, there will be pileups of bottles, accompanied by breaking glass, spilled beer, a big cleanup job, and expensive down-time on the production line.

QUEUE DISCIPLINE

In our queuing examples we have tacitly assumed a first-come, first-served queue discipline. This assumption is not always correct. Nowhere is this more evident than in time-sharing computer systems. A form of last-come, first-served queue discipline is practiced because users newly signing on are frequently served before those who have been computing for some time. This is done because the vast majority of users have such short jobs that they can be served in one "quantum," or elementary time unit. Thus, many users can be satisfied at the expense of a few.

In inventory systems, the usual discipline is last in, first out, or LIFO. The reverse of this discipline—first in, first out, or FIFO—is used when prices are rising rapidly. This arrangement makes profits as stated in accounting records agree with actual cash flow, because sales are closely related to the current cost of goods sold.

A common form of queue discipline depends upon some system of priorities: women and children first into the lifeboats when a ship sinks; officers first in a military chow line; triaging emergency medical patients (treating first those who require treatment and have the best chance for recovery); emergency vehicles have the right of way; police respond first to major crimes in progress.

Simulation of a priority queing system requires that arrivals be generated that have attached to them the attributes upon which the queue priority depends. These attributes may be assigned according to the proportions in which they occur and cooccur in the customer population. The priorities will be expressed in terms of logic rules, and the indicated priority will be assigned to each arrival. After each arrival it may be necessary to sort the queue by priority tag and by arrival time within priority class. Thus, each queue member may have to be tagged with arrival time as well as priority.

Priority queues are a form of preemption of those with the lower priorities. In some systems, absolute preemption occurs. Here the customer currently receiving service is booted out of the service facility when a preempting customer arrives. An example exists in the case of a port with one pier. If a cargo vessel is being unloaded and a passenger ship arrives, the freighter is towed out to a buoy and moored there until the passenger ship has been unloaded.

MULTIPLE POPULATIONS

Obviously, all customers are not created equal. Some will possess special needs; for example, some customers entering a bank may be doing so to open a new account, and this service is very different from that usually rendered on the teller line. Some customers may possess particular entitlements such as queue priorities because they are special in some way, such as military officers in chow lines.

Therefore the universe of customers, which is sometimes known as the calling population, may consist of several subpopulations. It may be necessary to create these subpopulations and to establish rules for sampling from them. The proportions of the subpopulations may vary depending upon the simulated time of day.

STATE DETERMINED SERVICE

In queuing theory the term *state* refers to the number of customers in the waiting line. In some systems the number of customers in the waiting line affects the service time. Usually it speeds it up because the server is working under pressure and omits some of the usual pleasantries of conversation. This can be represented in program logic by selecting a service-time multiplier between zero and one whose magnitude depends upon the length of the waiting line.

In some systems, line length can increase service time when the server becomes fatigued. To simulate this effect you would have to use a formula that added a variable that incorporated information about how long the system had been operating and allowed the service-time multiplier to exceed one.

WAITING-LINE BEHAVIOR

Another factor that tends to nullify the cost advantage of analytic solutions is that customers in waiting lines do not always behave predictably. Although few of us surrender to the impulse to strangle the creep who engages the server in a long and pointless conversation, some balk, some renege, and others jockey; we shall discuss jockeying in the next section.

Balking means that the customer takes one look at the length of the waiting line and decides to go to another store, use an automatic-teller machine, or put off that haircut until next month. This kind of behavior can be described by assigning a balking probability whose magnitude depends upon the length of the queue and drawing a random number to determine whether or not a customer balks.

Reneging is similar to balking except that the customer initially joins the waiting line and then becomes tired of waiting and leaves. The probability of reneging is usually determined by the values of two variables: how long the customer has waited and how many customers are ahead.

MULTIPLE SERVICE FACILITIES

Many, if not most, waiting-line systems have more than one service facility. You can observe this in any large bank, airline ticket concourse, or supermarket. The existence of multiple servers opens many design choices. You can have a separate queue in front of each service facility. This gives rise to a queue-behavior phenomenon called jockeying, where impatient customers wait in one line for a while, then leave to join another that they perceive is shorter or moving faster.

Banks and airlines often eliminate jockeying by making customers form a single queue and go to the first free server when they get to the head of the line. I have simulated both the single queue and multiple queues using various logical descriptions of the jockeying behavior. Overall, I have found that neither arrangement has any effect on total customer throughput, although the multiple-queue situation leads to wider differences in individual waiting times.

Another design variation is to differentiate between the kinds of service offered by the different facilities. This approach is very common. We observe lines at bridge toll plazas for "Trucks & Campers" and for "Exact Change Only"; in airline ticket concourses there are lines marked "Purchase Tickets Only" and "Ticketed Passengers with Baggage"; and supermarkets have express lines for "1 to 6 Items" and "7 to 12 Items." Customers still try to join the line that they perceive affords them the greatest advantage, however. A supermarket manager in Cambridge, Massachusetts, claimed this happened in his store because MIT students couldn't read and Harvard students couldn't count.

Figure 7–1 is a logic flow chart of a program that simulates a waiting-line system with two servers; the program is modularized so that any number of servers can be simulated. The multiple-server program has a separate queue

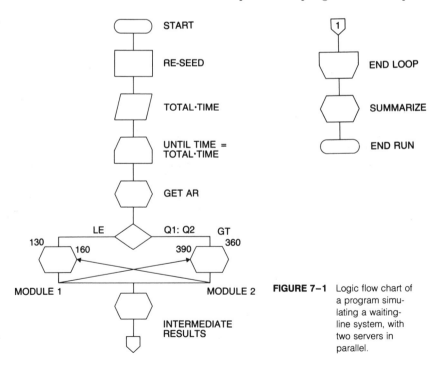

FIGURE 7–1   Logic flow chart of a program simulating a waiting-line system, with two servers in parallel.

before each facility. It consists of two time-oriented simulation modules that process two customers at one time; thus, it simulates a computer system with parallel processors. Modularization of the service-facility routine permits creating networks of many facilities in parallel and in series. This capability is useful when simulating a metalworking factory in which jobs are routed to different kinds of machines according to predetermined sequences and in which there exist several machines of each type.

Figure 7–2 is a listing of the multiple-server program. The program consists of a main section (statements 10 to 120) and six subroutines. Two of the subroutines (statements 130 to 350 and 360 to 600) are identical time-oriented simulation modules. On a hardware system with parallel computing capabilities, these modules could execute simultaneously on separate processors.

```
LIST -200
10 ' TIME ORIENTED SIMULATION
20 RANDOMIZE TIME
30 CLS: INPUT "ENTER TOTAL TIME TO BE SIMULATED ";TOTAL.TIME
40 FOR I=1 TO TOTAL.TIME
50 ' GET ARRIVALS
60 GOSUB 960 ' ARRIVAL GENERATOR
70 TOTAL.ARRIVALS=TOTAL.ARRIVALS+ARRIVALS
80 IF QUEUE1<=QUEUE2 THEN GOSUB 130: GOSUB 390: GOTO 100
90 GOSUB 160: GOSUB 360
100 NEXT I
110 GOSUB 780
120 END
130 ' MODULE #1
140 ' PUT ARRIVALS ON WORK QUEUE
150 QUEUE1=QUEUE1+ARRIVALS
160 ' TEST FOR NO QUEUE
170 IF QUEUE1=0 THEN 290
175 ' TEST FOR SERVICE COMPLETE
180 IF SERVICE.TIME1>0 THEN 310
190 ' TEST FOR SERVICE JUST COMPLETED
200 IF SERVICE.INDICATOR1=0 THEN 220
Ok


Ok
LIST 210-400
210 EXIT.QUEUE=EXIT.QUEUE+1
220 ' FILL THE SERVICE FACILITY
230 QUEUE1=QUEUE1-1
240 IF QUEUE1=0 THEN NO.WAIT=NO.WAIT+1
250 SERVICE.INDICATOR1=1
260 ' GET SERVICE TIME
270 GOSUB 1020 ' SERVICE TIME GENERATOR
280 SERVICE.TIME1=NEW.SERVICE.TIME
290 ' TEST FOR SYSTEM EMPTY
300 IF SERVICE.TIME1>0 THEN 310 ELSE 340
310 SERVICE.TIME1=SERVICE.TIME1-1
320 TOTAL.SERVICE.TIME=TOTAL.SERVICE.TIME+1
330 TOTAL.QUEUE=TOTAL.QUEUE+QUEUE1
340 GOSUB 610
350 RETURN
360 ' MODULE #2
370 ' PUT ARRIVALS ON WORK QUEUE
380 QUEUE2=QUEUE2+ARRIVALS
390 ' TEST FOR NO QUEUE
400 IF QUEUE2=0 THEN 540
Ok
```

FIGURE 7–2 Program listing of a waiting-line simulation with two parallel servers.

```
Ok
LIST 410-600
410 ' TEST FOR SERVICE COMPLETE
420 IF SERVICE.TIME2>0 THEN 560
430 ' TEST FOR SERVICE JUST COMPLETED
440 IF SERVICE.INDICATOR2=0 THEN 470
450 SERVICE.INDICATOR2=0
460 EXIT.QUEUE=EXIT.QUEUE+1
470 ' FILL THE SERVICE FACILITY
480 QUEUE2=QUEUE2-1
490 IF QUEUE2=0 THEN NO.WAIT=NO.WAIT+1
500 SERVICE.INDICATOR2=1
510 ' GET SERVICE TIME
520 GOSUB 1020 ' SERVICE TIME GENERATOR
530 SERVICE.TIME2=NEW.SERVICE.TIME
540 ' TEST FOR SYSTEM EMPTY
550 IF SERVICE.TIME2>0 THEN 560 ELSE 590
560 SERVICE.TIME2=SERVICE.TIME2-1
570 TOTAL.SERVICE.TIME=TOTAL.SERVICE.TIME+1
580 TOTAL.QUEUE=TOTAL.QUEUE+QUEUE2
590 GOSUB 610
600 RETURN
Ok
```

```
Ok
LIST 610-770
610 ' DISPLAY RESULTS
620 CLS: LOCATE 1,16: PRINT "***** RESULTS OF TIME-ORIENTED SIMULATION *****"
630 LOCATE 3,1: PRINT "TIME PERIOD #"I" OF"TOTAL.TIME
640 LOCATE 5,5: PRINT "WORK QUEUE #1      ";:
    FOR J=1 TO QUEUE1: PRINT "*";: NEXT J
650 LOCATE 5,75: PRINT QUEUE1
660 LOCATE 7,5: PRINT "WORK QUEUE #2      ";:
    FOR J=1 TO QUEUE2: PRINT "*";:NEXT J
670 LOCATE 7,75: PRINT QUEUE2
680 IF SERVICE.INDICATOR1=1 THEN FLAG1$="*" ELSE FLAG1$=""
690 LOCATE 10,5: PRINT "SERVICE FACILITY #1";: PRINT FLAG1$
700 LOCATE 10,75: PRINT SERVICE.INDICATOR1
710 IF SERVICE.INDICATOR2=1 THEN FLAG2$="*" ELSE FLAG2$=""
720 LOCATE 12,5: PRINT "SERVICE FACILITY #2";: PRINT FLAG2$
730 LOCATE 12,75: PRINT SERVICE.INDICATOR2
740 LOCATE 15,5: PRINT "EXIT QUEUE        ";:
    FOR J=1 TO EXIT.QUEUE: PRINT "*";: NEXT J
750 LOCATE 15,75: PRINT EXIT.QUEUE
760 LOCATE 20,5: INPUT "TYPE <RETURN> OR <ENTER> TO CONTINUE ";X
770 RETURN
Ok
```

```
Ok
LIST 780-970
780 ' SUMMARIZE RESULTS
790 CLS
800 LOCATE 1,25: PRINT "***** SUMMARY OF RESULTS *****"
810 LOCATE 4,1: PRINT "ARRIVAL RATE="TOTAL.ARRIVALS/TOTAL.TIME
820 LOCATE 4,40: PRINT "SERVICE RATE="EXIT.QUEUE/TOTAL.SERVICE.TIME
830 LOCATE 7,1: PRINT "ARRIVAL TIME="TOTAL.TIME/TOTAL.ARRIVALS
840 LOCATE 7,40: PRINT "SERVICE TIME="TOTAL.SERVICE.TIME/EXIT.QUEUE
850 LOCATE 10,1: PRINT "TOTAL QUEUE="TOTAL.QUEUE
860 LOCATE 10,40: PRINT "AVERAGE QUEUE="TOTAL.QUEUE/TOTAL.TIME
870 LOCATE 13,1: PRINT "AVERAGE WAIT="TOTAL.QUEUE/TOTAL.ARRIVALS
880 LOCATE 13,40:PRINT"MEAN TIME IN QUEUE="TOTAL.QUEUE/(TOTAL.ARRIVALS-NO.WAIT)
890 LOCATE 16,1: PRINT "BUSY TIME="TOTAL.SERVICE.TIME
900 LOCATE 16,40: PRINT "IDLE TIME="TOTAL.TIME-TOTAL.SERVICE.TIME
910 LOCATE 19,1: PRINT "TOTAL ARRIVALS="TOTAL.ARRIVALS
```

FIGURE 7-2 (continued)

```
920 LOCATE 19,40: PRINT "TOTAL SERVICES="EXIT.QUEUE
930 LOCATE 22,1: PRINT "LEFT IN QUEUE="QUEUE1+QUEUE2
940 LOCATE 22,40: PRINT "LEFT IN SERVICE="SERVICE.INDICATOR1+SERVICE.INDICATOR2
950 RETURN
960 ' ARRIVAL GENERATOR
970 X=RND
Ok


Ok
LIST 980-
980 IF X<=.7 THEN ARRIVALS=0: GOTO 1010
990 IF X<=.9 THEN ARRIVALS=1: GOTO 1010
1000 ARRIVALS=2
1010 RETURN
1020 ' SERVICE-TIME GENERATOR
1030 X=RND
1040 IF X<=.3 THEN NEW.SERVICE.TIME=1: GOTO 1090
1050 IF X<=.7 THEN NEW.SERVICE.TIME=2: GOTO 1090
1060 IF X<=.8 THEN NEW.SERVICE.TIME=3: GOTO 1090
1070 IF X<=.9 THEN NEW.SERVICE.TIME=4: GOTO 1090
1080 NEW.SERVICE.TIME=5
1090 RETURN
Ok
```

FIGURE 7-2 (continued)

The display subroutine (statements 610 to 770) graphically shows the conditions of both waiting-line queues and both service facilities at the end of every time slice. It also shows the condition of a combined exit queue. For long simulation runs, this subroutine should be "commented out."

The summary subroutine (statements 780 to 950) reports the results of each simulation run. It calculates arrival rate and time and service rate and time. It reports combined queue statistics; that is, queue statistics that regard the separate queues in front of each service facility as a single queue. It reports service-facility loading, and total arrivals and services also on a consolidated basis.

The program has only one arrival generator (statements 960 to 1010) and one service-time generator (statements 1020 to 1090), although it could just as well have had a separate pair of generators for each simulation module, or more if we were interested in simulating different conditions. The generators both produce empirically distributed values. The arrival generator has a designed mean arrival rate of 0.4 per day (or whatever you care to define the time slice to be—interarrival time is 2.5). The service-time generator has a designed mean service time of 2.3 (service rate is .435). Thus the system is stable inasmuch as the service rate exceeds the arrival rate.

There are two entries to both simulation modules. The first entries are the starting statements (130 and 360, respectively). The second entries (statements 160 and 390) bypass the instructions that place the current arrival on the waiting-line queue.

The main program randomizes the generators, then accepts an input message establishing the total time of the current simulation run. This parameter becomes the extent of a FOR-NEXT loop. The main program next calls the arrival generator and adds the value of the returned variable to the count of TOTAL.ARRIVALS. Then it tests whether QUEUE #1 is less than or equal to QUEUE #2. If this test is true, the main program makes a normal entry to the first simulation module and, upon returning from the first simulation module, makes the bypass entry to the second module. This sequence of instructions establishes the queuing logic for the two servers: An arrival always joins the shortest queue, and in case the queues are equal, joins QUEUE #1. If the test of queue length is false, the main program makes a bypass entry to the first simulation module and upon return makes a normal entry to the second simulation module. After exiting the FOR-NEXT loop, the main program calls the summary report module and terminates.

The service-time generators are called from within the simulation modules, making it easy to install separate service-time generators and thus provide differentiated services (such as an express checkout and a normal checkout if we were writing a supermarket simulation). Just before returning to the main program, each simulation module can call the display subroutine so the user can have a step-by-step graphical representation of the simulation. Each simulation module updates common exit statistics and common counts of TOTAL.QUEUE and TOTAL.SERVICE.TIME.

We programmed the generators of the single time-oriented simulation program the same way that the generators of the two-server program were programmed, and made several comparative runs with these results:

SINGLE-SERVER PROGRAM

Days	Arr Rate	Svc Rate	Avg Queue	Loading	Arrivals
10	.5	3.	1.1	.90	5
100	.47	2.25	2.11	.99	47
1,000	.43	2.31	7.82	.99	426
10,000	.4	2.28	4.05	.92	4044

TWO-SERVER PROGRAM

Days	Arr Rate	Svc Rate	Avg Queue	Loading	Arrivals
10	.2	5.	.3	.5	2
100	.37	2.54	.33	.84	37
1,000	.4	2.29	.49	.91	398
10,000	.4	2.31	.51	.92	3990

You can see the dramatic reduction in average queue length, which means a reduction in the time customers waste waiting in line, and a consequent increase in both the number of customers that can be served and in customer satisfaction. These improvements come at the cost of adding a second server. The more servers, the better the service.

However, in all systems there is a design trade-off between service level and slack resources—in this case, employing more servers than we really need. Usually the trade-off is resolved in economic terms. The question is: Can we make enough money from the increased throughput of customers to pay the cost of additional servers and return some predetermined increase in overall profit, called our return on investment?

Return on investment is the usual criterion in determining design choices for stores, factories, and service-oriented establishments such as barbershops, banks, and ticket counters. In designing systems that have to respond to life-threatening emergencies, such as those for fire protection, police protection, national defense, air-traffic control, hospital emergency rooms, and flood control, different assessment criteria may be employed.

Here it has become popular to use Risk Analysis. We establish an Annual Loss Expectancy (ALE) based upon the probability of a threat (such as a flood), our current vulnerability to it, and the value of assets threatened by it. Then we try to balance the ALE against the annualized cost of countermeasures (for instance, a new dam).

Intangible items such as loss of life are usually evaluated on the basis of how much somebody could successfully sue you for if the loss occurred. This leads to inequities such as evaluating an American life at $200,000 and the life of a resident of India at $2,500 or less.

SUMMARY

In this chapter we have paid attention to the complexities that exist in simulations of real-life waiting-line systems.

The first of these was that calling populations are finite rather than infinite. We may run out of customers; or our customers may return for repeated services, at which times their needs may be conditioned by the services they have previously received.

Then we considered the fact that waiting-line queues may have imposed on them an upper limit of length, as is the case with waiting rooms, bridge toll plazas, theater lobbies, and, especially, buffer areas between two or more sequential production processes.

We observed that queuing discipline is not always first-come, first-served. It may be just the reverse, or it may be determined by a sometimes complex system of priorities. These may be conditioned upon the innate characteristics of each customer or determined by the current state or past history of the waiting-line system itself.

We considered the existence of two or more subpopulations within the calling populations, the proportions of which may vary depending upon the time of day, week, or year or other exogenous or endogenous factors. These subpopulations may be entitled to different priorities and require different kinds of services—such as express customers versus regular customers in a supermarket.

We noted that the size and sometimes the composition of the waiting line can influence the performance of the servers for either good or bad.

The performance of waiting-line systems can also be influenced by the behavior of customers waiting in line. They can balk (refuse to join the line), renege (quit the line), or jockey (leave one line and join another).

Finally, we presented a time-oriented simulation in modular form. This permits one to simulate multiple servers working in parallel, as tellers in a bank; multiple servers rendering service in sequence, such as production operations in a factory; or combinations of these arrangements.

CHAPTER EIGHT

Simulation Examples

One of the most useful applications of simulation on personal computers turns on the ability of a programmer to reproduce the essential characteristics of mainframe simulations so as to carry out operational or training exercises. We shall examine two examples: a program that predicts hourly crime occurrences in a city of 300,000 people, and one that simulates shadowing a hostile submarine. The first can be used to give police watch commanders some idea of what they may expect on the basis of historical statistics. The second is a pursuit game that gives some training in relating transverse Mercator map projections quickly to latitude and longitude.

POLICE SIMULATION

The police simulation derives from a study we did in London, Canada, to rationalize police patrol-car areas. The original study is described in Chapter Ten. Our input consisted of crime-occurrence reports that had been collected in computer-readable form. Over a three-year period we detected a stability in the hourly, daily, and monthly pattern of the occurrences of criminal incidents.

On an hourly basis, crime seems to peak in the early evening and drop off in the early-morning hours. We were able to fit our historical data with a curve of the form:

$$\text{HOURLY EVENTS} = (\text{SIN}(\text{HOUR} * .130927 - 1.4724))^2$$

where the variable HOUR is given as a 24-hour clock. Figure 8–1 shows the

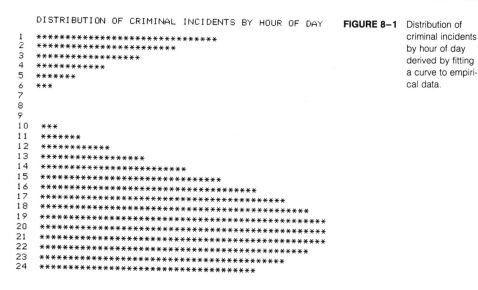

```
DISTRIBUTION OF CRIMINAL INCIDENTS BY HOUR OF DAY
1   *******************************
2   ***********************
3   ******************
4   *************
5   *******
6   ***
7
8
9
10  ***
11  *******
12  ************
13  *****************
14  ***************************
15  ********************************
16  *******************************************
17  **************************************************
18  ****************************************************
19  *******************************************************
20  ******************************************************
21  *****************************************************
22  ****************************************************
23  **************************************************
24  **************************************
```

FIGURE 8–1 Distribution of criminal incidents by hour of day derived by fitting a curve to empirical data.

distribution of incidents on an hourly basis—1 is set equal to 50 for display purposes.

On a daily basis, crime appears to rise steadily from a low on Sunday to a maximum on Saturday. We were able to fit our historical data with a straight line:

DAILY EVENTS = DAY.OF.WEEK/7

where DAY.OF.WEEK equals 1 for Sunday and 7 for Saturday. Figure 8–2 shows the distribution of incidents on a day-of-week basis.

On a monthly basis, crime seems to decline in the winter and peak in August. We were able to fit our historical data with a curve of the form:

MONTHLY EVENTS = $ABS(SIN(MONTH*.261854 - .52362))$

where months are numbered beginning with January = 1. Figure 8–3 shows the distribution of incidents on a monthly basis.

We obtained a base crime rate by dividing the number of crimes forecast for the current year by 8,760, the number of hours in a year (8,784 if it is a

```
DISTRIBUTION OF CRIMINAL INCIDENTS BY DAY OF WEEK
1   *******
2   *************
3   *********************
4   ***************************
5   **********************************
6   ******************************************
7   *************************************************
```

FIGURE 8–2 Distribution of criminal occurrences by day of week.

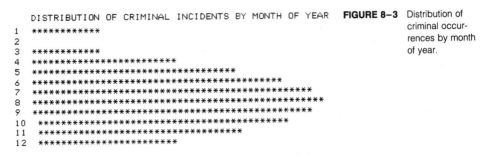

FIGURE 8–3 Distribution of criminal occurrences by month of year.

leap year). The number of crimes forecast is usually obtained by plotting a line of regression based upon experience in, say, the past three years.

We multiplied the base rate by:

MULTIPLIER = HOURLY EVENTS + DAILY EVENTS + MONTHLY EVENTS

and normalized the result by multiplying by .6470435, so that the sum of events for all the hours of the year equaled the yearly forecast.

The only randomization we did was to use a random-number draw to decide, with a probability of .5, whether to integerize or round up the number of crimes forecast in each hour.

The simulation consists of a main program and four subroutines: an initialization ("housekeeping") subroutine, one that establishes the starting time of the simulation, another that generates hourly occurrences, and an annotation subroutine. Figure 8–4 is a logic flow chart for this simulation program. Figure 8–5 is a complete listing.

The housekeeping subroutine is called first. It clears the screen, initializes the random-number generator, and loads three vectors. The FIRST.DAY vector contains the number of the day of the week for January 1, 1984 to January 1, 1993. (For example, New Year's Day 1985 falls on a Tuesday, so FIRST.DAY(2) is equal to 3.) The index is equal to current year minus the base year of 1983.

The DAYS.IN.MONTH vector is used to convert Year/Month/Day dates (YY,MM,DD) to Month/Day (MM,DDD) dates. These are called "Julian dates" here, perpetuating a common misnomer. (Another date representation, called Julian, keeps dates in days since the beginning of the Christian era. This format simplifies date arithmetic and can be converted easily to American style: MM/DD/YY, European style: DD/MM/YY, or international standard: YY/MM/DD.) The vector contains the cumulative days in the month for each month of the year—in a normal year, January = 0, February = 31, March = 59, and so on. In a leap year, March = 60. There are 24 components; the first 12 are selected for a normal year, the last 12 for a leap year. The DAY.OF.WEEK string vector contains the names of the days of the week, as opposed to their numbers.

The main program asks the user to enter the forecast number of occurrences for the year to be simulated (OCCUR), and the date and time at which the simulation is to start (YY, MM, DD, HH); then it calls the "Julian" date

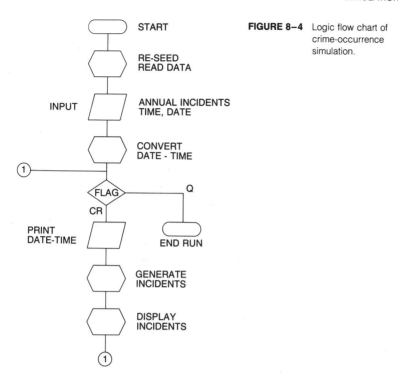

FIGURE 8–4 Logic flow chart of crime-occurrence simulation.

subroutine. This subroutine first finds the INDEX. Then it tests whether the current year is a leap year or not (that is, whether or not it is evenly divisible by 4. We're not going to worry about the year 2000 in this book; we'll save that for the second edition.) If the current year is a leap year, we equate an offset for the DAYS.IN.MONTH vector to 12; otherwise it is 0. The offset is called ADD.

The subroutine calculates the hourly crime rate (RATE) for either a normal year or a leap year. Then it lives up to its name and calculates the Julian date; this is simply the value of the DAYS.IN.MONTH vector indexed by the month number (MONTH) plus the offset (ADD), added to the day (DAY).

The Julian subroutine determines which day of the week (DAY.OF.WEEK) it is by adding the current-year component of the FIRST.DAY vector less one to the Julian date modulo, then taking the sum module-7. It determines which hour of the year (HOUR.INDEX) it is by adding the Julian date less one times 24 to the starting time (HOUR). Then control is returned to the main program.

The main program then enters a WHILE-WEND loop that is terminated when FLAG$ is set equal to "Q," for QUIT. For each iteration of the loop, it increments the HOUR.INDEX, calls the Crime Occurrence subroutine, and calls the Annotation subroutine. The main program terminates with the loop.

The Occurrence subroutine uses the functions of curves fitted to historical statistical data to calculate the number of crimes expected to occur during the current simulated hour.

```
Ok
LIST -490
10 GOSUB 500 '   HOUSEKEEPING SUBROUTINE
20 INPUT "ENTER ANNUAL NUMBER OF OCCURRENCES "; OCCUR
30 INPUT "ENTER DATE/TIME: YY, MM, DD, HH "; YEAR, MONTH, DAY, HOUR
40 GOSUB 700 '   DATE CONVERSION SUBROUTINE
50 WHILE FLAG$ <> "Q"
60 INPUT "TO ADVANCE PROGRAM TYPE 'RETURN' OR 'ENTER'; TYPE 'Q' TO QUIT"; FLAG$
70 PRINT
80 HOUR.INDEX = HOUR.INDEX+1
90 GOSUB 1000 '   CRIME OCCURRENCE SUBROUTINE
100 GOSUB 2000 '   ANNOTATION SUBROUTINE
110 WEND
120 END
130 '
Ok




Ok
LIST 500-900
500 '   HOUSEKEEPING SUBROUTINE
510 CLS: RANDOMIZE TIME
520 DIM FIRST.DAY(10),DAYS.IN.MONTH(24),DAY.OF.WEEK$(7)
530 FOR I=1 TO 10:READ FIRST.DAY(I):NEXT I
540 FOR I=1 TO 24:READ DAYS.IN.MONTH(I):NEXT I
550 FOR I=1 TO 7:READ DAY.OF.WEEK$(I):NEXT I
560 DATA 1,3,4,5,6,1,2,3,4,6
570 DATA 0,31,59,90,120,151,181,212,243,275,304,334
580 DATA 0,31,60,91,122,152,182,213,244,276,305,335
590 DATA "SUNDAY","MONDAY","TUESDAY","WEDNESDAY","THURSDAY","FRIDAY","SATURDAY"
600 RETURN
700 '   DATE CONVERSION SUBROUTINE
710 INDEX=YEAR-83
720 IF YEAR/4-INT(YEAR/4)=0 THEN ADD=12 ELSE ADD=0
725 RATE=OCCUR/((ADD/12)*24+8760)
730 RATE=OCCUR/((ADD/12)*24+8760)
740 JULIAN.DATE=DAYS.IN.MONTH(ADD+MONTH)+DAY
750 DAY.OF.WEEK=(FIRST.DAY(INDEX)-1+JULIAN.DATE MOD 7) MOD 7
760 HOUR.INDEX=(JULIAN.DATE-1)*24+HOUR
770 RETURN
Ok




Ok
LIST 1000-
1000 '   CRIME OCCURRENCE SUBROUTINE
1010 HOUR=(HOUR.INDEX MOD 24)
1020 HOUR.EVENT=(SIN(HOUR*.130927-1.04724))^2
1030 JULIAN.DATE=INT(HOUR.INDEX/24)
1040 DAY.OF.WEEK=((FIRST.DAY(INDEX)-1+JULIAN.DATE MOD 7) MOD 7)+1
1050 DAY.EVENT=DAY.OF.WEEK/7
1060 FOR I=1+ADD TO 12+ADD
1070 IF JULIAN.DATE<(DAYS.IN.MONTH(I)+1) THEN MONTH=I-ADD-1:GOTO 1090
1080 NEXT I
1090 MONTH.EVENT=ABS(SIN(MONTH*.261854-.52362))
1100 EVENT=(HOUR.EVENT+DAY.EVENT+MONTH.EVENT)*.6470435
1110 CRIME=EVENT*RATE
1120 IF RND >=.5 THEN CRIME=INT(CRIME+.5) ELSE CRIME=INT(CRIME)
1125 PRINT "CRIMES = "CRIME
1130 RETURN
2000 '   ANNOTATION SUBROUTINE
2010 PRINT "'JULIAN' DATE IS: 19"YEAR"/"JULIAN.DATE"/"HOUR":00"
2020 PRINT"DAY OF WEEK IS "DAY.OF.WEEK$(DAY.OF.WEEK)
2030 PRINT"HOUR INDEX IS:"HOUR.INDEX
2040 RETURN
Ok
```

FIGURE 8-5 Complete program listing of crime-occurrence simulation.

```
ENTER ANNUAL NUMBER OF OCCURRENCES ? 80000
ENTER DATE/TIME: YY, MM, DD, HH ? 85,02,01,19
TO ADVANCE PROGRAM TYPE 'RETURN' OR 'ENTER'; TYPE 'Q' TO QUIT?

CRIMES =  12
'JULIAN' DATE IS: 19 85 / 31 / 20 :00
DAY OF WEEK IS FRIDAY
HOUR INDEX IS: 764
TO ADVANCE PROGRAM TYPE 'RETURN' OR 'ENTER'; TYPE 'Q' TO QUIT?

CRIMES =  12
'JULIAN' DATE IS: 19 85 / 31 / 21 :00
DAY OF WEEK IS FRIDAY
HOUR INDEX IS: 765
TO ADVANCE PROGRAM TYPE 'RETURN' OR 'ENTER'; TYPE 'Q' TO QUIT?

CRIMES =  12
'JULIAN' DATE IS: 19 85 / 31 / 22 :00
DAY OF WEEK IS FRIDAY
HOUR INDEX IS: 766
TO ADVANCE PROGRAM TYPE 'RETURN' OR 'ENTER'; TYPE 'Q' TO QUIT?
```

FIGURE 8–6   Output from crime-occurrence simulation showing control statements.

The Annotation subroutine prints out the Julian date, hour (on a 24-hour clock), day of the week, and hour of the year (HOUR.INDEX).

Thus the program starts at the time the user enters and, using the total annual criminal occurrences for that year, generates the number of crimes for that year. This program can be augmented by logic statements that differentiate the occurrences by offense and by geographical area, provided historical statistics are available from which appropriate logic rules can be written. Figures 8–6 and 8–7 are examples of output from this program.

The program can support people-machine simulations for training watch commanders and communications personnel. It can also provide input to simulations whose objective would be rationalizing patrol-area assignments, de-

FIGURE 8–7   Additional output from crime-occurrence simulation.

```
CRIMES =  9
'JULIAN' DATE IS: 19 85 / 32 / 2 :00
DAY OF WEEK IS SATURDAY
HOUR INDEX IS: 770
TO ADVANCE PROGRAM TYPE 'RETURN' OR 'ENTER'; TYPE 'Q' TO QUIT?

CRIMES =  8
'JULIAN' DATE IS: 19 85 / 32 / 3 :00
DAY OF WEEK IS SATURDAY
HOUR INDEX IS: 771
TO ADVANCE PROGRAM TYPE 'RETURN' OR 'ENTER'; TYPE 'Q' TO QUIT?

CRIMES =  7
'JULIAN' DATE IS: 19 85 / 32 / 4 :00
DAY OF WEEK IS SATURDAY
HOUR INDEX IS: 772
TO ADVANCE PROGRAM TYPE 'RETURN' OR 'ENTER'; TYPE 'Q' TO QUIT?

CRIMES =  6
'JULIAN' DATE IS: 19 85 / 32 / 5 :00
DAY OF WEEK IS SATURDAY
HOUR INDEX IS: 773
TO ADVANCE PROGRAM TYPE 'RETURN' OR 'ENTER'; TYPE 'Q' TO QUIT?
```

ployment of backup forces, and rules of engagement to cover patrol areas when the primary unit is busy.

Up until now these simulations have demanded the use of mainframe computers, because of the voluminous statistical data required. However, new models of personal computers with megabyte main memories and 20-megabyte hard-disk secondary storage will overcome these deficiencies. Of course, execution time may be a problem if an interpreted language, such as BASIC is employed. Compilers are now available, however, for BASIC and other popular personal-computer languages. These compilers offer a ten-to-one advantage in execution time. Their use does restrict the portability of programs among different makes of personal computers.

SUBMARINE PURSUIT

The next, and last, example is primarily a pursuit game, although it possesses some tutorial qualities. It is a skeletonized version of a program one of my students wrote in a graduate course in simulation. The program was intended to simulate one console of the U.S. Navy's Ocean Surveillance Information System (OSIS).

OSIS is a major command, control, and intelligence system with facilities in Spain; Japan; Pearl Harbor, Hawaii; and Norfolk, Virginia that the Navy uses to keep track of worldwide ocean traffic. It has eight sites, with four consoles at each one. We simulated one of these to see whether we could improve the autocorrelator program. This is a computer program that OSIS uses to link up new contact sightings with preexisting tracks of vessels or aircraft. Our simulation was done on a Digital Equipment Corp. System 1091 equipped with Tektronics graphic terminals. My skeletonized version is much less grand, but it does present some of the elements of computer graphics in a simulation context. Figure 8–8 is a logic flow chart of the simulation. Figure 8–9 is a complete program listing.

The program we shall examine presents a display that is 720 nautical miles from east to west and 300 nautical miles from north to south. The scale is one pixel (the elementary unit of computer graphics) equals one nautical mile. The southwest corner is 29 degrees (deg) north latitude, 82 degrees west longitude. The northwest corner is 34 deg N, 82 deg W. The southeast corner is 29 deg N, 67.54 W; and the northeast corner, taking into account the Mercator correction for the earth's spherical surface, is 34 deg N, 68.29 W. Annotations are shown in yellow.

The display depicts the shoreline of the southeastern United States from Norfolk, Virginia, to Daytona, Florida, although the graphical routines are sufficiently generalized that other features can be programmed in if desired. The coastal region is "painted" green; the black screen represents the ocean.

The program only handles two ships: a frigate based at Norfolk, represented by a blue circle; and a hostile submarine, represented by a red circle.

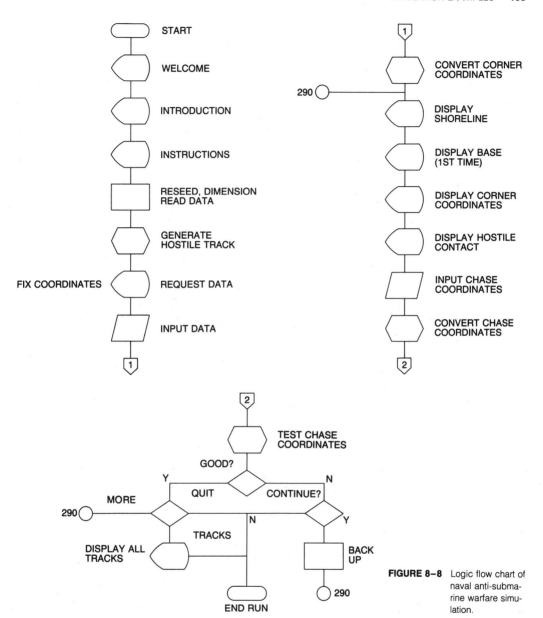

FIGURE 8–8 Logic flow chart of naval anti-submarine warfare simulation.

The initial location of the submarine is determined by two random-number draws. Actually, a random course of ten positions is preloaded before an engagement begins. The logical rules of movement for both ships provide for a 100-mile guard band along the left-hand margin of the display, to keep the ships from driving up US highway 13 or doing something equally silly. Furthermore, the hostile ship cannot move more than 100 miles north or south, east or west, at one time; that is, no more than 141.4 miles in a straight line. The friendly

```
LIST -201
10 ´
20 CLS: FOR I=1 TO 80: PRINT "*";:NEXT I
30 LOCATE 2,1: FOR I=1 TO 19: PRINT "*": NEXT I
40 FOR I=1 TO 19: LOCATE 1+I,80: PRINT "*": NEXT I
50 LOCATE 20,1: FOR I=1 TO 80: PRINT "*";: NEXT I
60 LOCATE 4,22: PRINT "***** WELCOME TO ´SUBCATCHER´ *****"
70 LOCATE 8,29: PRINT "COPYRIGHT C-CIRCLE 1984"
80 LOCATE 12,31: PRINT "BY JOHN M. CARROLL"
90 LOCATE 16,31: PRINT "ALL RIGHTS RESERVED"
100 LOCATE 22,1: INPUT "TYPE <RETURN> OR <ENTER> TO ADVANCE PROGRAM ";X
110 ´
120 CLS: FOR I=1 TO 80: PRINT "*";:NEXT I
130 LOCATE 2,1: FOR I=1 TO 19: PRINT "*": NEXT I
140 FOR I=1 TO 19: LOCATE 1+I,80: PRINT "*": NEXT I
150 LOCATE 20,1: FOR I=1 TO 80: PRINT "*";: NEXT I
160 LOCATE 4,22: PRINT "THIS PROGRAM SIMULATES PURSUIT OF A"
170 LOCATE 8,32: PRINT "HOSTILE SUBMARINE"
180 LOCATE 12,29: PRINT "OFF THE U.S. COASTLINE"
190 LOCATE 16,24: PRINT "FIELD IS 720 X 300 NAUTICAL MILES"
200 LOCATE 22,1: INPUT "TYPE <RETURN> OR <ENTER> TO ADVANCE PROGRAM ";X
201 CLS: FOR I=1 TO 80: PRINT "*";:NEXT I
Ok


LIST 202-325
202 LOCATE 2,1: FOR I=1 TO 19: PRINT "*": NEXT I
203 FOR I=1 TO 19: LOCATE 1+I,80: PRINT "*": NEXT I
204 LOCATE 20,1: FOR I=1 TO 80: PRINT "*";: NEXT I
205 LOCATE 4,18: PRINT "MOVE THE FRIGATE (BLUE DOT) FROM NORFOLK BY"
206 LOCATE 8,25: PRINT "BY ENTERING ITS LATITUDE AND"
207 LOCATE 12,25: PRINT "LONGITUDE AFTER STEAMING IN A"
208 LOCATE 16,22: PRINT "STRAIGHT LINE FOR 100 NAUTICAL MILES"
209 LOCATE 22,1: INPUT "TYPE <RETURN> OR <ENTER> TO ADVANCE PROGRAM ";X
210 REM INITIALIZATION
220 CLS:DIM XS(16),YS(16),XC(100),YC(100),XH(100),YH(100)
230 N=1:M=1
240 FOR I=1 TO 16:READ YS(I):NEXT I
250 FOR I=1 TO 16:READ XS(I):NEXT I
260 RANDOMIZE TIME
270 GOSUB 960´GET HOSTILE TRACK
280 GOSUB 710´FIX GEOGRAPHICAL COORDINATES
290 GOSUB 630´DRAW SHORELINE
300 GOSUB 550´SHOW HOME BASE
310 GOSUB 890´PRINT GEOGRAPHICAL COORDINATES
320 GOSUB 1250´SHOW HOSTILE CONTACT
325 FOR I=1 TO 3000: NEXT I
Ok


LIST 330-610
330 ´
340 REM CHASE HOSTILE CONTACT
440 LOCATE 10,25:INPUT"ENTER LATEST POSITION <LATITUDE,LONGITUDE>";Y,X
450 YP=(YN-Y)*60:XP=(XW-X)*COS(Y*.017454)*60.03
460 IF YP<0 OR YP>299 OR XP<0 OR XP>719, THEN GOSUB 1100
470 IF SQR(ABS(YP-YC(N))^2+ABS(XP-XC(N))^2)>200 THEN GOSUB 1100
480 GOSUB 1180
490 LOCATE 24,1:INPUT"TO GET ANOTHER CONTACT TYPE <2>;TO SEE TRACKS <1>;QUIT<0>"
:C$
500 IF C$="0" THEN CLS: END
510 IF C$="2" THEN 290
520 IF C$="1" THEN GOSUB 1320
530 GOTO 490
540 END
550 ´
```

FIGURE 8–9 Complete program listing of naval anti-submarine warfare simulation.

```
560 IF N>1 THEN 610
570 XB=110:YB=60
580 CIRCLE (XB,YB),5,1
590 PAINT (XB,YB),1,1
600 XC(1)=XB:YC(1)=YB
610 RETURN
Ok



LIST 620-820
620 '
630 REM DRAW SHORELINE
640 CLS:COLOR 6,0,0,32
650 FOR I=1 TO 15
660 LINE (XS(I),YS(I))-(XS(I+1),YS(I+1)),4
670 NEXT I
680 PAINT (0,0),4,4
690 RETURN
700 '
710 REM ROUTINE TO GET LATITUDE & LONGITUDE OF DISPLAY
720 CLS: FOR I=1 TO 80: PRINT "*";:NEXT I
730 LOCATE 2,1: FOR I=1 TO 19: PRINT "*": NEXT I
740 FOR I=1 TO 19: LOCATE 1+I,80: PRINT "*": NEXT I
750 LOCATE 20,1: FOR I=1 TO 80: PRINT "*";: NEXT I
760 LOCATE 4,15: PRINT "BUILT-IN MAP SHOWS SOUTHEASTERN COAST OF THE U.S."
770 LOCATE 8,23: PRINT "ROUGHLY NORFOLK, VA TO ORLANDO, FA"
780 LOCATE 12,23: PRINT "ENTER 29 DEG N X 82 DEG W (29,82)"
790 LOCATE 16,24: PRINT "AS THE SOUTHWESTERN CORNER OF MAP"
800 LOCATE 22,1: INPUT "TYPE <RETURN> OR <ENTER> TO ADVANCE PROGRAM ";X
810 CLS: LOCATE 10,5
820 INPUT"ENTER LATITUDE & LONGITUDE OF SW CORNER IN DECIMAL DEGREES";YS,XW
Ok



Ok
LIST 830-1020
830 YN=YS+5
840 XSE=XW-11.99/COS(YS*.017454)
850 XNE=XW-11.99/COS(YN*.017454)
860 CLS:COLOR 6,0,0,32
870 RETURN
880 '
890 REM PRINT COORDINATES
900 LOCATE 2,17:PRINT YN"N";"XW"W"
910 LOCATE 2,55:PRINT YN"N";"XNE"W"
920 LOCATE 22,1:PRINT YS"N";"XW"W"
930 LOCATE 22,55:PRINT YS"N";"XSE"W"
940 RETURN
950 '
960 REM HOSTILE TRACK
970 FOR I=1 TO 10
980 XH(I)=RND*719
990 IF XH(I)<=100 THEN XH(I)=XH(I)+100
1000 IF I=1 THEN 1020
1010 IF ABS(XH(I)-XH(I-1))>100 THEN 980
1020 NEXT I
Ok



Ok
LIST 1030-1220
1030 FOR I=1 TO 10
1040 YH(I)=RND*299
1050 IF I=1 THEN 1070
1060 IF ABS(YH(I)-YH(I-1))>100 THEN 1040
```

FIGURE 8-9 (continued)

```
1070 NEXT I
1080 RETURN
1090 '
1100 REM POSITION OUT OF BOUNDS
1110 LOCATE 15,1
1120 INPUT"POSITION OUT OF BOUNDS; TYPE <1> TO CONTINUE, <0> TO QUIT";C$
1130 IF C$="0" THEN END
1140 IF C$="1" THEN M=M-1:GOSUB 630:GOSUB 890:GOSUB 1250:GOTO 340
1150 GOTO 1120
1160 RETURN
1170 '
1180 REM GOOD POSITION
1190 GOSUB 890
1200 CIRCLE (XP,YP),5,1
1210 PAINT (XP,YP),1,1
1220 N=N+1:XC(N)=XP:YC(N)=YP
Ok
```

```
1230 RETURN
1240 '
1250 REM HOSTILE CONTACT
1260 GOSUB 890
1270 CIRCLE (XH(M),YH(M)),5,2
1280 PAINT (XH(M),YH(M)),2,2
1290 M=M+1
1300 RETURN
1310 '
1320 REM PRINT TRACKS
1330 GOSUB 630
1340 GOSUB 890
1350 FOR I=1 TO N-1
1360 LINE (XC(I),YC(I))-(XC(I+1),YC(I+1)),1
1370 NEXT I
1380 FOR I=1 TO M-2
1390 LINE (XH(I),YH(I))-(XH(I+1),YH(I+1)),2
1400 NEXT I
1410 RETURN
1420 '
1430 DATA 0,20,40,60,80,100,120,140,160,180,200,220,240,260,280,299
1440 DATA 100,95,85,90,75,60,55,40,35,22,18,15,10,7,5,0
Ok
```

FIGURE 8–9 (continued)

ship has an advantage. It can move up to 200 miles. The main program first calls a screen with program title and copyright notice (statements 20–100; see Figure 8–10). Then look at Figure 8–11, a screen that gives the objective of the exercise (statements 120–200); and finally Figure 8–12, a screen that gives the rules for playing it (statements 201–209).

Then the main program initializes itself (statements 210–260). It sets up three pairs of vectors. One (XS, YS) holds the coordinates of 16 points used to draw the shoreline. The other two pairs save the positions of the hostile submarine (XH, YH) and of the defending frigate (XC, YC). The initialization routine sets to 1 the movement counters for the hostile craft (M) and the friendly craft (N). It reads in the shoreline vectors and seeds the random-number generator from the real-time clock.

Next the main program calls two subroutines that can also be regarded as part of the initialization process. The Hostile Track subroutine (statements 960–1080) preloads the random positions of the hostile submarine. In addition to observing the shoreline guard band (statement 990), this subroutine keeps

```
***********************************************************************************
*                                                                                 *
*                                                                                 *
*                      ***** WELCOME TO 'SUBCATCHER' *****                         *
*                                                                                 *
*                                                                                 *
*                                                                                 *
*                         COPYRIGHT C-CIRCLE 1984                                  *
*                                                                                 *
*                                                                                 *
*                                                                                 *
*                           BY JOHN M. CARROLL                                     *
*                                                                                 *
*                                                                                 *
*                                                                                 *
*                          ALL RIGHTS RESERVED                                     *
*                                                                                 *
*                                                                                 *
*                                                                                 *
***********************************************************************************

TYPE <RETURN> OR <ENTER> TO ADVANCE PROGRAM ?
```

FIGURE 8-10 Copyright and welcoming panel.

the submarine within the surveillance area by multiplying the E-W random number by 719 miles (statement 980) and multiplying the N-S random number by 299 miles (statement 1040). It observes the 100-mile orthogonal-movement limitation as well (statements 1010 and 1060).

The Fix Geographical Coordinates subroutine (statements 710–870) is included in case you want to program in some other location. It presents a panel, Figure 8–13, that orients the user (statements 720–800); and another, Figure 8–14, that accepts the latitude and longitude of the southwest corner of the display (statements 810–820), converts latitude and longitude to positions on the Mercator projection map (statements 840–850); and colors the annotation (statement 860).

Statements 290 to 540 make up the heart of this simulation. Statements 290 to 325 set up the problem display, which consists of a map with latitude and

FIGURE 8-11 Introductory panel of "Subcatcher."

```
***********************************************************************************
*                                                                                 *
*                                                                                 *
*                     THIS PROGRAM SIMULATES PURSUIT OF A                          *
*                                                                                 *
*                                                                                 *
*                                                                                 *
*                           HOSTILE SUBMARINE                                      *
*                                                                                 *
*                                                                                 *
*                                                                                 *
*                         OFF THE U.S. COASTLINE                                   *
*                                                                                 *
*                                                                                 *
*                                                                                 *
*                    FIELD IS 720 X 300 NAUTICAL MILES                             *
*                                                                                 *
*                                                                                 *
*                                                                                 *
***********************************************************************************

TYPE <RETURN> OR <ENTER> TO ADVANCE PROGRAM ?
```

```
****************************************************************************
*                                                                          *
*                                                                          *
*              MOVE THE FRIGATE (BLUE DOT) FROM NORFOLK BY                  *
*                                                                          *
*                                                                          *
*                                                                          *
*                    BY ENTERING ITS LATITUDE AND                          *
*                                                                          *
*                                                                          *
*                                                                          *
*                  LONGITUDE AFTER STEAMING IN A                           *
*                                                                          *
*                                                                          *
*                                                                          *
*              STRAIGHT LINE FOR 100 NAUTICAL MILES                        *
*                                                                          *
*                                                                          *
*                                                                          *
****************************************************************************

TYPE <RETURN> OR <ENTER> TO ADVANCE PROGRAM ?
```

FIGURE 8–12 Instructions for playing "Subcatcher."

longitude annotated in each corner, the shoreline, the frigate at its home base, and the hostile submarine somewhere offshore. This involves calling the subroutines Draw Shoreline (statements 630–690); Show Home Base (statements 550–610); Print Geographical Coordinates (statements 890–940); Show Hostile Contact (statements 1250–1300); and a timing loop for program synchronization (statement 325). The Show Home Base subroutine is executed only during the first iteration of an engagement. The Chase Hostile Contact routine (statements 340–480) carries out the actual operation; and statements 490–530 make up the main control switch. These displays are shown in photographs of the color monitor screen.

The Draw Shoreline subroutine simply draws a line connecting the 16 points in vectors XS and S, and paints the enclosed area green.

The Show Home Base subroutine is by-passed if N, the movement counter

FIGURE 8–13 Geographical orientation of naval anti-submarine warfare simulation.

```
****************************************************************************
*                                                                          *
*                                                                          *
*          BUILT-IN MAP SHOWS SOUTHEASTERN COAST OF THE U.S.               *
*                                                                          *
*                                                                          *
*                                                                          *
*                  ROUGHLY NORFOLK, VA TO ORLANDO, FA                      *
*                                                                          *
*                                                                          *
*                                                                          *
*                  ENTER 29 DEG N X 82 DEG W (29,82)                       *
*                                                                          *
*                                                                          *
*                                                                          *
*                  AS THE SOUTHWESTERN CORNER OF MAP                       *
*                                                                          *
*                                                                          *
*                                                                          *
****************************************************************************

TYPE <RETURN> OR <ENTER> TO ADVANCE PROGRAM ?
```

ENTER LATITUDE & LONGITUDE OF SW CORNER IN DECIMAL DEGREES? 29,82

FIGURE 8-14 Entering latitude and longitude of southwestern corner of map display.

for the frigate, is greater than one; that is, on every iteration in an engagement except the first. The subroutine draws a blue circle at graphical coordinates 110, 60; corresponding roughly to 33 deg N, 79.8 deg W. It enters the X, Y coordinates of the home base as the first component of the friendly craft's movement history vectors (XC, YC).

The Print Geographical Coordinates subroutine prints the pairs of values: YN (Y − NORTH), XW (X − WEST); YS (Y − SOUTH), XW; YN, XNE (X − NORTHEAST); and YS, XSE (X − SOUTHEAST) obtained in the Geographical Coordinates subroutine.

The Show Hostile Contact subroutine unstacks the first set of preloaded coordinates from the XH, YH vectors using the subscript M (hostile-craft movement counter), draws a red circle at that point, and increments M by one.

ACTUAL ENGAGEMENT

The Chase Hostile Contact routine (statements 240 to 530) invites the user to enter the latitude and longitude of where the frigate is supposed to be at the end of the iteration (statement 440). Ideally, this should be directly over the submarine. If the user is sufficiently skilled in relating map position to latitude and longitude, it should then be possible to "shadow" the submarine by staying directly over it no matter what maneuvers it executes.

The hardest part of the exercise is initially catching the intruder, who may be more than 200 miles away. Moreover, it is not easy to relate map position to latitude and longitude, since there is no grid on the map.

The program converts the latitude and longitude to map coordinates (statement 450). Then it checks to see whether the point selected is on the map (statement 460), and whether the point is less than or equal to 200 miles from the last position of the friendly vessel (statement 470). If either of these checks fails, control is transferred to the Position-Out-Of-Bounds subroutine (statements 1100 to 1160). If the point fulfills both criteria, control is transferred to the Good Position subroutine (statements 1180 to 1230).

The Good Position subroutine increments counter N, pushes the point's coordinates onto the XC and YC vectors, and paints a blue circle at that point. Control is returned to the master switch (statement 490).

The master switch has three positions: 0, 1, and 2. Position 0 concludes the engagement immediately. Position 1 transfers control to the Print Tracks subroutine (statements 1320 to 1410). Position 2 transfers control back to statement 290. It causes another iteration displaying the map and moving the hostile submarine to the next prestored random position. If none of these answers is selected, control is returned to statement 490 and the user is invited to respond again.

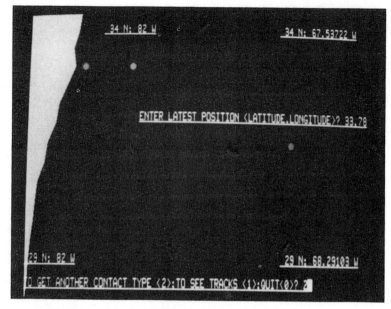

Start of an engagement. The coastline is shown in green. Home base (Norfolk, VA) is a blue circle. The initial position of the hostile submarine is shown as a red circle. The first position taken by the friendly frigate is shown as a blue circle.

End of the engagement. The frigate is shown closing with the submarine.

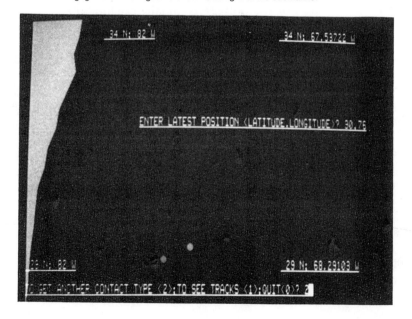

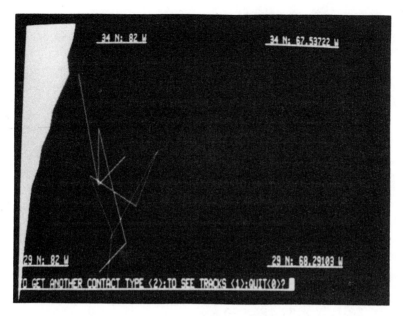

This display recalls and displays all the tracks made by the frigate and the submarine during an engagement.

If the selected point is determined to be out of bounds, the Position-Out-Of-Bounds subroutine handles things differently. A message: "Position out of bounds" is displayed and the user is invited to enter the response "0" to quit or "1" to try again. If the user elects to try again, the M counter is decremented by one to make the hostile submarine execute its last maneuver again. Then three subroutines are called: Draw Shoreline, Print Geographical Coordinates, and Show Hostile Contact; and control is transferred to statement 340 so the user can execute the Chase Hostile Contact routine again. Notice that we don't have to decrement the N counter, because the Out-Of-Bounds position never was stacked on the XC, YC vectors.

If the user elects the "Print Tracks" option, the Print Tracks subroutine first redraws the shoreline and then reprints the geographical coordinates. The subroutine then reads out the XC and YC vectors, drawing blue lines from XC(I), YC(I), to XC(I + 1), YC(I + 1). Then it reads out the XH and YH vectors, drawing red lines from XH(I), YH(I) to XH(I + 1), YH(I + 1)—but stops one location short of the current value of M to put the counters back into step. Upon returning to the main program, the engagement is terminated.

MAKING MOUNTAINS

It often is convenient to include a terrain display in a simulation. Random-number techniques can be used to generate randomly different terrain displays.

Our first example involves using Fourier synthesis (making a complex wave form out of the sums of sine and/or cosine waves) to generate the ridge line of a mountain range.

This is part of an artillery-training simulator that we shall describe in Chapter Ten. The program is written in the dialect of BASIC used by the Tandy TRS-80 computers:

```
10 G = RND(30) 'THIS RANDOMIZES THE PATTERN
20 'COMMENT OUT STEP 10 TO GET THE SAME
PATTERN EVERY TIME
30 FOR X = 1 TO 127 ' TRS-80 GRAPHICS USE A 128
X 80 PIXEL DISPLAY
40 Y = 28 - 3 *SIN(X*6.28/90) + 2 *
SIN(3*X*6.28/90 + G + 15) + 2 * SIN(5*X*6.28/90 - 30) +
SIN(7*X*6.28/90) + 30) + 3 * SIN(2*X*6.28/90)
50 IF Y < 19 THEN 90
60 IF Y > 37 THEN 90
70 Y(X) = Y
80 SET (X,Y)
90 NEXT X
```

FIGURE 8–15 Equilateral triangle divided into 3 levels of fractiles: 4 triangles. In the lower left apex is shown how we get 16 and 64 triangles.

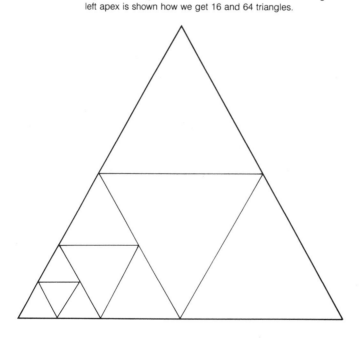

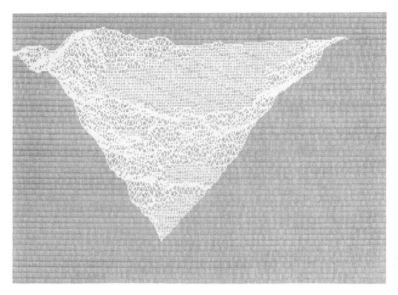

FIGURE 8–16   Three-dimensional picture of mountainous terrain produced by randomized fractiles of a triangle.

A complex three-dimensional terrain pattern can be generated using the geometric concept of fractiles. This concept is illustrated in Figure 8–15.

We start with an equilateral triangle and connect the midpoints of the three sides. This gives us 4 equilateral triangles and we have descended one level of fractiles. Now we can descend another level and do the same thing to each of our 4 equilateral triangles, to obtain 16 triangles. By descending to the third level, we obtain 64 triangles. These little triangles are fractiles of the big one we started with.

Now we bring simulation into the picture. Instead of drawing our lines that subdivide triangles from the midpoints of the sides of the bigger ones, we use our random-number generator to pick a random point on each side. The result is not the regular geometric pattern we had before, but one that, after we add some random shading and/or color, produces the simulated aerial photograph of mountainous terrain shown in Figure 8–16.

The program to generate pictures like this (every picture will be differ-

FIGURE 8–17   Basic program for producing three-dimensional pictures by randomized fractiles.

```
20   DIM D(64,32)
30   INPUT "Number of levels >> ";LE
40  DS = 2: FOR N = 1 TO LE
45  DS = DS + 2 ^ (N - 1): NEXT N
50  MX = DS - 1:MY = MX / 2:VPI = 3.1416
55  RH = VPI * 30 / 180:VVT = RH * 1.2
60   FOR N = 1 TO LE:L = 10000 / 1.8 ^ N
70   PRINT " Working on level ";N
80  IB = MX / 2 ^ N:SK = IB * 2
85   REM *** Assign heights along X in array ***
```

```
90    GOSUB 150
95    REM *** Assign heights along Y in array ***
100   GOSUB 220
105   REM *** Assign heights along diagonal in array ***
110   GOSUB 290
120   NEXT N
130   GOTO 640: REM  *** Draw ***
140   REM  * Heights along X ***
150   FOR YE = 0 TO MX - 1 STEP SK
160   FOR XE = IB + YE TO MX STEP SK
170   AX = XE - IB:AY = YE: GOSUB 370
175   D1 = D:AX = XE + IB: GOSUB 370:D2 = D
180   D = (D1 + D2) / 2 + RND * L / 2 - L / 4
185   AX = XE:AY = YE: GOSUB 420
190   NEXT XE
200   NEXT YE: RETURN
210   REM  * Heights along Y *
220   FOR XE = MX TO 1 STEP  - SK
230   FOR YE = IB TO XE STEP SK
240   AX = XE:AY = YE + IB: GOSUB 370
245   D1 = D:AY = YE - IB: GOSUB 370:D2 = D
250   D = (D1 + D2) / 2 +  RND   * L / 2 - L / 4
255   AX = XE:AY = YE: GOSUB 420
260   NEXT YE
270   NEXT XE: RETURN
280   REM  * Heights along diagonal *
290   FOR XE = 0 TO MX - 1 STEP SK
300   FOR YE = IB TO MX - XE STEP SK
310   AX = XE + YE - IB:AY = YE - IB: GOSUB 370:D1 = D
320   AX = XE + YE + IB:AY = YE + IB: GOSUB 370:D2 = D
330   AX = XE + YE:AY = YE
332   D = (D1 + D2) / 2 +  RND   * L / 2 - L / 4
334   GOSUB 420
340   NEXT YE
350   NEXT XE: RETURN
360   REM  *** return data from array ***
370   IF AY > MY THEN 390
380   VBY = AY:BX = AX: GOTO 400
390   VBY = MX + 1 - AY:BX = MX - AX
400   D = D(BX,VBY): RETURN
410   REM  *** Put data into array ***
420   IF AY > MY THEN 440
430   VBY = AY:BX = AX: GOTO 450
440   VBY = MX + 1 - AY:BX = MX - AX
450   D(BX,VBY) = D: RETURN
460   REM  *** Put in sea level here ***
470   IF X0 <> - 999 THEN 500
480   IF ZZ < 0 THEN  GOSUB 1070:Z2 = ZZ:ZZ = 0: GOTO 620
490   GOSUB 1090: GOTO 610
500   IF. Z2 > 0 AND ZZ > 0 THEN 610
510   IF Z2 < 0 AND ZZ < 0 THEN Z2 = ZZ:ZZ = 0: GOTO 620
520   W3 = ZZ / (ZZ - Z2)
522   X3 = (X2 - XX) * W3 + XX
524   Y3 = (Y2 - YY) * W3 + YY
526   Z3 = 0
530   ZT = ZZ:YT = YY:XT = XX
540   IF ZZ > 0 THEN 590
550   REM  *** going into water ***
560   ZZ = Z3:YY = Y3:XX = X3: GOSUB 950
570   GOSUB 1070:ZZ = 0:YY = YT:XX = XT:Z2 = ZT: GOTO 620
580   REM  *** comming up out of water ***
590   ZZ = Z3:YY = Y3:XX = X3: GOSUB 950
600   GOSUB 1090:ZZ = ZT:YY = YT:XX = XT
610   Z2 = ZZ
620   X2 = XX:Y2 = YY: RETURN
630   REM  *** display here ***
635   REM ** set up plotting device or screen ***
640   GOSUB 1110
```

FIGURE 8-17 (continued)

```
645  REM *** scaling factors ***
650  XS = .04:YS = .04:ZS = .04
660  FOR AX = 0 TO MX:XO = - 999: FOR AY = 0 TO AX
670  GOSUB 370
672  ZZ = D
674  YY = AY / MX * 10000
676  XX = AX / MX * 10000 - YY / 2
680  GOSUB 940: NEXT AY: NEXT AX
690  FOR AY = 0 TO MX:XO = - 999: FOR AX = AY TO MX
700  GOSUB 370
702  ZZ = D
704  YY = AY / MX * 10000
706  XX = AX / MX * 10000 - YY / 2
710  GOSUB 940: NEXT AX: NEXT AY
720  FOR EX = 0 TO MX:XO = - 999: FOR EY = 0 TO MX - EX
730  AX = EX + EY
732  AY = EY: GOSUB 370
736  ZZ = D
738  YY = AY / MX * 10000
740  XX = AX / MX * 10000 - YY / 2
745  GOSUB 940: NEXT EY: NEXT EX
750  GOTO 1130: REM  *** Done plotting goto end loop **
760  REM  *** rotate ***
770  IF XX <> 0 THEN 800
780  IF YY <= 0 THEN RA = - VPI / 2: GOTO 820
790  RA = VPI / 2: GOTO 820
800  RA = ATN (YY / XX)
810  IF XX < 0 THEN RA = RA + VPI
820  R1 = RA + RH:RD = SQR (XX * XX + YY * YY)
830  XX = RD * COS (R1):YY = RD * SIN (R1)
840  RETURN
850  REM  *** Tilt down **
860  RD = SQR (ZZ * ZZ + XX * XX)
870  IF XX = 0 THEN RA = VPI / 2: GOTO 900
880  RA = ATN (ZZ / XX)
890  IF XX < 0 THEN RA = RA + VPI
900  R1 = RA - VVT
910  XX = RD * COS (R1) + XX:ZZ = RD * SIN (R1)
920  RETURN
930  REM  *** Move or plot to (XP,YP) ***
940  GOSUB 470
950  XX = XX * XS:YY = YY * YS:ZZ = ZZ * ZS
960  GOSUB 770: REM  *** rotate ***
970  GOSUB 860: REM  *** Tilt up ***
980  IF XO = - 999 THEN PR$ = "M"
985  IF XO <> - 999 THEN PR$ = "D"
990  XP = INT (YY) + CX:YP = INT (ZZ)
1000  GOSUB 1030
1010  RETURN
1020  REM  *** Plot line here ***
1030  XP = XP * .625:YP = 33.14 - .663 * YP
1040  IF PR$ = "M" THEN X8 = XP:Y8 = YP:XO = X
1045  IF Y8 > 179 OR Y8 < 0 OR YP > 179 OR YP < 0 THEN  RETURN
1050  LINE (X8,Y8)-(XP,YP),CL
1060  REM  *** switch to sea colour ***
1064  X8 = XP:Y8 = YP: RETURN
1070  CL = 1
1075  RETURN
1080  REM  *** switch to land colour ***
1090  CL = 3
1095  RETURN
1100  REM  *** Setup plotting device or screen ***
1110  SCREEN 1
1112  COLOR 0,1
1115  RETURN
1120  REM  *** End looooop ***
1130  INPUT A$
1140  END
```

FIGURE 8-17 (continued)

ent, as long as you reseed the random-number generator) is given in Figure 8–17. It is written in MS/BASIC for IBM/PC graphics.

SUMMARY

We have examined two simulation programs that were skeletonized from mainframe simulations to run on personal computers.

The first simulated the occurrence of criminal incidents in a medium-sized city. The main point of this program was the rationalization of time to correspond to curves fitted to historical statistics.

The second program simulated a two-vessel encounter. Its main point was the creation of a colored map upon which to carry out the engagement.

In both cases, the personal computer was turned into a convenient training system based upon a person-machine simulation.

Then we presented two ways to use random-number techniques to produce randomly different terrain representations: One uses Fourier synthesis to create the line of a mountain ridge; the other uses fractiles to create a three-dimensional picture of mountains, and islands if desired.

CHAPTER NINE

GPSS for Personal Computers

Most users of computer simulation programs today use special simulation languages, of which there are a large number. Three popular ones are SIMULA, SIMSCRIPT, and GPSS. Some of these languages are available only on mainframe computers, and sometimes on only certain makes and/or models. Others are available on personal computers.

GPSS, which stands for General Purpose Systems Simulator, is a widely used simulation language. It was originally an IBM product, but its instruction set has been implemented on many different computers. At the University of Western Ontario, we use a version written by David Martin, of the Department of Computer Science systems support group; it was originally called GPSS-10 to suggest that it ran on the Digital Equipment Corporation (DEC) PDP-10. A later version of this program, written with C. Bruce Richards, is called GPSSR (revised).

Bruce Richards, a former student of mine, has written and is marketing a version of GPSSR that runs on personal computers compatible with the IBM-PC. It is called GPSSR/PC.

GPSSR/PC is a General Purpose Simulation System that runs under MDOS-V2.0. The MDOS operating system is supplied for the IBM/PC line of personal computers. Many other personal computers are compatible with the IBM/PC and can also run GPSSR/PC.

GPSSR/PC concepts do not vary from other popular GPSS implementations. It has been designed to be a substantial subset of both GPSS/360 on IBM systems and GPSS10 on DEC systems 10 and 20. These two systems were used as guidelines to produce a language that is familiar to GPSS users and compatible with most textbooks.

INTRODUCTION TO GPSS

by C. Bruce Richards
Department of Computer Science
The University of Western Ontario
London, Ontario, Canada

INTRODUCTION TO GPSS

Unlike a conventional general-purpose programming language such as FORTRAN or PASCAL, GPSS does not have a sequential flow of control. Conceptually there may be numerous portions of a GPSS program being executed simultaneously. GPSS is event-oriented, and at any given moment in simulated time, numerous different events may take place: It is natural to think of them as happening at one instant in time.

This concept of concurrency may be explained with a car-wash example. At one instant it is possible that one car is leaving the car wash, another is entering, and yet another is joining the queue waiting outside. (These are events.)

The basic element in the multiple flow of control in GPSS is the "transaction." Transactions flow through a model sequentially from block to block in much the same manner that the flow of control in a FORTRAN program passes from statement to statement. The main difference is that a GPSS model can have many transactions flowing through it simultaneously, while a FORTRAN program has only one element in its flow of control.

The flow of control in a conventional program starts at the begining of the program and continues sequentially from there. A transaction in a GPSS program starts at a GENERATE block and continues into the system. The single flow of control in a conventional program continues until the program comes to its logical conclusion and is halted. A GPSS transaction passes from block to block until it reaches a TERMINATE, which removes the transaction from the model. However, this does not necessarily halt the model. Execution of the model is halted only after a specified number of transactions have been terminated.

There may be numerous GENERATE blocks in a GPSS program. This gives rise to the concept of multiple starting locations, with many transactions leaving GENERATE blocks in the same simulated time interval. It is also possible for many transactions to leave a GENERATE block before any reaches a TERMINATE block. This results in a model having possibly only one GENERATE block but many active transactions moving simultaneously.

Novice GPSS programmers often have the misconception that a transaction transfers from the TERMINATE block back to the GENERATE block that it originated from, similar to a FORTRAN-style GOTO. This is not the case. Transactions leaving a GENERATE block are completely independent from the transactions being removed by a TERMINATE block.

CASE STUDY I (CAR WASH)

Scenario

Johnny Canuck, owner of the Great Polish—Sparkling Shine Car Wash, wants to increase his profits. It seems a little risky to build an extension to his facility without knowing beforehand how large it should be. He feels that adding more capacity would increase his throughput, but if it is too large the facilities would be underutilized, thereby decreasing profits.

Analysis

The first step in designing a simulation is to specify the goals and objectives. To make a decision regarding the expansion of the car-wash facilities, information pertaining to queue lengths and waiting times, along with facility utilization, should suffice.

Identification of the different components and control points of the system in question with respect to the foregoing information requirements is the next phase. Obviously the main component of our system is the washing mechanism. In the current car wash this is a facility that can wash one car at a time. Another, possibly less obvious, component is the lineup of cars waiting to enter the car wash, better known as a queue. This queue does not directly affect the operation of the car wash, but resultant information regarding queue lengths and waiting times is invaluable when studying the model. The rate at which cars to be washed join the queue and the time it takes to wash a car are the third and fourth components.

Next, the appropriate times and rates must be measured. The two timings that are important in this system are the rate at which cars arrive and the length of time needed to wash a car. A measure of actual queue lengths will be useful for model validation.

The arrival rate is best calculated by measuring the elapsed time between successive arrivals (the interarrival rate). The number of cars arriving per time unit can be useful if an appropriate time unit is chosen (traffic seldom arrives at a constant rate). By measuring the interarrival times, we can calculate the average, minimum, and maximum interarrival times. Using this information, a uniformly distributed random interarrival rate can be very easily programmed into the model with GPSS. GPSS is structured such that this is the distribution of choice in GENERATE and ADVANCE blocks.

Raw Data

By analyzing the raw data in Tables 9–1 and 9–2, we may derive the following system characteristics. The average time between arrivals at the wash is 5.2 minutes. The shortest time interval is 1.4 minutes and the longest is 9.0

Table 9–1 Interarrival Times (Minutes) of
Consecutive Arrivals

4.4	3.6	2.3	5.2
6.8	5.4	5.9	6.1
4.5	4.9	5.3	1.7
7.5	4.2	8.3	3.5
3.3	6.3	6.0	7.5
2.5	2.0	9.0	3.5
7.1	2.5	5.0	4.4
6.3	1.4	8.2	3.2
5.0	7.5	2.7	4.1
4.0	3.5	5.6	2.0
5.0	4.6	7.7	8.9
5.8	6.8	5.7	5.6
8.8	5.9	8.7	7.5

minutes. To simplify things, the interarrival times could be stated as 5 plus or minus 4 minutes. The time a car spends inside the car wash is between 3.2 and 4.9 minutes, with an average time of 4.1 minutes. Similarly, this time spread could be stated as 4 plus or minus 1 minute.

The observed queue lengths can be summarized as a maximum length of 12 and an average length of 6.8 cars.

Simulation

GPSS has entities and block definitions to represent the different types of components in a system. The manner in which transactions are to enter the model (in our example, cars entering the car-wash system) is represented by the GENERATE block. The different options of the GENERATE block allow the programmer to specify the rate at which transactions are to enter the system. The first subfield (field A) specifies the mean interarrival time, and the next subfield (field B) is the spread of times.

The GPSS statements QUEUE and DEPART respectively insert and remove transactions from the specified queue. The QUEUE entity type also generates queue statistics by automatically accumulating pertinent information about the queue's behavior.

Equipment entities may be represented by a FACILITY or a STORAGE. A STORAGE entity may be defined to contain a maximum of one or many

Table 9–2 Random Sample of Car-wash Times
(Minutes) Observed During the
Same Time Period as Table 9–1

4.2	3.5	3.6	4.5
4.0	4.2	3.2	4.9
3.7	4.0	3.5	3.4

Table 9-3 Random Sample of Car-wash Queue Lengths Observed During the Same Time Period as Table 9-1

3	7	6	7
6	5	3	2
9	12	8	7
7	9	11	8

transactions. A FACILITY may contain only one at a time. The single car wash in our example will be represented by a FACILITY. The SEIZE and RELEASE statements cause a transaction to gain control of the specified facility if the facility is free, and relinquish control when finished.

A time delay is represented by an ADVANCE block. The time delay may be constant or variable, depending on the options used. ADVANCE 4,1 represents a random time delay uniformly distributed between 3 and 5 units in duration. This time delay may represent the length of time that a transaction keeps control of a piece of equipment (i.e., the time it takes to wash a car).

The TERMINATE block removes transactions from the model. As a transaction enters a TERMINATE block, it is conceptually destroyed. We are no longer interested in a car after it exits the car wash. Therefore it is terminated. Figure 9-1 relates the activities of the car-wash system to the different GPSS blocks.

Verification and Validation

Verification that the GPSS program matches the designed model is of utmost importance. This is similar to program debugging. In GPSS the interactive debugger allows the user to single-step through a model to check transaction flow. Other debugger features allow examination of entities and setting of break points in the model. (Further information can be found in the reference manual.)

Once the GPSS program is running correctly, the model should be validated. Model validation involves tests to determine if samples of simulated output statistics belong to the same population as the actual system statistics. Figure 9-2 shows the actual output of a GPSS simulation run. By comparing the output to the performance of the actual system it is possible to determine if the model is simulating the car wash correctly. If, for example, the queue lengths in the model and the actual car wash bear no resemblance to one another, it is possible that there is still a bug in the GPSS program or the model design is incorrect.

Three possible causes of an incorrect model are: oversimplification, invalid data analysis, or insufficient raw data. Oversimplification may be caused by using too crude a time measure or by combining too many components of the actual system into one entity in the model. Not obtaining enough raw data may result in a sample that is not a true representation of the real system. Poor data analysis may result in an incorrect assumption regarding the distribution of timings. What may at first appear to be a uniform distribution may actually be a normal distribution.

Figure 9–2 contains the output of our GPSS car-wash simulation. The information that is of interest to us is the automatically generated statistics regarding queue length and facility utilization. The .78 utilization means that in our model the carwash was busy 78 percent of the time. This does not mean the actual car wash is this busy. The maximum and average queue lengths of 5

FIGURE 9–1   Car wash simulation using GPSS.

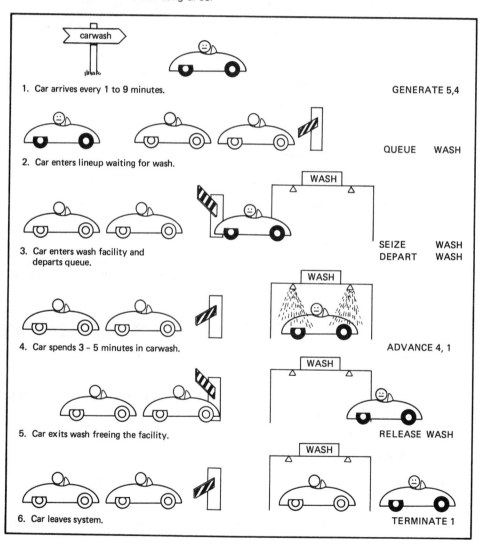

1. Car arrives every 1 to 9 minutes.   GENERATE 5,4

2. Car enters lineup waiting for wash.   QUEUE   WASH

3. Car enters wash facility and departs queue.   SEIZE   WASH   DEPART   WASH

4. Car spends 3 – 5 minutes in carwash.   ADVANCE 4, 1

5. Car exits wash freeing the facility.   RELEASE WASH

6. Car leaves system.   TERMINATE 1

```
     GPSSR/PC   V1.1                9-FEB-1985   18:26                    PAGE 1
     carwash1.LST=carwash1.gps

LINE     BLOCK

1                    *
2                    *       CAR WASH EXAMPLE 1
3                    *
4                            RMULT       31415
5            WASH    EQU     1          ;WASH EQUATED TO A NUMERIC VALUE
6                            SIMULATE
7        1           GENERATE   5,4     ;CAR ENTERS SYSTEM
8        2           QUEUE      WASH    ;CAR LINES UP FOR WASH
9        3           SEIZE      WASH    ;CAR GAINS CONTROL OF WASHER
10       4           DEPART     WASH    ;CAR LEAVES LINEUP
11       5           ADVANCE    4,1     ;TIME TO WASH CAR
12       6           RELEASE    WASH    ;CAR EXITS WASHER
13       7           TERMINATE  1       ;CAR EXITS SYSTEM
14                   START      1000    ;RUN MODEL FOR 1000 TERMINATIONS
15                   END
```

```
          SYMBOL     VALUE          SYMBOL     VALUE
          ======     =====          ======     =====

          WASH         1
```

```
     GPSSR/PC   V1.1                9-FEB-1985   18:26                    PAGE 2
     carwash1.LST=carwash1.gps

     RELATIVE CLOCK        5112    ABSOLUTE CLOCK          5112

     BLOCK COUNTS
     BLOCK CURRENT   TOTAL      BLOCK CURRENT   TOTAL      BLOCK CURRENT   TOTAL

       1      1      1002         2      1      1001         3      0      1000
       4      0      1000         5      0      1000         6      0      1000
       7      0      1000

     FACILITY         AVERAGE       NUMBER        AVERAGE      SEIZING      PREEMPTING
                    UTILIZATION    ENTRIES      TIME/TRAN    TRANS.NO.     TRANS.NO.
            1          0.78         1000          3.99
```

```
     QUEUE MAXIMUM AVERAGE   TOTAL     ZERO    PERC.   AVERAGE *AVERAGE TABLE CURRENT
           CONTENT CONTENT ENTRIES ENTRIES    ZERO   TIME/TR  TIME/TR NUMBR CONTENT
       1      5     0.34    1001     513    51.25     1.74     3.56              1
```

FIGURE 9–2 GPSS output listing with (default) queue and facility statistics.

and .34 do not appear to be close to our observed queue lengths. There may be a problem in our model.

CASE STUDY PART II

Scenario

The observed queue lengths are substantially longer than those generated by the GPSS model. What is wrong?

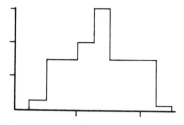

FIGURE 9–3 Histogram of interarrival rates (ap-
proximately nor-
mal).

Analysis

A further analysis of the interarrival-rate data produces the conclusion that the distribution is not uniform. The first step toward a better understanding of the interarrival distribution is to create a frequency table (Table 9–4).

The relative frequency represents the percentage of cars that arrive in that range of times. A histogram of the raw data (Figure 9–3) visually demonstrates the similarity between the observed data and a normal distribution.

Two different simulations, one with the observed distribution of interarrival times and the other based on a normal distribution, will be run. A standard normal distribution has a mean of 0 and a standard deviation of 1. The standard deviation is a statistic representing the measure of spread in the data. The standard deviation of the observed interarrival rates is 2.

Simulation

The GPSS block GENERATE 5,4 (Figure 9–2) creates one transaction every one to nine time units with equal probability (i.e., uniform distribution). To modify the program to use a different distribution, a FUNCTION is required.

Table 9–4 Frequency Table of Interarrival Times

INTERARRIVAL TIME	OBSERVED FREQUENCY	RELATIVE FREQUENCY	CUMULATIVE RELATIVE FREQUENCY
1–2	2	.038	.038
2–3	6	.113	.151
3–4	6	.113	.264
4–5	8	.152	.416
5–6	12	.226	.642
6–7	6	.113	.755
7–8	6	.113	.868
8–9	6	.113	.981
9–10	1	.019	1.00

The GENERATE block may reference a predefined function to specify the arrival rate.

A function is defined with a FUNCTION statement and is referenced via the FN standard numeric attribute (SNA). (There are a number of SNAs in GPSS that can be used to reference information pertaining to the different entities in the model.)

To produce a random interarrival time, one of the random-number generators will be declared to be the independent variable for this function. The actual shape of the function is described by a function-follower statement.

```
INTERVL    FUNCTION    RN$2,C9
```

The preceding function statement declares INTERVL to be a continuous function using random-number generator 2 as the independent variable and having 9 points in the definition.

```
.038,1/.151,2/.264,3/.416,4
.642,5/.755,6/.868,7/.981,8/1,9
```

Note that in the foregoing function-follower statement, a slash (/) separates pairs of values. The first value of each pair is the cumulative relative frequency, and the second is the lower limit of the corresponding range of times from Table 9–4.

The function-follower statement contains 9 pairs of values that define the curve of the function. The value of RN$2 is compared to the first value of each pair until a match or the correct interval between two points is found. If the independent value lies between two defined points, an interpolation is performed to calculate the value to be used. For example, if the random number is between .038 and .151, the interarrival rate will be between two and three time units. The probability of the random number's falling into the range .038 to .151 is equal to the relative frequency of this range 11.3 percent.

It is possible to define either a discrete (histogram) or continuous (smooth curve) function to represent any desired distribution.

```
GENERATE    FN$INTERVL
```

In the preceding GENERATE block, the function INTERVL specifies the interarrival rate.

FN$INTERVL is a function standard numeric attribute. Each reference to FN$INTERVL will return a value that depends on the random number RN$2 specified in the function definition.

```
GPSSR/PC  V1.1              9-FEB-1985   18:43                    PAGE 1
carwashb.LST=carwashb.gps

LINE     BLOCK

1                  *
2                  *        CAR WASH EXAMPLE 2A
3                  *
4                  WASH      EQU           1        ;WASH EQUATED TO A NUMERIC VALUE
5                  INTERVL   EQU           1
6                  *
7                  INTERVL   FUNCTION      RN#2,C9
8                            .038,1/.151,2/.264,3/.416,4
9                            .642,5/.755,6/.868,7/.981,8/1,9
10                 *
11                           SIMULATE
12        1                  GENERATE      FN$INTERVL  ;CAR ENTERS SYSTEM
13        2                  QUEUE         WASH       ;CAR LINES UP FOR WASH
14        3                  SEIZE         WASH       ;CAR GAINS CONTROL OF WASHER
15        4                  DEPART        WASH       ;CAR LEAVES LINEUP
16        5                  ADVANCE       4,1        ;TIME TO WASH CAR
17        6                  RELEASE       WASH       ;CAR EXITS WASHER
18        7                  TERMINATE     1          ;CAR EXITS SYSTEM
19                           START         1000       ;RUN MODEL FOR 1000 TERMINATIONS
20                           END


           SYMBOL      VALUE        SYMBOL      VALUE
           ======      =====        ======      =====

           INTERVL       1          WASH          1



GPSSR/PC  V1.1              9-FEB-1985  18:43                     PAGE 2
carwashb.LST=carwashb.gps

RELATIVE CLOCK        3993    ABSOLUTE CLOCK         3993

BLOCK COUNTS
BLOCK CURRENT   TOTAL    BLOCK CURRENT  TOTAL    BLOCK CURRENT   TOTAL

   1      1     1029       2     28     1028       3     0       1000
   4      0     1000       5     0      1000       6     0       1000
   7      0     1000


FACILITY        AVERAGE       NUMBER        AVERAGE     SEIZING      PREEMPTING
               UTILIZATION    ENTRIES     TIME/TRAN    TRANS.NO.    TRANS.NO.
      1          1.00          1000          3.98


QUEUE MAXIMUM AVERAGE   TOTAL    ZERO    PERC.   AVERAGE $AVERAGE TABLE CURRENT
      CONTENT CONTENT ENTRIES ENTRIES    ZERO   TIME/TR  TIME/TR NUMBR CONTENT
   1     35    16.72    1028      12     1.17    64.95    65.72           28
```

FIGURE 9–4 GPSS program using empirically distributed interarrival rates.

In the second model a standard normal function will be used to approximate the distribution of observed interarrival times.

```
NORM   FUNCTION   RN$2,C12
```

The preceding GPSS statement defines NORM to be a continuous function using random-number generator 2 as its independent variable and having 12 points in the definition.

.006, −2.5/.066, −1.5/.158, −1/.274, − .6/.420, − .2
.5,0/.579, .2/.725, .6/.841,1/.933,1.5/.993,2.5/1,3.5

The function NORM is defined to return a value between −2.5 and +3.5, depending on the value between 0 and 1 of the independent variable RN$2.

By definition the standard normal distribution function has a mean of 0 and standard deviation of 1. To obtain a mean of 5 and a standard deviation of 2, a variable is defined.

```
RATE   FVARIABLE   2*FN$NORM+5
```

The foregoing variable-definition statement declares RATE to be a floating-point variable to multiply the function NORM by 2 and add 5. The

FIGURE 9–5 GPSS program listing using normally distributed interarrival rates.

```
GPSSR/PC  V1.1                 9-FEB-1985  18:36                    PAGE 1
carwash2.LST=carwash2.gps

LINE    BLOCK

1                    *
2                    *       CAR WASH EXAMPLE 2B
3                    *
4              WASH      EQU          1         WASH EQUATED TO
5              NORM      EQU          1         A NUMERIC VALUE
6              RATE      EQU          1
7                    *
8              NORM      FUNCTION     RN$2,C12
9                        .006,-2.5/.066,-1.5/.158,-1/.274,-.6/.420,-.2
10                       .5,0/.579,.2/.725,.6/.841,1/.933,1.5/.993,2.5/1,3.5
11                   *
12             RATE      FVARIABLE    2*FN$NORM+5
13                   *
14                       SIMULATE
15      1                GENERATE     V$RATE ;CAR ENTERS SYSTEM
16      2                QUEUE        WASH   ;CAR LINES UP FOR WASH
17      3                SEIZE        WASH   ;CAR GAINS CONTROL OF WASHER
18      4                DEPART       WASH   ;CAR LEAVES LINEUP
19      5                ADVANCE      4,1    ;TIME TO WASH CAR
20      6                RELEASE      WASH   ;CAR EXITS WASHER
21      7                TERMINATE    1      ;CAR EXITS SYSTEM
22                       START        1000   ;RUN MODEL FOR 1000 TERMINATIONS
23                       END
```

SYMBOL	VALUE	SYMBOL	VALUE
NORM	1	RATE	1
WASH	1		

```
GPSSR/PC   V1.1                    9-FEB-1985   18:36                       PAGE 2
carwash2.LST=carwash2.gps


RELATIVE CLOCK          4431     ABSOLUTE CLOCK          4431

BLOCK COUNTS
BLOCK CURRENT   TOTAL     BLOCK CURRENT   TOTAL     BLOCK CURRENT   TOTAL
  1      1      1002        2      1      1001        3      0      1000
  4      0      1000        5      0      1000        6      0      1000
  7      0      1000


FACILITY        AVERAGE       NUMBER          AVERAGE     SEIZING      PREEMPTING
               UTILIZATION    ENTRIES        TIME/TRAN   TRANS.NO.     TRANS.NO.
     1           0.90          1000            3.98


QUEUE MAXIMUM AVERAGE   TOTAL     ZERO     PERC.   AVERAGE  ●AVERAGE TABLE CURRENT
      CONTENT CONTENT ENTRIES ENTRIES    ZERO   TIME/TR  TIME/TR NUMBR CONTENT
   1      4     0.44    1001     379    37.86    1.96     3.15              1
```

FIGURE 9-5 (continued)

interarrival rates of our model should now match the mean and spread of our observed data.

An FVARIABLE uses floating-point arithmetic to return an integer value, whereas a VARIABLE does integer calculations to return an integer result. Both floating-point and integer functions are referenced via the "V" standard numeric attribute.

GENERATE   V$RATE

The preceding generate statement uses the value returned by the variable RATE as the interarrival time.

Verification and Validation

A comparison of the queue statistics generated by the GPSS model (Figure 9–4) and the observed queue lengths (Table 9–3) reveals a discrepancy. The simulation produced a maximum queue length of 35 and an average length of 16.72. These values are substantially higher than those observed in the actual system. The second simulation (Figure 9–5) produced very different queue statistics. With a maximum queue length of 4 and average of .44, it appears that neither model simulates the desired system.

CAR WASH PART III

Scenario

A more in-depth analysis of the observed interarrival rates did not result in a correct model. It is possible that the sample size of the data is too small to produce a true representation of the actual system. The next step in solving the problem would be a further analysis of the original system. This would involve more data collection and a more detailed investigation of system traffic flow.

Analysis

The two components of the system that most obviously affect queue lengths are arrival rate and service rate. If either of these timings is incorrect, the model would be invalid. It may also be advantageous to collect more queue-length data to ensure that our sample is a true representation of the system. It would be a gross error to attempt to validate the model against invalid data.

Figure 9–6 is the resultant histogram, after the increase in interarrival-rate observations. It does not resemble the distribution of our original data; therefore, the original sample was not a true representation. The new larger sample of interarrival-rate data resembles an exponential distribution curve. A simple arithmetic calculation results in a mean of 3.6 and a standard deviation of 4.2. A system with an exponentially distributed interarrival rate will have a Poisson-distributed arrival rate. A comparison between the cumulative distribution of the empiral data and the chosen theoretical function should be done to validate the choice. (These distributions are very common in traffic simulations and are discussed in detail in most simulation textbooks.)

The more in-depth analysis of the car-wash system uncovered a traffic-flow situation not previously taken into consideration. The previous model assumed all cars remained in the queue and received a wash. In the actual system, drivers did not wait if the queue was too long. (The maximum queue length in which a driver would wait was 11 or 12 cars, oneself included.) The interarrival rate incorporated into the model includes cars that left the system without getting washed. Therefore, a test of the queue length must also be built into the model.

To help solve the original problem regarding expansion of the car wash, the number of cars that leave because of queue length and the amount of time spent by cars that receive a wash would be helpful.

Simulation

GPSS has readily available the procedures necessary to generate trans-actions with an exponentially distributed interarrival rate. It is defined by a

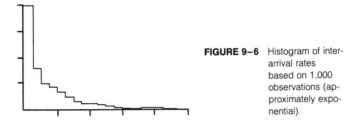

FIGURE 9–6 Histogram of inter-arrival rates based on 1,000 observations (approximately exponential).

FUNCTION statement in much the same way that the normal function was defined in the previous model.

```
   EXPON  FUNCTION  RN2,C12
0,0/.2,.222/.4,.509/.6,.915/.75,1.38/.84,1.83
.9,2.3/.94,2.81/.96,3.2/.98,3.9/995,5.3/.999,7
```

The foregoing GPSS statements define EXPON to be an inverse negative exponential function with a mean of 1 using random-number generator 2 as the independant variable. (Standard deviation and mean are equal in this distribution.) This function will be referenced by the generate block to produce transactions with the desired Poisson-distributed arrival rates.

In the GENERATE (and ADVANCE) block, if field B is a function reference, the departure time is the product of field A and field B.

```
GENERATE  4,FN$EXPON
```

In the preceding generate block, the values of function EXPON are multiplied by 4 to produce an interarrival rate with a mean of 4 and a Standard Deviation of 4.

A decision mechanism must be built into the model to decide if a driver waits for a car wash or leaves prematurely. Three GPSS statements for altering a transactions flow through the model are: GATE, TEST, and TRANSFER. The GATE block is used to test the status of entities, the TEST block is used to compare two standard numeric attributes, and the TRANSFER block alters transaction flow depending on the subfields specified.

A TEST block is used in the model to compare queue length against a constant. If the queue is less than the specified value, the transaction enters the queue; otherwise, the transaction's flow will be altered such that it does not enter the queue.

```
TEST  L  Q$WASH,12,EXITW
```

The preceding TEST block allows the current transaction to enter the next block if the length of queue WASH is less than 12. If the queue is equal to or greater than 12, the transaction is transferred to the block labeled EXITW.

Q$WASH is a standard numeric attribute whose value is the current contents of the queue WASH.

The analysis of the system informed us that drivers do not become frustrated and leave when the queue is exactly 12 cars long, but 11 or 12. In order to build this into the model, a VARIABLE will be used. Rather than reference the constant 12 in the TEST block, an integer variable, whose value is 11 or 12 based on a random number, will be incorporated.

```
LNGTH  VARIABLE   Q$WASH< 11+(RN$3*2)/1000
```

The preceding GPSS statement defines an integer variable, labeled LNGTH. The expression 11+(RN$3*2)/1000 is evaluated on every reference to the foregoing variable and compared to the current queue length. If the queue length is less than the arithmetic expression, the result is true (1). The foregoing expression will return the value 0 or 1, depending on the random number generated and the current queue length. RN$3 is a random integer value between 0 and 999. A variable expression may contain SNA references (including other variables) and constants combined with arithmetic, logical, and boolean operators.

```
TEST_NE   V$LNGTH,0,EXITW
```

This modified TEST block references the variable LNGTH rather than the constant 12. V$LNGTH is the standard numeric attribute whose value is computed using the variable LNGTH. If V$LNGTH is equal to zero (false), the transaction transfers to the block EXITW.

To facilitate calculating the total number of cars that do not wait for a car wash, a means of accumulating and saving numeric information must be employed. GPSS has two different entities designed for this purpose: PARAMETERS and SAVEVALUES.

Each transaction has a number of PARAMETERS associated with it. The concept of a car's having a luggage compartment that is attached to the car and every car's having its own unique compartment is similar to the concept of every transaction's having its own unique parameters. If a transaction enters a block that references a parameter, it is the parameter of that individual transaction that is affected. The P standard numeric attribute is used to reference a parameter.

SAVEVALUES are a more global storage location. If a transaction enters a block that references a particular SAVEVALUE, it is the same SAVEVALUE that every other transaction that enters that block will access. The XH or XF standard numeric attributes refer to half-word or full-word SAVEVALUES respectively. Unlike parameters, SAVEVALUES are not associated with individual transactions.

To total the number of transactions (cars) that do not queue up for a wash but exit the system, a global counter must be used. Each transaction that does not wait must be able to access the same counter; therefore, a SAVEVALUE is used to accumulate the total.

```
EXITW   SAVEVALUE    1+,1
```

The GPSS statement labeled EXITW adds 1 to SAVEVALUE 1. Field A specifies which SAVEVALUE is to be affected, and field B specifies the value to be stored. If field A has a plus sign (+) following the SAVEVALUE number, the value in field B is added to the current contents of the SAVEVALUE. If field A is not followed by a sign, the field B value replaces the contents of the savevalue. (A plus + or minus [−] sign may be used in field A to denote addition or subtraction respectively.)

In order to obtain information regarding the total amount of time cars spend to get a wash, a frequency-distribution table is defined. A distribution table of any SNA may be obtained at any point in the model. The TABLE statement describes what a table is to contain, and a TABULATE statement specifies at what point in the model an entry is to be made into the table.

```
1  TABLE  M$1,15,5,12
```

Table 1 is defined to be a frequency distribution of transaction transit times M$1. The first cell of the table accumulates transit times of 15 or less, and subsequent cells have upper limits in increments of 5 for a maximum of 12 cells total.

```
TABULATE  1
```

The foregoing statement enters into Table 1 the amount of clock time that has passed since the current transaction was generated. Field A of the tabulate block identifies into which table an entry is to be made. What is entered into the table is defined by the TABLE statement, not the TABULATE.

```
RMULT   31415,31415,31415
```

The RMULT statement initializes the seed of one or more of the 8 random-number generators in GPSS. The preceding statement sets the seeds of RN$1, RN$2, and RN$3 to 31415.

Verification and Validation

The simulated average queue length of 6.63 is close to the observed average of 6.8, and the maximum lengths are equal. This would lead us to believe that the model is valid. To be reasonably certain that the model simulates the system correctly, a number of different simulation runs using a variety of random-number seeds should be examined. Statistical tests (using the already mentioned GPSS runs) designed to verify whether the model's behavior and the real system's behavior belong to the same population group could prove or disprove the model's validity.

After the model's correctness has been validated, it can be used to test

FIGURE 9-7 GPSS program and output listing using exponentially distributed interarrival rates.

```
GPSSR/PC  V1.1              9-FEB-1985   18:17              PAGE 1
carwash3.LST=carwash3.gps


LINE    BLOCK


1               *
2               *     CAR WASH EXAMPLE 3
3               *
4                     RMULT         31415,31415,31415
5               WASH  EQU           1         SYMBOLS EQUATED TO
6               EXPON EQU           1         NUMERIC VALUES
7               LNGTH EQU           1
8               *
9               EXPON FUNCTION      RN$2,C12
10                    0,0/.2,.222/.4,.509/.6,.915/.75,1.38/.84,1.83
11                    .9,2.3/.94,2.81/.96,3.2/.98,3.9/.995,5.3/.999,7
12              *
13              LNGTH VARIABLE       Q$WASH < 11+(RN$3*2)/1000 )
14              *
15          1         TABLE         M$1,15,5,12 TABLE TRANSIT TIMES
16                    SIMULATE
17      1             GENERATE      4,FN$EXPON  CAR ENTERS SYSTEM
18      2             TEST_NE       V$LNGTH,0,EXITW
19      3             QUEUE         WASH        CAR LINES UP FOR WASH
20      4             SEIZE         WASH        CAR GAINS CONTROL OF WASHER
21      5             DEPART        WASH        CAR LEAVES LINEUP
22      6             ADVANCE       4,1         TIME TO WASH CAR
23      7             RELEASE       WASH        CAR EXITS WASHER
24      8             TABULATE      1
25      9             TERMINATE     1           CAR EXITS SYSTEM
26      10      EXITW SAVEVALUE     1+,1        COUNT CARS THAT DON'T WAIT
27      11            TERMINATE     1
28                    START         1000        RUN FOR 1000 TERMINATIONS
29                    END
```

SYMBOL	VALUE	SYMBOL	VALUE
EXITW	10	EXPON	1
LNGTH	1	WASH	1

```
GPSSR/PC   V1.1                9-FEB-1985  17:34                    PAGE 2
carwash3.LST=carwash3.gps
```

RELATIVE CLOCK   3558   ABSOLUTE CLOCK   3558

BLOCK COUNTS

BLOCK	CURRENT	TOTAL	BLOCK	CURRENT	TOTAL	BLOCK	CURRENT	TOTAL
1	1	1011	2	0	1010	3	10	877
4	0	867	5	0	867	6	0	867
7	0	867	8	0	867	9	0	867
10	0	133	11	0	133			

FACILITY	AVERAGE UTILIZATION	NUMBER ENTRIES	AVERAGE TIME/TRAN	SEIZING TRANS.NO.	PREEMPTING TRANS.NO.
1	0.98	867	4.02		

QUEUE	MAXIMUM CONTENT	AVERAGE CONTENT	TOTAL ENTRIES	ZERO ENTRIES	PERC. ZERO	AVERAGE TIME/TR	$AVERAGE TIME/TR	TABLE NUMBR	CURRENT CONTENT
1	12	6.63	877	13	1.48	26.91	27.31		10

CONTENTS OF (NONZERO) FULLWORD SAVEVALUES

XF LOC	VALUE	LOC	VALUE	LOC	VALUE	LOC	VALUE
1	133						

```
GPSSR/PC   V1.1                9-FEB-1985  17:34                    PAGE 3
carwash3.LST=carwash3.gps
```

TABLE NO. 1

ENTRIES IN TABLE	MEAN ARGUMENT	STANDARD DEVIATION	SUM OF ARGUMENTS
867	31.00	13.28	26881.0

UPPER LIMIT	OBSERVED FREQUENCY	PER CENT OF TOTAL	CUMULATIVE PERCENTAGE	CUMULATIVE REMAINDER	MULTIPLE OF MEAN	DEVIATION FROM MEAN
15	137	15.80	15.80	84.20	0.48	-1.20
20	82	9.46	25.26	74.74	0.65	-0.83
25	78	9.00	34.26	65.74	0.81	-0.45
30	93	10.73	44.98	55.02	0.97	-0.08
35	83	9.57	54.56	45.44	1.13	0.30
40	135	15.57	70.13	29.87	1.29	0.68
45	136	15.69	85.81	14.19	1.45	1.05
50	100	11.53	97.35	2.65	1.61	1.43
55	23	2.65	100.00	0.00	1.77	1.81

REMAINING VALUES ARE ZERO

FIGURE 9–7 (continued)

system changes. In the car-wash example, it could be tested with more than one washer or a faster washer. Changes in arrival rates could also be tested in anticipation of future traffic flow.

Once a valid model has been developed, it becomes very simple and inexpensive to test different ideas. A new car wash is vastly more expensive than a run of a GPSS model.

APPENDIX A

The following is a brief description of different GPSSR/PC statements divided into functional categories.

Queue

A queue is used to measure the time delay of transactions waiting for an entity to become available. A transaction may join a queue prior to seizing a facility or entering a storage in order to produce statistics on output regarding the amount of time transactions spent waiting.

Statement	Meaning
QUEUE	start measuring time delay
DEPART	stop measuring time delay

Table

A frequency-distribution table may be created using any standard numeric value. A special queue table may be defined to measure queue-delay times.

Statement	Meaning
QTABLE	define a queue table
TABLE	define a distribution table
TABULATE	add entry to a distribution table

Decisions and Flow Alteration

The transaction flow through a model may be altered unconditionally or be conditional on the state of the model.

Statement	Meaning
GATE	check entity status
LOOP	iterate through a portion of model
TEST	compare two SNA values
TRANSFER	GOTO block
TRANSFER SBR	goto subroutine
TRANSFER P	return from subroutine

Create and Destroy a Transaction

A transaction is the basic entity that flows through the system. A communications message, a railway train, or an assembly-line part may be represented via a transaction.

Statement	*Meaning*
GENERATE	create a transaction
JOBTAPE	transation from a disk file
TERMINATE	destroy a transaction

Also see Assembly Set, which follows Changing Values.

Changing Values

Values may be stored in transaction parameters and SAVEVALUES. SAVEVALUES are global storage locations available for all transactions, and parameters are local areas associated with each individual transaction.

Statement	*Meaning*
SAVEVALUE	augment SAVEVALUE
ASSIGN	augment parameter

Assembly Set

A single transaction may be split into many transactions, which may be rejoined into a single transaction. Members of a set may be synchronized in the model by being gathered at one point or being matched with members of the same set at different points in the model.

Statement	*Meaning*
ASSEMBLE	combine members of set onto one transaction
GATHER	members wait for one another before proceeding
MATCH	synchronize members at two different blocks
SPLIT	create many transactions from one

Time Delay

A transaction may be stopped at a specific point in the model for a period of time. This time may represent transmission time or time to complete a process. A time distribution may be specified via a function.

Statement	*Meaning*
ADVANCE	transaction stops for a period of time

Alternate Queue Strategy

By default, GPSS deals in a first-in, first-out strategy. A user chain may be used to create a last-in, first-out or a priority-queue discipline. Model efficiency may also be improved by placing transactions onto a user chain. User-chain transactions are not on the future-events chain, thereby decreasing the computer time necessary to process the future-events chain.

Statement	Meaning
LINK	add transaction to chain
UNLINK	take transaction off chain

Debugging Model

A transaction's process through the model may be traced from block to block. The contents of any standard numeric attribute may also be printed out at specific points in the model. GPSSR/PC's interactive mode allows a more dynamic look at the model during execution, to help locate problems.

Statement	Meaning
PRINT	output SNA contents
TRACE	follow transaction through model
UNTRACE	turn off tracing of a transaction

CHAPTER TEN

Applications of Simulation

This chapter will depart from the pattern of using programming examples to illustrate principles of simulation and will describe a few actual applications. One reason for not discussing all of the programs that implement these applications is that many of the programs are large—1,000 lines of source code is a small simulation. Another reason is that many of the program routines, such as random-number generators, probability functions, and queues, have already been covered, and a large application often consists of an aggregation of these elementary steps plus a great many mundane routines for handling input and output of data.

Most of the examples covered so far have had to do with finding out how fast people or things can be moved through a waiting line. That is because competition for limited resources is a predominant feature of modern life. Some of the applications in this chapter will deal with waiting lines, although their presence may not be immediately apparent. Other applications will have nothing to do with them.

PART 1—INDUSTRIAL APPLICATION

Case 1—How to Find Defects
in Printed Wiring Boards [1]

DOA—"Dead on Arrival." Too often that describes computers or other kinds of electronic hardware.

Usually the reason why is trivial: a glob of solder where it shouldn't be, a missing or faulty part, or an unsoldered connection. Or we have the legendary

$1.25 part that causes a space mission to abort, or provokes a false alarm about incoming intercontinental ballistic missiles.

Generally the assemblies that fail have been given a 100 percent inspection. Then how come the defects weren't found in the factory?

We were doing an in-depth study of factory testing practices for a major electronics company and had to know what percentage of faulty products human inspectors were allowing to escape. This knowledge would help decide whether we had to tolerate a certain proportion of defective products, train our inspectors better, or automate the human inspectors out of the process.

Role of Simulation

We had to take our study out of the factory because the International Brotherhood of Electrical Workers objected to it. We couldn't take the product out of the plant and test it elsewhere because the National Security Agency objected (we were making government cryptographic equipment). So we had to resort to simulation. We wound up using two kinds of simulation: iconic simulation to model the process and computer-based stochastic simulation to make the icons.

Iconic Simulation

The product was nine-layer printed circuit boards measuring 4.5 by 4.8 inches. They were made from individual printed circuits that were inspected under large magnifying glasses and then pressed together with interleaved sheets of plastic.

Printed circuit patterns are made up of pads to which connections are made and traces that connect the pads. Four things could go wrong: cracks that totally severed a trace or pad; pinholes where etchant had eaten away parts of pads or traces; notches that were like pinholes, only worse; and spurs where pads or traces were shorted together because the etchant hadn't removed enough copper.

The icons were full-sized photographs of perfect printed circuit boards (taken from the masks) on which artists had added cracks, pinholes, notches, and spurs.

The iconic simulation consisted of setting up a dummy production line in a local technical high school and finding out how many defects the students, who were given the usual factory training by supervisors, would catch and how many would get by them.

Computer Simulation

The computer simulation told the artist what and how many defects to draw and where to draw them, so as to reproduce the actual situation in the factory. We knew from having a sample of 90 boards checked out in the engineering laboratory that there were on average .322 defects per board.

We assumed defects were Poisson-distributed among boards. This gave us the following distribution:

Number of Defects	Percent of Boards
0	70.00
1	24.90
2	4.52
3	0.54
4	0.03
5	0.01

The lab had observed that the four types of defect occurred with this distribution:

Kind of Defect	Percent of Defects
crack	60
pinhole	20
notch	15
spur	5

To locate the defects after random draws had determined how many defects a board would contain and what kind they should be, we covered just the traces and pads with a pattern of 1/10-inch squares and numbered each one on a transparent overlay of the photo. For example, for one type of board there were 609 squares; for another, 503. We assumed the defects were uniformly distributed on the boards, so in the first case we located defects by making random draws in the range 1 to 609. The computer printed out instructions to the artist that were later used to score the performance of the students pretending to be inspectors.

Results

On average, the students (there were eight of them) accepted 10 percent of the defective boards as being good. Moreover, they rejected 3 percent of the good boards as being bad. As a consequence, we started development of automatic test equipment in which a platen with spring-loaded fingers would make contact with every trace and pad, while a computer program would test for either connectivity or isolation between each pair of fingers. This equipment caught all the cracks and spurs, but the pinholes and notches remained as incipient defects. We tried blowing them out with 800-volt D.C. pulses. It worked sometimes on notches and large pinholes, but most of these defects remain a source of potential failure.

Case 2—What's the Cost of Bad TV Sets? [2]

Our client's competitor offered a six-month warranty on parts and labor for his line of TV sets. Our client went him one better and offered a full year's warranty. He budgeted $2 million to cover the cost but after three months became alarmed and called us in for an estimate. We wrote a simulation model in which we "built" a year's production of TV sets with defects in them such as our prior experience would lead us to predict and totaled up the cost of warranty. It came to $15 million. The client was not happy. By year's end he was even more unhappy. The actual cost came to $17 million. Next year he moved his TV-manufacturing operations to Taiwan.

The set consisted of eight phenolic circuit boards, four ceramic modules, and individual parts, such as VHF and UHF tuners, a built-in antenna, picture tube, power transformer, and picture-tube yoke. We simulated building the boards and modules, then assembling the TV chassis from boards, modules, and other parts. To avoid boring repetition, we shall describe how we simulated building a module. Building a chassis is a similar operation; the modules are regarded as basic parts of the chassis. The idea is to predict which TV sets will leave the factory with defects that will cause them to fail within the warranty period.

Simulating the Building of Modules

To make a module, say 10 basic parts are selected. Each has a probability of being defective (about 1.5 percent). Every module with a defective basic part is tagged as defective by the simulation program.

Modules may also be defective because of workmanship errors. The probability of a workmanship error is about 10 percent, but the rate tends to vary depending on the day of the week and other factors. This variation in rate can be described by a beta distribution. The beta distribution ranges from zero to one. It has two shaping parameters, A and B, that are related to the mean and variance in a somewhat complicated way. We produced appropriate distributions by simulation: holding the mean and allowing the variance to vary while displaying the plot and picking those that seemed most appropriate for different days of the week and times of day.

We sampled from the appropriate beta distribution to get a percent defective, then made random draws to see which modules should be tagged as defective.

Testing the Modules

The module next is exposed to the testing operation. There is a 2 percent chance that a good module will be labeled bad and go on to the troubleshooting function, and a 14 percent chance that a bad module will be labeled good and go on to the chassis-assembly step.

The first time a troubleshooter sees a particular module, there is a 50 percent chance he or she will incorrectly diagnose the problem.

After troubleshooting, the module goes to the repair person. There is a 10 percent chance that the repair person will fail to fix the problem and a 2 percent chance that the repair work will ruin the module, so that it has to be scrapped.

The module now goes back through the testing operation, and modules labeled bad go back to the troubleshooter. Now the troubleshooter has a 30 percent chance of failing to diagnose the problem correctly. The third time the troubleshooter sees the same module, the diagnosis will be correct.

Results

Overall, we found that 3 percent of the modules that found their way into chassis were defective and 11 percent of the TV sets shipped from the factory contained defects serious enough to impel the customer to claim on the warranty agreement. (In 1974 these TV sets were probably the best ones made in the United States. By way of comparison, the engineering lab determined that the worst Japanese sets were 10 percent defective; the best Japanese sets were less than 2 percent defective.)

PART 2—SIMULATION IN EMERGENCY PLANNING

Case 1—Restructuring Police Patrol Zones [3]

The objective of this study was to redraw the boundaries of 29 police patrol zones in a city of 226,000 people so as to minimize driving time when answering calls for service, thereby leaving more time for crime-repression patrolling.

We redrew the zones this way: The smallest political unit of the city was the Polling Sub-Division, an area in which an average of 430 people live. There are 524 of them. Statistics on incidents requiring police response are kept by PSD. Our redrawing program took each PSD in turn as the center of a patrol zone and added adjacent PSDs around it until a zone was formed that produced roughly 3241 incidents a year (1/29 of the 94,000 occurring annually in the city).

For every PSD we counted the number of zones in which it appeared. Then for every zone we totaled the counts of the PSDs it contained. We retained the 29 zones out of 524 that had the lowest overlap and resolved any remaining overlap manually. Now we had to use simulation to find out whether the new boundaries would result in less driving time when answering calls for service.

Frequency and Location of Incidents

We knew the annual number of incidents per PSD (call it $Y(p)$), so we could divide it by 8760 hours in a year and use it as the mean of a Poisson distribution to simulate hour by hour how many incidents occurred in that PSD; by doing this for all 524 PSDs we could simulate incidents throughout the city. This would not be realistic, however, because incident occurrence is highly time-dependent; and it would take a great deal of computer time to simulate every hour of, say, ten years.

Incident occurrence depends upon month of the year.

Month	Incidents
January	8,400
February	7,500
March	7,400
April	6,700
May	6,900
June	6,800
July	7,200
August	9,000
September	8,800
October	8,600
November	8,500
December	8,300

Incident occurrence also depends upon the hour of the day.

Hour	Incidents
24:00	4,800
01:00	4,400
02:00	3,300
03:00	2,400
04:00	1,000
05:00	900
06:00	700
07:00	1,900
08:00	3,800
09:00	3,900
10:00	3,800
11:00	4,400
12:00	4,800
13:00	4,300
14:00	3,400
15:00	4,300
16:00	4,900
17:00	5,100

Hour	Incidents
18:00	5,500
19:00	5,500
20:00	5,700
21:00	5,400
22:00	5,000
23:00	4,800

And incident occurrence depends upon the day of the week.

Day	Incidents
Sunday	11,500
Monday	12,000
Tuesday	12,500
Wednesday	12,400
Thursday	13,600
Friday	15,900
Saturday	16,100

We used the technique of Fourier synthesis to express these data as three wave forms, each developed as a constant plus the sum of six cosine terms and five sine terms. We added the wave forms:

$$K(t) = (F(month) + F(hour) + F(day))/3$$

The values of K for each hour of the year (t) were multiplied by the Poisson means Y(p) for each PSD to correct for time-dependent changes in incident-occurrence frequency:

$$lambda(t,p) = K(t)*Y(p)/8760$$

To reduce the length of the simulation, we first made a histogram out of the K function.

Range of K	Number of Hours
.5 to .6	80
.6 to .7	300
.7 to .8	700
.8 to .9	1,000
.9 to 1	1,700
1 to 1.1	2,600
1.1 to 1.2	1,900
1.2 to 1.3	400
1.3 to 1.4	80

In each class interval we drew a 1 percent random sample. This gave us a total sample of 88 hours that would represent a whole year for the purpose of comparing two patrol-zone designs.

Duration of Incidents

We knew the distribution of length of incidents.

Length in Minutes	Number of Incidents
0 to 30	36,000
30 to 60	33,000
60 to 90	16,000
90 to 120	5,000
120 to 150	2,000
150 to 180	1,000
180 to 210	500
210 to 240	200
240 to 300	100
300 to 360	100
Over 360	100

For each hour of the simulation we simulated two hours and only counted the last hour to wash out any start-up bias. We located each of the 29 patrol cars by drawing for each zone a random number in the range of the number of PSDs in the zone and assumed the car to be at the geographical center of the PSD selected. We sampled every PSD using the Poisson distribution with the appropriate time-adjusted mean to find out how many incidents occurred. We assumed the incident to occur at the geographical center of the PSD. Then we made random draws on 1 to 60 to determine when each incident began. Finally, we made a random draw from the incident-duration distribution to find out how long each incident would last.

Servicing Incidents

We used data obtained in a prior study to determine driving speed. We assumed the speed to be normally distributed, with a mean of 17.7 miles per hour and a standard deviation of 5.8 mph. In servicing incidents we first sent the zone car. We knew the distance from its current location to the incident and obtained its speed by sampling from the driving-speed distribution. We posted the car as being unavailable for the duration of the incident plus driving time.

When the zone car was unavailable we serviced subsequent incidents in the zone by sending the nearest out-of-zone car.

Results

We averaged the results from ten simulation runs and found the new patrol-zone layout reduced the average driving time from six to four minutes.

This allowed officers to spend 45 percent of their time on repressive patrol, rather than 44 percent. Inasmuch as this fell short of the 50 percent repressive-patrol time targeted by the department, these results were used to substantiate a recommendation for additional personnel and vehicles to permit assigning second and third cars to particularly active zones at peak incident periods.

Case 2—Deciding Where to Put a Fire Station [4]

This case involved simulating the operation of a municipal fire department. One application of the simulator was determining how to relocate resources to get better fire protection. The city is the same one we studied in the police patrol-zone problem. There are nine fire stations and 15 pieces of active apparatus. On average there were 3,351 fires a year for the three years on which our data are based.

Because of the relatively few incidents as compared with the police situation, we decided to simulate ten full years of activity and average the results instead of resorting to importance sampling. We used a time-oriented simulation with 15-minute intervals. Our basic Y(t) is therefore equal to 3351/4*24*365, or 0.1 fire every quarter hour.

Time Dependence of Fires

Fires are distributed in time according to the month of the year.

Month	Number of Fires
January	247
February	237
March	276
April	320
May	305
June	289
July	336
August	288
September	271
October	276
November	247
December	258

Fire occurrences also depend upon the time of day.

Time	Number of Fires
24:00	161
1:00	136

Time	Number of Fires
2:00	135
3:00	96
4:00	70
5:00	56
6:00	41
7:00	51
8:00	69
9:00	80
10:00	106
11:00	115
12:00	142
13:00	143
14:00	163
15:00	156
16:00	181
17:00	199
18:00	197
19:00	192
20:00	214
21:00	238
22:00	214
23:00	196

We shall normalize fire-occurrence frequencies with respect to their expected value. We illustrate this in the case of the day-of-week distribution where the expected value is 3,351/7, or 479.

Day of Week	Number of Fires	Normalized Value
Sunday	461	.96
Monday	473	.99
Tuesday	437	.91
Wednesday	473	.99
Thursday	456	.95
Friday	497	1.04
Saturday	554	1.16

Frequencies are adjusted with respect to time to obtain Poisson means.

$$\text{lambda}(t) = Y(t) * N(\text{month}) * N(\text{hour}) * N(\text{day})$$

For example, between 21:00 and 22:00 on a Saturday in July, the city-wide Poisson mean for each of the four 15-minute periods is .1*1.2*1.7*1.16, or .237; while between 6:00 and 7:00 on a Tuesday in February, the city-wide Poisson mean for each of the four 15-minute periods is .1*.85*.29*.91, or .02.

Geographical Distribution of Fires

The probabilistic geographical distribution of fires by district (the area served from a station) is:

Station Number	Percent of Fires
1	18
2	14
3	10
4	8
5	11
6	6
7	13
8	8
9	12

Multiple-Alarm Fires

So far, the problem of fire simulation is similar to that of the police—perhaps easier, because there are fewer incidents. However, in more than one third of fires, more than one station responds. Moreover, the needs for apparatus are highly specific. The probability distribution of station calls is:

Number of Stations Called	Number of Fires
1	2,078
2	536
3	562
4	160
5	12
6 or more	3

Duration of Fires

The duration of a fire is related to the number of stations called. Durations are exponentially distributed. The relationship between mean duration and number of stations called is:

Number of Stations Called	Mean Duration in Minutes
1	21.2
2	31.9
3	33.2
4	35
5	39.1
6 or more	50

In addition, there is a small probability that a fire will take a very long time to extinguish (as when a tire warehouse burned down). To simulate such a fire, we draw a random number, and if it exceeds 0.99933, we make a random draw from an exponential distribution having a mean of 80 and add it to 300 minutes.

Station Backup and Substitution

Responding to multiple alarms is by no means as easy as sending an engine from the nearest station; a particular kind of apparatus may be needed. We created a backup matrix by entering how many times in three years each station was backed up by every other station and put these data on a percentage basis. For example, station #1 was backed up by station #3 27 percent of the time; by #5, 21 percent; by #4, 18 percent; by #9, 9 percent; by #6, 8 percent; by #8, 7 percent; by #2, 6 percent; and by #7 in 4 percent of fires in which station #1 was called first.

To simulate which station or stations backed up the one called first (that is, the one in whose district the fire occurred), we made a random draw from the cumulative distribution of backup probabilities in the appropriate row of the backup matrix. If we found the chosen station was engaged, we made another draw and so on until the requirements were satisfied or until we determined that the required resources were not available.

Driving-Time Distributions

We had no data on how fast a fire engine goes. However, we had very accurate data on how long it took a fire company to reach a fire scene. We plotted these data and found that there was a different distribution for each fire district but that they all were approximately normal.

Fire Station	Driving-Time Mean (Minutes)	Standard Deviation
1	3.9	2.8
2	5.2	2.6
3	3.8	2.2
4	4.3	2.5
5	3.4	1.7
6	5.2	2.7
7	4.6	2
8	5.3	2.7
9	4.7	2.3

Implementation

To implement the simulation, we first wrote an Events file; then we ran it against a Simulate program. The following steps were used to create the Events file:

1. If not end of simulation, then :-.
2. Advance clock 15 minutes.

3. If new month, get N(month).
4. If new day, get N(day).
5. If new hour, get N(hour).
6. Calculate lambda.
7. Sample Poisson distribution; get number of fires.
8. For each fire, get geographical location (district).
9. For each fire, get number of stations called.
10. If not a long-duration fire :-.
11. Get mean duration.
12. Sample exponential distribution; get actual duration.
13. If a long-duration fire, get duration.
14. Write fire parameters to Event file.
15. If end of simulation, close Events file.

The Simulate program calculates three negative measures of merit:

1. Resources unavailable :- neither a station called nor a substitute is available.
2. Interference :- a station called is already engaged and a substitute must be called.
3. Primary interference :- the first (or only) station called is engaged and a substitute must be called. These events are tagged as to the district in which they occur.

The Simulate program proceeds as follows:

1. If not end of Events file :-.
2. Advance file one record.
3. If district company not engaged :-.
4. Sample appropriate driving-time distribution. (The normal driving-time distributions are regarded as truncated, since negative driving time would be meaningless.)
5. Post selected company engaged for duration + driving time.
6. If selected company engaged, select substitute.
7. Increment interference count.
8. Increment primary interference count.
9. If selected company not engaged :-.
10. Perform steps 4 and 5; jump to step 12.
11. If substitute company engaged, and no companies left, increment resources-lacking count; otherwise, perform steps 6–9.
12. For each backup company required :-.
13. Select backup company.
14. Perform steps 6, 7, and 9.
15. If no more resources available or required, return to step 1.
16. At end of Events file, report outcome.

Results

The results of ten year-long runs were:

1. Incidents of resources unavailable, 1.6 per year.
2. Total incidents of interference, 467.3 per year.
3. Incidents of primary interference, 188.2 per year.

Fire Station	Yearly Primary Interference
1	61.4
2	27.3
3	17.2
4	5.9
5	10.0
6	2.7
7	25.7
8	6.9
9	36.3

These results were useful in making a decision about how to improve fire protection in district #7. One proposal was to move station #2 into district #7; the other was to build a new station, effectively dividing the district in two.

It is apparent that moving company #2 would put a heavier burden on company #1 and exacerbate an already bad situation in the city's core area. This supported the option of building a new station.

Case 3—Modeling a Hospital Emergency Department [5]

This simulation models the emergency department of a 421-bed hospital. The department handles 25,000 patients annually. The simulation model was used to forecast the effects of increased demand or augmented facilities. This is essentially a waiting-line model. The (negative) measure of merit is patient waiting time. Our empirical data were gathered by a study of 100 percent of patient records for one month and 10 percent of patient records for five months. The department consisted of a resuscitation room with three trauma beds and six treatment/examination rooms. It is staffed around the clock by two doctors and four nurses.

Patient Arrivals

The frequency of patient arrivals was found to be independent of the month of the year but highly dependent in a complex manner on time of day and day of the week. We modeled patient arrivals by exponential distributions of times between arrivals. We divided the week into 84 two-hour periods each with its own mean in minutes between arrivals:

DAY	TWO-HOUR PERIODS											
	24–2	–4	–6	–8	–10	–12	–14	–16	–18	–20	–22	–24
Sun	24	60	60	60	30	12	8	12	12	12	13	17
Mon	60	120	120	60	24	10	12	15	17	19	17	17
Tue	40	120	120	60	40	15	20	17	17	13	20	24
Wed	30	120	120	120	24	17	13	13	15	12	15	15
Thu	60	60	120	60	20	20	20	17	24	15	13	24
Fri	24	120	120	60	20	15	15	15	17	17	15	40
Sat	30	40	120	120	40	8	12	11	17	12	11	20

The smaller the number, the busier the hospital.

Patient Service Time

We performed a stepwise linear regression of patient histories against total patient service time. This resulted in an equation with seven terms that were added and used to predict each patient's service time in minutes.

1. Class of patient: Critical = 42.12; Urgent = 41.16; Other = 40.14
2. Age of patient in years times .144
3. Hematology test done? 33.84 if YES; 0 if NO
4. X rays taken? 37.92 if YES; 0 if NO
5. Microbiology test done? 7.68 if YES; 0 if NO
6. Patient admitted to hospital? −2.22 if YES; 0 if NO
7. Subtract minutes since last patient arrived times .12

Patients' Characteristics

The probabilities of a patient's belonging to one of the three classes were:

Critical	9%
Urgent	53%
Other	38%

Patients' ages followed a truncated (no negative ages) normal distribution, with a mean of 29 years and a standard deviation of 15 years.

The probabilities that tests were performed were:

Class	Hematology	X ray	Microbiology
Critical	60%	45%	5%
Urgent	20%	30%	17%
Other	10%	20%	2%

The probabilities that patients would be admitted to hospital depended upon their class.

Critical	80%
Urgent	20%
Other	2%

Utilization of Facilities

Use of emergency-department facilities depended upon the class of the patient. Patients used either one of the examination/treatment rooms or one of the trauma beds in the resuscitation room. The probabilities of using trauma beds were:

Critical	67%
Urgent	15%
Other	none

The time doctors spend with patients also depended on class.

Critical	25 + or − 10 minutes
Urgent	20 + or − 10 minutes
Other	15 + or − 10 minutes

The time nurses spend with patients depended on class.

Critical	60 + or − 20 minutes
Urgent	15 + or − 10 minutes
Other	10 + or − 5 minutes

Implementation

This simulation was written in GPSS, which was appropriate, since it was event-oriented. We kept a clock to determine which mean to use with the exponential distribution of time between arrivals. When a patient arrived, we made a random draw from the cumulative empirical distribution of class probabilities to find whether the patient would be classed as critical, urgent, or other. Using that information, we determined the tests to be performed and the requirements for hospital facilities. Then we sampled the age distribution and substituted values into the regression equation to find the patient's total service time.

We posted either a trauma bed or an examination room as engaged for the patient's entire stay in the emergency department and posted a doctor and a nurse as busy for a length of time determined by a draw from the appropriate uniform distribution. We kept track of the time patients had to wait because needed resources were not available.

We ran the simulation under four sets of conditions:

1. Current demand.
2. Ten years at a 1.8 percent annual growth rate in patient service demand.
3. A sustained 50 percent increased demand for service.
4. A bus crash at 18:00 Sunday, bringing 55 additional patients.

Results

We found that under existing conditions, acceptable service could be rendered with the following schedule:

7:00–15:00	2 doctors, 4 nurses
15:00–23:00	2 doctors, 4 nurses
23:00–7:00	1 doctor, 2 nurses

The existing level of service can be maintained with present staff and facilities for ten years of 1.8 percent annual growth of the service area population.

To cope with a 50 percent increase in work load, one more examination/ treatment room would be needed; and the following schedule:

7:00–15:00	2 doctors, 6 nurses
15:00–23:00	2 doctors, 6 nurses
23:00–7:00	1 doctor, 2 nurses

Handling a disaster like the one postulated would require that one doctor and three nurses be on call. Also, five more trauma beds and five more examination beds would be needed. Five sets of portable resuscitation equipment could be used in existing examination rooms. The examination beds could be set up in a large room (possibly in the pharmacy area) with curtain separators.

PART 3—SOCIOLOGICAL SIMULATION
PREDICTING SIZE OF HOUSEHOLDS [6]

Long-range planners often find it more useful to tie predictions of future population size to the size and composition of households rather than to raw population statistics that deal with people as individuals. Clearly, household-size information is vital to land developers and manufacturers of consumer durable goods such as washing machines and refrigerators.

This simulation works on data available from the census bureau and projects it into the future by applying the expected rates of birth, death, and marriage. We worked with Canadian data, but our technique can be used anywhere comparable census data are available.

We knew that between 1851 and 1971, the size of the average Canadian household declined from 6.2 persons to 3.42 persons. The 1976 census reported it at 3.2 persons; the 1981 census reported 2.75 persons. Our task was to estimate the average size of the Canadian household in 1991.

Input Data

Our source of data was the Public Use Files that Statistics Canada makes available for research. They are 1-in-10,000 samples of the national census stratified on a provincial basis. The most important of these tapes to us was the Household Census Data tape for 1971. It contained information about 601 households consisting of a total of 2,054 persons.

Our game plan was to follow these two thousand people and their descendants for 20 years, simulating births, marriages, and deaths, as well as the occasional importation of a bride or groom. To do this we first had to create a file listing for each person: sex, age in completed years, place in the household (that is, head, spouse, child, or other person), and a tag linking that person to a household.

The household file did not give the sex of children and other persons. Moreover, it gave their ages only in five-year classes. Only the sex of the spouse was given. We had to simulate the missing data.

We assigned gender to children and other persons by assuming a 485/515 chance of their being male or female. We assigned ages in single years of completed age by assuming a uniform age distribution within the given five-year age brackets. To get the age of spouse, we consulted another public-use census file: the Provincial Family File. Here the ages of both spouses were given. We determined that the age difference between wife and husband was normally distributed with a mean of -4.35 years and a standard deviation of 3.06 years. For each household, we sampled from this distribution and applied the result to the given age of the head of household to obtain the age of spouse.

Implementation

Our simulation was time-oriented. For each year, we exposed each individual to the sex- and age-specific probabilities of death, birth, and marriage.

We obtained these probabilities from Canadian census data. The simulation consisted of these steps:

1. Expose each person to mortality.
2. If dead, cancel individual's record: report −1 person.
3. Expose each married female 15 to 50 to married fertility.
4. Expose each single female 15 to 50 to single fertility (about 1/10 married fertility).
5. If birth results, create an individual's record, determine gender.
6. Expose new individual to newborn mortality.
7. If dead, cancel individual's record; otherwise, report +1 person.
8. Expose each single female to female nuptiality.
9. If nubile, add to marriage roster.
10. Expose each single male to male nuptiality.
11. If nubile, add to marriage roster.
12. Apply criteria to match females to males.
13. If match found, create new household; adjust bride's family; adjust groom's family.
14. Otherwise, import a bride (or groom); create new household; adjust groom's (or bride's) family; report +1 person.

We matched couples by making a draw from our age-difference distribution for each prospective groom in turn and picked the bride whose age was closest to the groom's age minus the selected age difference. For the leftover brides, we imported grooms and assigned them ages from our age-difference distribution. We similarly imported brides if there were leftover grooms.

After matching couples, we adjusted the households they came from by subtracting out the spouses and any children belonging to them, to form a new household.

For each simulated year, we cycled through the file of individuals. Afterward we updated our household file by using the tags in each person's record. Then we calculated household statistics describing size and composition.

We did this for 20 simulated years for each run. We made ten runs and calculated the mean and standard error of our statistics.

Results

Our simulation suggested that by 1991 the average Canadian household will consist of 2.3 persons. Moreover, by doing this kind of simulation instead of just extrapolating a curve of household size, we can not only forecast average household size but also predict how many households of 1, 2, . . . to 10 or more persons will exist and how many of these people will be children of various ages or other persons. This is far more useful planning information than household size alone.

OTHER SIMULATIONS

Training Fire Dispatchers [7]

We turned the fire-department resource-allocation simulation into a "video game" for training fire-department dispatchers. It was written with graphical displays and runs on a microcomputer.

The relative locations of fire districts are shown as a three-by-three matrix display. They are identified by large Arabic numerals. Stylized symbols show the location of fire stations within districts, and fires, when they occur. A legend at the top of the display shows date and time, legends in each cell give the status of that district's fire company, and a legend at the bottom gives the number of companies needed to fight the current fire. Figure 10–1 shows the display.

The game begins at a selected date and time and proceeds in fifteen-minute increments. There is no backup matrix; the dispatcher must assign companies. The objective of the game is to minimize fire loss in dollars.

The heaviest penalty is incurred if the driving time of the first company called is longer than it could be. This is because any delay during the first critical

FIGURE 10–1   Display for fire-dispatch simulator.

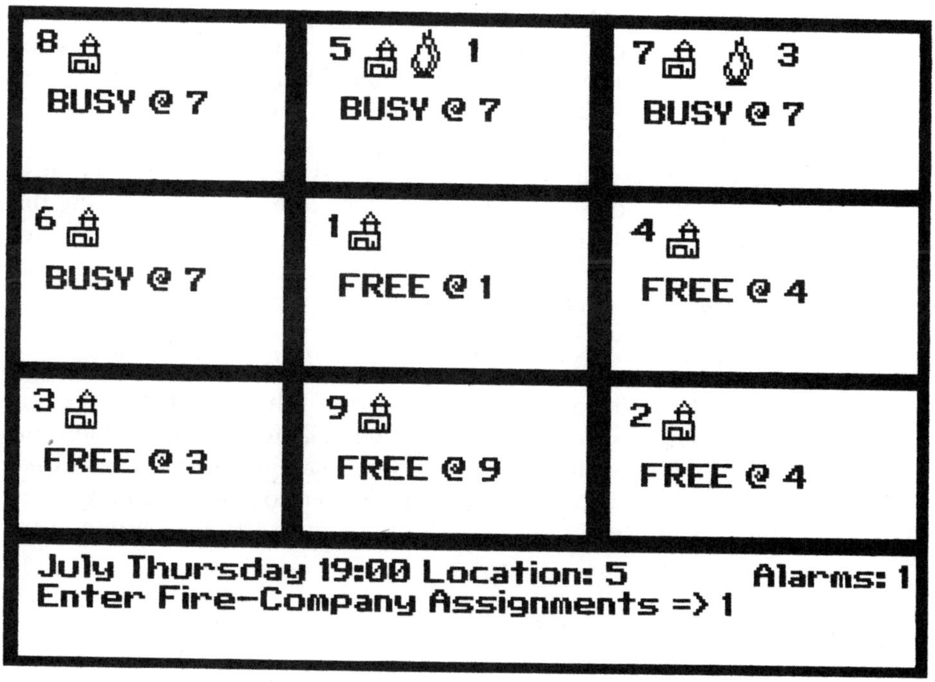

minutes of a fire will greatly exacerbate the ultimate damage. The penalty is calculated by this formula:

$$\text{Loss} = \text{Value} * \{1/(1 + 99 * \exp[-\text{Driving-time} * .17])\}$$

This equation is derived from the well-known logistic, or Pearl-Reed, curve of growth.

Value is found from this equation:

$$\text{Value} = \text{Man-property-value-in-district} * \log(\text{Random-number})$$

This means a heavier penalty will be exacted if the student dispatcher lets a fire in a rich neighborhood get out of control despite the fact that more lives may be lost if the same adverse event occurs in a poor neighborhood. This may not be nice, but it is reality; and that's what simulation is all about—depicting reality.

Driving time is found by sampling from the driving-time distribution of every district through which the first company called must drive and adding these random variates.

The second kind of penalty is incurred when the dispatcher fails to assign enough companies. The effect of this penalty is to tie up the companies assigned for a longer time than would be required if the needed resources had been assigned. To get fire-fighting time under penalty conditions, we first sample from the time distribution appropriate to the total number of companies required. Then we sample from the time distribution appropriate to the number of companies not available and add these two random variates.

Increasing fire-fighting time will make apparatus unavailable for subsequent fires. This situation will be reflected in property loss because in subsequent fires the closest company is unlikely to be free and driving time of the first company called will therefore be increased. To find the number of fires in each fifteen-minute period, we sample from a Poisson distribution whose mean is found from the equation:

$$\text{lambda} = .1 * N(\text{month}) * N(\text{day}) * N(\text{hour}) * \text{Difficulty-factor}$$

The difficulty factor is a number greater than one that the student selects. This feature enables the student to test his skill as he becomes more proficient. (The masculine pronoun reflects the fact that fire dispatchers in this city are male, unlike police dispatchers. The job is used to give continuing employment to firefighters injured in the line of duty.) Figure 10–2 is a listing of the source code of the program.

Training Artillery Gunners [8]

This working game was designed to train gunners in the use of graphical firing tables (GFT). A GFT is a special slide rule that helps gunners aim their

```
.10 '
20 'FIRE DISPATCH SIMULATION
30 'COPYRIGHT 1982
40 'BY JOHN M. CARROLL
50 'ALL RIGHTS RESERVED
55 CLS
60 PRINT CHR$(23):PRINT:PRINT:PRINT
70 PRINT"WELCOME TO FIRE DISPATCH"
72 PRINT:PRINT"    COPYRIGHT 1982"
75 PRINT:PRINT"   BY JOHN M. CARROLL"
77 PRINT:PRINT"  ALL RIGHTS RESERVED"
78 FOR I=1 TO 1000:NEXT I:CLS
85 PRINT:PRINT"             INTRODUCTION"
86 PRINT:PRINT"==>ENTER STARTING DATE IN FORMAT YY/MM/DD/HH."
87 PRINT
88 PRINT "==>YOU WILL SEE A MAP OF 9 FIRE DISTRICTS SHOWING"
89 PRINT "THE STATUS OF EACH FIRE COMPANY, THE LOCATION OF A"
90 PRINT "FIRE AND THE NUMBER OF COMPANIES NEEDED TO FIGHT IT."
91 PRINT
92 PRINT"==>SELECT COMPANIES WHEN ASKED; ENTER AS '1,2,3,...'"
95 PRINT:PRINT"==>WHEN YOU SEE THE SYMBOL '?', TYPE 'ENTER'."
97 C$="":PRINT:INPUT"==>TYPE 'C' TO CONTINUE; 'Q' TO QUIT";C$
98 IF C$="Q" THEN 4000
99 IF C$<>"C" THEN 97
100 '
110 '              INDEX
120 '  900 INITIALIZATION
130 ' 1000 DIMENSIONS
140 ' 2000 READ  DATA
150 ' 3000 MAIN
160 ' 7800 END-OF-SIMULATION SUBROUTINE
170 ' 7900 END-OF-PERIOD SUBROUTINE
180 ' 8000 END-OF-FIRE SUBROUTINE
190 ' 8100 FIRE LOSS SUBROUTINE
200 ' 8200 PROPERTY VALUE SUBROUTINE
210 ' 8300 FIRE DURATION SUBROUTINE
220 ' 8400 FIRE-DURATION PARAMETER SUBROUTINE
230 ' 8500 EXPONENTIAL SUBROUTINE
240 ' 8600 DRIVING TIME SUBROUTINE
250 ' 8700 NORMAL SUBROUTINE
260 ' 8800 DRIVING-TIME PARAMETERS SUBROUTINE
270 ' 8900 RESOURCE AVAILABILITY SUBROUTINE
280 ' 9000 RESOURCE ASSIGNMENT SUBROUTINE
290 ' 9100 NUMBER-OF-ALARMS SUBROUTINE
300 ' 9200 FIRE-LOCATION SUBROUTINE
310 ' 9300 POISSON SUBROUTINE
320 ' 9400 GRAPHICAL SUBROUTINE
330 ' 9600 POISSON MEAN SUBROUTINE
340 ' 9700 MONTH-OF-YEAR SUBROUTINE
350 ' 9800 DAY-OF-WEEK SUBROUTINE
360 ' 9900 HOUR-OF-DAY SUBROUTINE
370 '10000 DATA
500 '
510 '              GLOSSARY
520 'AA MULTIPLE-ALARM VECTOR    PP AVERAGE FIRES/15 MINUTES
525 'C$ COMMAND STRING
530 'CA$ # DISTRICTS CROSSED     R RANDOM VARIATE
535 'CC ENDING PERIOD            R ASSIGNMENT VECTOR
537 'D$ STARTING DAY
540 'DD DURATION-ALARM VECTOR    R$ ASSIGNMENT INPUT
550 'DM MEAN DRIVING TIME VEC    RD RESOURCE-DURATION VECTOR
560 'DS DRIVING TIME STD DEV V   RL RESOURCE-LOCATION VECTOR
570 'DT DRIVING TIME             S POISSON SUMMATION
575 'DY SIMULATION LENGTH (DAYS)
580 'EX STAT EXPECTATION         SD STAT STD DEVIATION
590 'FA # ALARMS                 SL STATION LOCATION VECTOR
600 'FD FIRE DURATION            SN NORMAL SUMMATION
```

FIGURE 10–2   Program listing of the fire-dispatch simulator.

```
610 'FF POISSON FACTORIAL      SS STARTING PERIOD
620 'FL FIRE LOCATION          V FIRE LOSS
630 'FP POISSON MEAN           VM MEAN PROPERTY VALUE VECTOR
640 'FT TOTAL FIRES            VT TOTAL FIRE LOSS
650 'H CURRENT HOUR            W CURRENT DAY
660 'H$ STARTING HOUR          WW DAY-OF-WEEK VECTOR
670 'HH HOUR-OF-DAY VECTOR      WW$ DAY NAME VECTOR
680 'HH$ HOUR NAME VECTOR       X HORIZONTAL COORDINATE
690 'I OUTER COUNTER           Y VERTICAL COORDINATE
700 'II INNER COUNTER          Y$ STARTING YEAR
710 'J FIRE  COUNTER           YY MONTH-OF-YEAR VECTOR
720 'LC STATION CONDITION VEC  YY$ MONTH NAME VECTOR
730 'LF FIRE SYMBOL VECTOR      YR CURRENT MONTH
740 'LL FIRE-LOCATION VECTOR   Z CURRENT PERIOD
750 'LS STATION-LOCATION VECTOR
760 'M$ STARTING MONTH
770 'ME EXPONENTIAL VARIATE
780 'MN NORMAL VARIATE
790 'NN POISSON VARIATE
800 'NS STATION NAME VECTOR
810 'PF PENALTY FACTOR
900 '
910 ' INITIALIZATION
920 CLEAR 1000:RANDOM:CLS
1000 '
1010 ' DIMENSION STATEMENTS
1020 '  DATA ARRAYS
1030 DIM  YY(12),WW(7),HH(24),LL(9),AA(9),DD(9),DM(9),DS(9)
1032 DIM VM(9),LS(9),LC(9),LF(9),NS(9)
1034 DIM  YY$(12),WW$(7),HH$(24),SL(9)
1040 '  WORKING-STORAGE ARRAYS
1050 DIM R(18),RL(9),RD(9)
2000 '
2010 ' READ DATA ARRAYS
2020 FOR I=1 TO 12:READ YY(I):NEXT I
2030 FOR I=1 TO 7:READ WW(I):NEXT I
2040 FOR I=1 TO 24:READ HH(I):NEXT I
2050 FOR I=1 TO 9:READ LL(I):NEXT I
2060 FOR I=1 TO 9:READ AA(I):NEXT I
2070 FOR I=1 TO 9:READ DD(I):NEXT I
2080 FOR I=1 TO 9:READ DM(I):NEXT I
2090 FOR I=1 TO 9:READ DS(I):NEXT I
2100 FOR I=1 TO 9:READ VM(I):NEXT I
2110 FOR I=1 TO 9:READ LS(I):NEXT I
2120 FOR I=1 TO 9:READ LC(I):NEXT I
2130 FOR I=1 TO 9:READ LF(I):NEXT I
2140 '
2150 READ PP
2160 '
2170 FOR I=1 TO 9:READ NS(I):NEXT I
2180 FOR I=1 TO 12:READ YY$(I):NEXT I
2190 FOR I=1 TO 7:READ WW$(I):NEXT I
2200 FOR I=1 TO 24:READ HH$(I):NEXT I
2210 FOR I=1 TO 9:READ SL(I):NEXT I
3000 '
3010 ' START
3020 'GET SIMULATED STARTING TIME (SS)
3030 PRINT:PRINT:PRINT:PRINT:PRINT:PRINT:PRINT
3040 INPUT"ENTER STARTING TIME AS YY/MM/DD/HH";Y$
3050 M$=MID$(Y$,4,2):D$=MID$(Y$,7,2):H$=MID$(Y$,10,2)
3060 SS=(VAL(M$)-1)*2920+(VAL(D$)-1)*(VAL(H$)-1)*4
3070 '
3080 'SET TIME PERIOD OF SIMULATION (CC)
3090 PRINT:INPUT"ENTER PERIOD OF SIMULATION IN DAYS";DY
3100 CC=DY*96+SS
3200 N=SS
3205 N=N+1:Z=N
```

FIGURE 10–2 (continued)

```
3210 IF N>=CC THEN 3995
3220 '
3230 GOSUB 9900 'GET HOUR-OF-DAY (H)
3240 GOSUB 9800 'GET DAY-OF-WEEK (W)
3250 GOSUB 9700 'GET MONTH-OF-YEAR (YR)
3260 GOSUB 9600 'GET POISSON MEAN FOR 15-MIN PERIOD (FP)
3270 GOSUB 9300 'GET NUMBER OF FIRES THIS PERIOD (NF)
3285 IF NF=0 THEN 3205
3290 FOR J=1 TO NF 'HANDLE FIRES FOR CURRENT PERIOD
3300 GOSUB 9200 'GET FIRE LOCATION (FL)
3310 GOSUB 9100 'GET NUMBER OF ALARMS (FA)
3320 GOSUB 9400 'PRINT FIRE MAP SHOWING CURRENT FIRE
3325 PRINT@896,YY$(YR)" "WW$(W)" "HH$(H)" LOCATION= "FL"
3327 PRINT@940,"ALARMS= "FA
3330 PRINT@960,"ENTER FIRE-COMPANY ASSIGNMENTS ==>";
3340 LINE INPUT R$
3345 GOSUB 9000 'GET RESOURCE ASSIGNMENTS (R)
3350 GOSUB 8900 'CHECK AVAILABILITY (RL)
3360 GOSUB 8800 'GET DRIVING-TIME PARAMETER (CA$)
3370 GOSUB 8600 'GET DRIVING TIME (DT)
3380 GOSUB 8400 'GET FIRE-DURATION PARAMETER (RD)
3390 GOSUB 8300 'GET FIRE DURATION (FD)
3400 GOSUB 8200 'GET MEAN VALUE OF PROPERTY THREATENED (VM)
3410 GOSUB 8100 'GET FIRE LOSS (V)
3420 GOSUB 8000 'END-OF-FIRE (Z,FT,FL,FA,FD,V)
3970 INPUT X
3975 '
3980 NEXT J
3985 GOSUB 7900 'END-OF-PERIOD (RD,RL)
3990 GOTO 3205
3995 GOSUB 7800 'END-OF-SIMULATION (SS,CC,FT,VT)
4000 END
7800 '
7810 'END-OF-SIMULATION SUBROUTINE (SS,CC,FT,VT)
7820 CLS:PRINT:PRINT:PRINT:PRINT:PRINT
7830 PRINT"SIMULATION FROM PERIOD # "SS" TO PERIOD # "CC
7840 PRINT:PRINT"NUMBER OF FIRES = "FT"    PROPERTY LOSS = "VT
7845 PRINT
7847 PRINT"                          THE END":PRINT
7850 RETURN
7900 '
7910 'END-OF-PERIOD SUBROUTINE (RD,RL)
7920 FOR I=1 TO 9:RD(I)=RD(I)-15
7930 IF RD(I)<0 THEN RD(I)=0
7940 IF RD(I)=0 THEN RL(I)=0
7950 NEXT I
7970 RETURN
8000 '
8010 'END OF FIRE SUBROUTINE (Z,FT,FL,FA,FD)
8020 FT=FT+1:VT=VT+V
8030 CLS:PRINT:PRINT:PRINT:PRINT:PRINT
8035 PRINT"                    FIRE AUDIT"1:PRINT
8040 PRINT"PERIOD #= "Z;" FIRE #= "FT;" LOCATION= "FL
8042 PRINT " # OF ALARMS= "FA
8045 PRINT"DURATION= "FD"    FIRE LOSS= "V
8050 PRINT
8090 FOR I=1 TO 18:R(I)=0:NEXT I
8095 RETURN
8100 '
8110 'FIRE-LOSS SUBROUTINE (V)
8120 EX=VM:GOSUB 8500
8130 V=ME-((ME*100*(2.172828[(-DT)))/14)
8135 IF V<0 THEN V=1000
8140 RETURN
8200 '
8210 'PROPERTY-VALUE-PARAMETERS SUBROUTINE (VM)
8220 VM=VM(FL)
```

FIGURE 10–2 (continued)

```
8240 RETURN
8300 '
8310 'FIRE-DURATION SUBROUTINE (FD)
8320 EX=RD:GOSUB 8500
8325 FD=DT+ME+PF*ABS(ME-RD)
8330 FOR I=1 TO FA:IF R(I)=0 THEN 8350
8335 FOR II=1 TO 9
8340 IF II=R(I) THEN RD(II)=FD
8345 NEXT II
8350 NEXT I
8360 RETURN
8400 '
8410 'FIRE-DURATION-PARAMETER SUBROUTINE (RD)
8420 RD=DD(FA)
8440 RETURN
8500 '
8510 'EXPONENTIAL-DISTRIBUTION SUBROUTINE (ME)
8520 ME=(-EX)*LOG(RND(0))
8530 RETURN
8600 '
8610 'DRIVING-TIME SUBROUTINE (DT)
8615 DT=0
8620 EX=DM(R(1)):SD=DS(R(1)):GOSUB 8700:DT=MN
8630 IF CA$="1" THEN 8670
8640 EX=DM(FL):SD=DS(FL):GOSUB 8700:DT=DT+MN
8650 IF CA$="2" THEN 8670
8660 EX=DM(1):SD=DS(1):GOSUB 8700:DT=DT+MN
8670 RETURN
8700 '
8710 'NORMAL-DISTRIBUTION SUBROUTINE (MN)
8720 SN=0:FOR I=1 TO 12
8730 SN=SN+RND(0)
8740 NEXT I
8750 MN=SD*(SN-6)+EX
8760 IF MN<=0 THEN 8720
8770 RETURN
8800 '
8810 'DRIVING-TIME-PARAMETERS SUBROUTINE (CA$)
8820 CA$="":IF R(1)=FL THEN CA$="1":GOTO 8850
8822 IF R(1)=1 OR FL=1 THEN CA$="2":GOTO 8850
8826 IF (R(1)=6 OR R(1)=8 OR R(1)=5) AND (FL=6 OR FL=8 OR FL=5)
     THEN CA$="2":GOTO 8850
8827 IF (R(1)=5 OR R(1)=7 OR R(1)=4) AND (FL=5 OR FL=7 OR FL=4)
     THEN CA$="2":GOTO 8850
8828 IF (R(1)=4 OR R(1)=2 OR R(1)=9) AND (FL=4 OR FL=2 OR FL=9)
     THEN CA$="2":GOTO 8850
8830 IF (R(1)=9 OR R(1)=3 OR R(1)=6) AND (FL=9 OR FL=3 OR FL=6)
     THEN CA$="2":GOTO 8850
8840 CA$="3"
8850 RETURN
8900 '
8910 'AVAILABILITY SUBROUTINE (PF)
8920 PF=0:FOR I=1 TO FA
8930 IF R(I)=0 THEN PF=PF+1
8940 NEXT I
8945 IF R(1)=0 THEN DT=300:GOTO 3400
8950 RETURN
9000 '
9010 'FIRE-COMPANY ASSIGNMENT SUBROUTINE (R)
9020 FOR I=1 TO LEN(R$)
9030 R(I)=VAL(MID$(R$,(I*2-1),1))
9035 FOR II=1 TO 9
9040 IF II=R(NS(I)) AND RD(II)<>0 THEN R(I)=0:GOTO 9060
9050 IF RL(II)=0 THEN RL(II)=FL
9060 NEXT II
9065 NEXT I
9070 RETURN
```

FIGURE 10-2 (continued)

```
9100 '
9110 'NUMBER OF ALARMS SUBROUTINE (FA)
9120 R=RND(0)
9130 FOR I=9 TO 1 STEP -1
9140 IF R>=AA(I) THEN NEXT I ELSE FA=I
9150 RETURN
9200 '
9210 'FIRE-LOCATION SUBROUTINE (FL)
9215 R=RND(0)
9220 FOR I=9 TO 1 STEP -1
9230 IF R>=LL(I) THEN NEXT I ELSE FL=I
9240 RETURN
9300 '
9310 'POISSON SUBROUTINE (NF)
9320 S=0:R=RND(0)
9330 FOR I=1 TO 100
9335 NF=I-1
9340 IF NF<>0 THEN 9360
9350 FF=1:GOTO 9370
9360 FF=NF*FF
9370 NN=((2.718282[(-FP))*(FP[NF])/FF:S=S+NN
9380 IF S>=R THEN RETURN ELSE NEXT I
9400 '
9410 ' GRAPHICAL (DRAW-FIRE-MAP) SUBROUTINE
9420 CLS:Y=0:FOR X=0 TO 127:SET(X,Y):NEXT X
9430 Y=15:FOR X=0 TO 127:SET(X,Y):NEXT X
9440 Y=30:FOR X=0 TO 127:SET(X,Y):NEXT X
9450 Y=47:FOR X=0 TO 127:SET(X,Y):NEXT X
9460 X=0:FOR Y=0 TO 47:SET(X,Y):NEXT Y
9470 X=42:FOR Y=0 TO 47:SET(X,Y):NEXT Y
9480 X=84:FOR Y=0 TO 47:SET(X,Y):NEXT Y
9490 X=127:FOR Y=0 TO 47:SET(X,Y):NEXT Y
9500 FOR I=1 TO 9
9502 PRINT@LS(I),NS(I)" "CHR$(188)CHR$(188)CHR$(191)
9505 NEXT I
9510 PRINT@LF(SL(FL)),CHR$(185)CHR$(182)" "          FA
9550 FOR I=1 TO 9
9555 IF RD(NS(I))=0 THEN PRINT@LC(I)," FREE @ "NS(I):GOTO 9570
9560 PRINT@LC(I)," BUSY @ "RL(NS(I))
9570 NEXT I
9580 RETURN
9600 '
9610 'POISSON-MEAN SUBROUTINE (FP)
9620 FP=PP*YY(YR)*WW(W)*HH(H)
9630 RETURN
9700 '
9710 'MONTH-OF-YEAR SUBROUTINE (YR)
9720 YR=(INT(Z/2920)+1)-INT((INT(Z/2920)+1)/12)*12
9730 IF YR=0 THEN YR=12
9740 RETURN
9800 '
9810 'DAY-OF-WEEK SUBROUTINE (W)
9820 W=(INT(Z/96)+1)-INT((INT(Z/96)+1)/7)*7
9830 IF W=0 THEN W=7
9840 RETURN
9900 '
9910 'HOUR-OF-DAY SUBROUTINE (H)
9920 H=(INT(Z/4)+1)-INT((INT(Z/4)+1)/24)*24
9930 IF H=0 THEN H=24
9940 RETURN
10000 '
10010 ' DATA STATEMENTS
10020 '  MONTH-OF-YEAR VECTOR @ 12 (YY)
10030 DATA .8848,.8490,.9887,1.1463,1.0925,1.0352,1.2036
10035 DATA 1.0316,.9787,.8848,.9241
10040 '  DAY-OF-WEEK VECTOR @ 7 (WW)
10050 DATA .9880,.9129,.9880,.9526,1.0382,1.1573,.9630
```

FIGURE 10–2 (continued)

```
10060 '  HOUR-OF-DAY VECTOR @ 24 (HH)
10070 DATA .9740,.9669,.6876,.5013,.4011,.2936,.3653,.4942
10072 DATA .5730,.7592,.8236,.1.0170,.1.0241,1.1674,1.1173
10075 DATA 1.2963,.1.4252,1.4109,1.3751,1.5327,1.7046,1.5327
10077 DATA 1.4038,1.1531
10080 '  LOCATION-OF-FIRE VECTOR @ 9 (LL)
10090 DATA 1.0,.8175,.6798,.5802,.5021,.3942,.339,.2193,.1418
10100 '  MULTIPLE-ALARM VECTOR @ 9 (AA)
10110 DATA 1.0,.3797,.2197,.052,.0042,.0005,.0004,.0001,.0
10120 '  DURATION-VS-ALARM FUNCTION TABLE @ 9 (DD)
10130 DATA 21.19,31.94,33.24,35.03,39.09,50.,300.,300.,300.
10140 '  DRIVING-TIME MEANS BY DISTRICT @ 9 (DM)
10150 DATA 3.904,5.1887,3.767,4.2998,3.3973,5.1726,4.562
10152 DATA 5.3022,4.7064
10160 '  DRIVING-TIME STANDARD DEVIATIONS BY DISTRICT @ 9 (DS)
10170 DATA 2.76,2.5943,2.1748,2.4825,1.6987,2.7017,2.0402
10172 DATA 2.6512,2.2756
10180 '  PROPERTY-VALUE MEANS BY DISTRICT @ 9 (VM)
10190 DATA 93881,63579,70923,57647,70923,74587,63821,82060
10191 DATA 63821
10200 '  MAP LOCATIONS OF FIRE STATIONS @ 9 (LS)
10210 DATA 65,87,109,385,407,429,705,725,749
10220 '  MAP LOCATION OF FIRE-STATION CONDITION FLAGS @ 9 (LC)
10230 DATA 130,152,174,450,472,494,770,792,814
10240 '  MAP LOCATION OF FIRE SYMBOLS @ 9 (LF)
10250 DATA 73,95,117,393,415,437,713,735,757
10260 '  AVERAGE NUMBER OF FIRES PER 15-MINUTE PERIOD (PP)
10270 DATA .0956335
10280 '  NUMERICAL DESIGNATIONS OF FIRE STATIONS @ 9 (NS)
10290 DATA 8,5,7,6,1,4,3,9,2
10300 '  NAMES OF MONTHS OF THE YEAR @ 12 (YY$)
10310 DATA "JANUARY","FEBRUARY","MARCH","APRIL","MAY","JUNE"
10312 DATA "JULY","AUGUST","SEPTEMBER","OCTOBER","NOVEMBER"
10314 DATA "DECEMBER"
10320 '  NAMES OF DAYS OF THE WEEK @ 7 (WW$)
10330 DATA "MONDAY","TUESDAY","WEDNESDAY","THURSDAY","FRIDAY"
10332 DATA "SATURDAY","SUNDAY"
10340 '  NUMERICAL DESIGNATIONS OF HOURS OF THE DAY @ 24 (HH$)
10350 DATA "01:00","02:00","03:00","04:00","05:00","06:00"
10352 DATA "07:00","08:00","09:00","10:00","11:00","12:00"
10354 DATA "13:00","14:00","15:00","16:00","17:00","18:00"
10356 DATA "19:00","20:00","21:00","22:00","23:00","24:00"
10360 '  MAP LOCATION EQUIVALENTS OF FIRE STATIONS @ 9 (SL)
10370 DATA 5,9,7,6,2,4,3,1,8
```

FIGURE 10–2 (continued)

cannons. The idea was to implement it on a cheap microcomputer that could be placed in the day rooms of barracks where trainees were billeted.

There are several variables in aiming a cannon:

First, what kind of cannon is it? We simulated a 155-millimeter self-propelled howitzer.

Second, what is the mode of fire? It could be direct, meaning the elevation is less than 45 degrees; or it could be high-angle, meaning the elevation is greater than 45 degrees and, of course, less than 90 degrees. We simulated high-angle fire. Different GFTs exist for different cannons and modes of fire.

Third, what is the charge; that is, how much propellant is used? We simulated only charge #3.

Fourth, what is the site; that is, the difference in elevation between the cannon and the target? We assumed no difference.

Fifth, what is the range? We simulated ranges between 4,000 and 6,000 yards by adding random draws on 0–2,000 to 4,000 yards.

Sixth, what is the chart deflection; that is, the bearing of the target from the initial direction of the cannon as shown on topographical charts? Incidentally, artillerymen measure bearings in artillery mils. There are 6,400 mils in a circle. We simulated chart deflection as 2,400 mils plus a random number drawn on 0–1,600.

The trainee had to use the GFT to calculate cannon elevation (called "quadrant") and actual deflection; both of these are nonlinear functions.

The game display consists of a horizontal gunline at the bottom of the screen with a stylized cannon at the midpoint. A jagged ridge line divides the screen vertically to simulate intervening high terrain. The target is a stylized tank at the top of the screen. Chart deflection and range are shown in a legend (see Figure 10–3).

The trainee enters quadrant and deflection from the GFT. The program calculates the correct values by interpolating between end values on the GFT using Newton's divided-difference polynomials. Then the program shows the trainee the effects of fire.

A parabolic arc is traced out on the screen. If the round misses, a white dot appears where the simulated shell landed: short, long, left, right, or some combination. If the round hit the target; a white glob obliterates it. The trainee gets another shot if he misses the target. After a hit, the trainee is given the option of getting another target or quitting the game. In addition to getting the results of each shot, the trainee gets a summary of hits and misses at the end of the exercise. Figure 10–4 is the program.

FIGURE 10–3 Display for the artillery fire-direction simulator showing a hit.

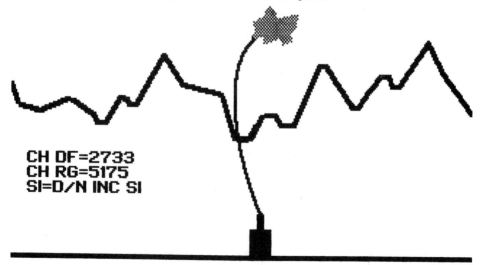

CH DF=2733
CH RG=5175
SI=D/N INC SI

```
100 'HIGH ANGLE
110 'COPYRIGHT 1981 BY JOHN M CARROLL
120 'ALL RIGHTS RESERVED
130 'CONTACT: BORGHAN REGISTERED
140 'RR#4, KOMOKA, ONTARIO, CANADA N0L 1R0
150 '
200 'A SIMULATOR IN VIDEO-GAME FORMAT FOR TRAINING
210 'ARTILLERYMEN IN FIRE-DIRECTION CONTROL USING
220 'A GRAPHICAL FIRING TABLE
230 '
300 'RUNS ON A RADIO SHACK MICROCOMPUTER TRS-80
310 'MODEL 1 LEVEL 2 WITH ONE DISK DRIVE AND
320 '16,000 BYTES OF RANDOM-ACCESS MEMORY
500 '
501 '           *****  GLOSSARY  *****
510 ' A=CONTINUE(CMD)           I=COUNTER
520 ' B$=BRANCH(STR)            I$=INITIALS(STR)
530 ' C$=COMMAND(SW)            M=RIGHT HOR LIMIT
540 ' CD=CHART DEFLECTION       N=LEFT HOR LIMIT
550 ' CG=CHARGE,GIVEN           N$=NAME(STR)
560 ' CH=CHARGE                 P=REPEAT(CMD)
570 ' D=CORRECTED DEFLECTION    Q=QUIT(CMD)
580 ' DF=DEFLECTION             QD=QUADRANT
590 ' DR=DRIFT                  R$=RANK(STR)
600 ' E=MISS                    RG=RANGE
610 ' EF$=EFFECT(SW & STR)      S=INTERMEDIATE VARIABLE
620 ' EL=ELEVATION              SI$=SITE(STR,DUMMY)
630 ' G=TERRAIN RANDOMIZER      Y=VERT COORDINATE
650 ' H=HIT                     Y(X)=VERT COORD,STORED
660 ' H$=ANOTHER SHOT(SW)       Z=TRY AGAIN
1000 '
1001 'MASTER CONTROL PROGRAM
1005 RANDOM:DIM Y(128)
1200 GOSUB 2000 'SIGN-IN
1210 IF C$="A" THEN C$="":CLS:GOTO 1300
1220 IF C$="Q" AND (H+E)>0  THEN C$="":CLS:GOTO 1900
1230 IF C$="Q" THEN CLS:END
1300 GOSUB 3000 'PROBLEM DESCRIPTION
1310 IF C$="A" THEN C$="":CLS:GOTO 1400
1320 IF C$="Q" AND (H+E)>0 THEN C$="":CLS:GOTO 1900
1325 IF C$="Q" THEN CLS:END
1330 IF C$="P" THEN C$="":CLS:GOTO 1200
1400 GOSUB 4000 'DRAW HIGH TERRAIN
1410 IF C$="A" THEN C$="":CLS:GOTO 1500
1420 IF C$="Q" AND (H+E)>0 THEN C$="":CLS:GOTO 1900
1425 IF C$="Q" THEN CLS:END
1430 IF C$="P" THEN C$="":CLS:GOTO 1300
1500 GOSUB 5000 'TARGET DISPLAY
1510 IF C$="A" THEN C$="":CLS:GOTO 1600
1520 IF C$="Q" AND (H+E)>0 THEN C$="":CLS:GOTO 1900
1525 IF C$="Q" THEN CLS:END
1530 IF C$="P" THEN C$="":CLS:GOTO 1400
1600 GOSUB 6000 'ENTER FIRING DATA
1610 IF C$="A" THEN C$="":CLS:GOTO 1700
1620 IF C$="Q" AND (H+E)>0 THEN C$="":CLS:GOTO 1900
1625 IF C$="Q" THEN CLS:END
1630 IF C$="P" THEN C$="":CLS:GOTO 1500
1700 GOSUB 7000 'EVALUATE FIRING
1750 GOSUB 5000 'TARGET DISPLAY-MODIFIED
1755 IF H$="ANOTHER SHOT" THEN 1600
1800 GOSUB 8000 'EFFECT OF FIRE
1810 IF C$="A" OR C$="Q" THEN C$="":CLS:GOTO 1900
1820 IF C$="P" THEN C$="":CLS:GOTO 1750
1900 GOSUB 9000 'SCORE ON EXERCISE
1910 IF C$="A" THEN C$="":EV$="":EF$="":CLS:GOTO 1500
1920 IF C$<>"Z" THEN GOTO 1950
1925 C$="":EF$="":EV$="":H$="ANOTHER SHOT":CLS:GOTO 1750
```

FIGURE 10–4 Program listing for the artillery fire-direction simulator.

```
1930 IF C$="Q" THEN C$="":CLS:GOTO 1950
1940 IF C$="P" THEN C$="":HX$="BACKUP":CLS:GOTO 1800
1950 GOTO 9500 'TERMINATION
2000 '
2001 'SIGN-IN
2005 CLS
2010 PRINT CHR$(23)
2020 PRINT:PRINT:PRINT
2030 PRINT"    WELCOME TO HIGH-ANGLE"
2040 PRINT" C CIRCLE 1981 BY JOHN M CARROLL":PRINT
2050 PRINT"      PLEASE SIGN IN"
2060 PRINT:INPUT"NAME,INITIALS";N$,I$
2070 PRINT:INPUT"RANK,BRANCH";R$,B$
2080 PRINT:INPUT"TYPE'A'TO CONTINUE,'Q'TO QUIT";C$
2100 IF C$="A" OR C$="Q" THEN 2200 ELSE 2080
2200 RETURN
3000 '
3001 'PROBLEM DESCRIPTION
3020 PRINT:PRINT
3030 PRINT"THIS GAME WILL TEST YOUR SKILL IN DIRECTING FIRE "
3032 PRINT"FOR THE M-109 SELF-PROPELLED 155-MM HOWITZER WHEN "
3034 PRINT"FIRING AT INTERMEDIATE RANGES WITH INTERVENING "
3036 PRINT"HIGH TERRAIN. "
3040 PRINT
3050 PRINT"        YOU WILL NEED YOUR GFT 155AMIHEM107."
3060 PRINT"        USE THE MANUFACTURER'S CURSOR."
3080 PRINT:PRINT:PRINT"            GOOD HUNTING!"
3090 PRINT
3092 PRINT
3094 INPUT"TYPE'A'TO CONTINUE,'Q'TO QUIT,'P'TO BACKUP";C$
3100 IF C$="A" OR C$="Q" OR C$="P" THEN 3200 ELSE 3090
3200 RETURN
4000 '
4001 'DRAW HIGH TERRAIN
4010 PRINT:PRINT"                AT EASE, SOLDIER"
4015 PRINT
4020 PRINT"        IN SIX DAYS GOD CREATED HEAVEN AND EARTH"
4025 PRINT
4030 PRINT" IT TAKES US 40.89 SECONDS TO MAKE THE WICHITA MTS"
4045 G=RND(30)
4050 FOR X=1 TO 127
4065 Y=28-3*SIN(X*6.28/90)+2*SIN(3*X*6.28/90+G+15)
4067 Y=Y+2*SIN(5*X*6.28/90-30)+SIN(7*X*6.28/90+30)
4068 Y=Y+3*SIN(2*X*6.28/90)
4070 IF Y<19 THEN 4100 'SET UPPER BOUND ON MOUNTAINS
4080 IF Y>37 THEN 4100 'SET LOWED BOUND ON MOUNTAINS
4085 Y(X)=Y
4090 SET(X,Y)
4100 NEXT X
4110 INPUT"TYPE'A'TO CONTINUE,'Q'TO QUIT,'P'TO BACKUP";C$
4200 IF C$="A" OR C$="Q" OR C$="P" THEN 4300 ELSE 4110
4300 RETURN
5000 '
5001 'GAME DISPLAY
5100 'GUNLINE AND HOWITZER
5105 FOR X=1 TO 127:Y=47:SET(X,Y):NEXT X
5107 FOR X=62 TO 67:FOR Y=46 TO 44 STEP -1:SET(X,Y):NEXT Y,X
5110 FOR X=64 TO 65
5120 FOR Y=47 TO 41 STEP -1
5130 SET(X,Y)
5140 NEXT Y,X
5200 'INTERVENING HIGH TERRAIN
5210 FOR X=1 TO 127
5220 IF Y(X)=0 THEN 5250 'AVOID FALSE ZEROS
5230 SET(X,Y(X))
5250 NEXT X
5300 'TARGET (TANK)
```

FIGURE 10-4 (continued)

```
5310 Y=2:FOR X=60 TO 68:SET(X,Y):NEXT X
5320 Y=3:FOR X=51 TO 68:SET(X,Y):NEXT X
5330 Y=4:FOR X=60 TO 75:SET(X,Y):NEXT X
5340 Y=5:FOR X=53 TO 75:SET(X,Y):NEXT X
5350 Y=6:FOR X=54 TO 74:SET(X,Y):NEXT X
5400 'GET CHART DATA
5405 'CHECK EVALUATE FLAG
5407 IF EV$="EVALUATE" OR HX$="ANOTHER SHOT" THEN 5500
5408 'MODIFICATION TO SUBROUTINE
5410 GOSUB 10000 'GET RANDOMIZED TARGET DATA
5500 PRINT@128,"CH DF="CD
5510 PRINT@192,"CH RG="RG
5520 PRINT@256,"SI="SI$
5550 IF EV$="EVALUATE" THEN RETURN 'MODIFICATION TO SUBROUTINE
5600 INPUT"TYPE'A'TO CONTINUE,'Q'TO QUIT,'P'TO BACKUP";C$
5610 IF C$="A" OR C$="Q" OR C$="P" THEN 5700 ELSE 5600
5700 RETURN
6000 '
6001 'FIRE DIRECTION
6010 CLS:PRINT:PRINT"CH DF="CD,"CH RG="RG,"SI="SI$
6015 PRINT
6020 PRINT:PRINT"          ***** YOUR  FIRE  DIRECTION *****"
6030 PRINT:PRINT:INPUT"ENTER CHARGE";CH
6040 PRINT:PRINT:INPUT"ENTER DEFLECTION";DF
6050 PRINT:PRINT:INPUT"ENTER QUADRANT";QD
6060 PRINT
6100 INPUT"'A'= CONTINUE,'Q'= QUIT,'Z'= REDO,'P'= BACKUP";C$
6200 IF C$="Z" THEN 6000
6210 IF C$="A" OR C$="Q" OR C$="P" THEN 6300 ELSE 6100
6300 RETURN
7000 '
7001 'EVALUATION
7010 EV$="EVALUATE" 'SET MODIFICATION MODE IN SUBROUTINE 5000
7020 HX$="" 'RESET 'ANOTHER SHOT' SWITCH
7100 'CHARGE
7110 IF CH<>CG THEN EF$="WRONG CHARGE-USE CHARGE 3":GOTO 7700
7115 'LINE 7700 IS MISS COUNTER
7200 'DEFLECTION
7210 S=(5500-RG)/250
7220 DR=55+S*6+(S*(S-1))/2+(S*(S-1)*(S-2)*(S-3)*.7)/24
7230 D=CD+DR
7240 IF DF=D THEN 7300
7250 IF DF-1>D THEN EF$="LEFT":GOTO 7700
7260 IF DF+1<D THEN EF$="RIGHT":GOTO 7700
7300 'QUADRANT
7305 IF RG>5220 THEN 7315 ELSE 7310
7310 EL=1117+.126*RG-.000024*RG*RG:GOTO 7320
7315 EL=1085+S*33+S*(S-1)*4/2+S*(S-1)*(S-2)/6
7317 EL=EL+S*(S-1)*(S-2)*(S-3)/24
7320 IF QD=EL THEN 7400
7330 IF QD-1>EL THEN EF$="SHORT ROUND":GOTO 7700
7340 IF QD+1<EL THEN EF$="LONG ROUND":GOTO 7700
7400 'SITE---RESERVED FOR EXPANSION OF GAME
7500 'SCORE A HIT
7510 EF$="STEEL ON TARGET!"
7520 H=H+1
7530 GOTO 7900
7700 'SCORE A MISS
7710 E=E+1
7900 RETURN
8000 '
8001 'EFFECT OF FIRE
8005 IF HX$="BACKUP" THEN 8905:OMIT TRAJECTORY DRAWING
8100 'DRAW PROJECTLE TRAJECTORY
8110 FOR Y=41 TO 7 STEP -1
8120 X=64.8389-.859335*Y+.0204604*Y*Y
8130 SET(X,Y)
```

FIGURE 10-4 (continued)

```
8140 NEXT Y
8150 HX$=""
8200 'WRONG CHARGE
8210 IF EF$="WRONG CHARGE-USE CHARGE 3" THEN 8900
8300 'LEFT
8310 IF EF$<>"LEFT" THEN 8400
8320 'DRAW LEFT IMPACT
8330 SET(48,3):GOTO 8900
8400 'RIGHT
8410 IF EF$<>"RIGHT" THEN 8500
8420 'DRAW RIGHT IMPACT
8430 SET(80,3):GOTO 8900
8500 'LONG ROUND
8510 IF EF$<>"LONG ROUND" THEN 8600
8520 'DRAW LONG ROUND IMPACT
8530 SET(65,0):GOTO 8900
8600 'SHORT ROUND
8610 IF EF$<>"SHORT ROUND" THEN 8700
8620 'DRAW SHORT ROUND
8630 SET(65,8):GOTO 8900
8700 'ON TARGET
8710 'DRAW ON TARGET IMPACT
8720 N=56:M=70
8730 FOR Y=1 TO 3
8740 N=N-2:M=M+2
8750 FOR X=N TO M
8760 SET(X,Y):NEXT X,Y
8770 FOR Y=4 TO 6
8780 N=N+2:M=M-2
8790 FOR X=N TO M
8800 SET(X,Y):NEXT X,Y
8900 FOR I=1 TO 500:NEXT I
8905 HX$=""
8910 'EFFECT OF FIRE PANEL
8915 CLS:PRINT:PRINT:PRINT:PRINT
8920 PRINT"                    EFFECT OF FIRE"
8925 PRINT:PRINT
8930 PRINT"         "R$", THE EFFECT OF YOUR SHOT WAS"
8935 PRINT:PRINT"              "EF$
8940 PRINT:PRINT:PRINT
8945 INPUT"TYPE'A'TO CONTINUE,'Q'TO QUIT,'P'TO BACKUP";C$
8950 IF C$="A" OR C$="Q" OR C$="P" THEN 8970 ELSE 8945
8970 RETURN
9000 '
9001 'SCORE ON EXERCISE
9010 PRINT:PRINT:PRINT:PRINT
9020 PRINT"                  SCORE ON EXERCISE"
9025 PRINT
9030 PRINT"     "R$" "I$" "N$", "B$": YOUR SCORE IS"
9040 PRINT:PRINT"              "H" HITS"
9045 PRINT"                   "E" MISSES"
9050 PRINT"                 "H+E" ROUNDS FIRED"
9060 PRINT:PRINT:PRINT:PRINT
9070 INPUT"'A'=NEW TARGET,'Z'=TRY AGAIN,'Q'=QUIT,'P'=BACKUP";C$
9080 IF C$="A" OR C$="Q" OR C$="Z" OR C$="P" THEN 9090 ELSE 9070
9090 RETURN
9500 '
9501 'TERMINATION
9510 PRINT:PRINT:PRINT:PRINT
9520 PRINT"            gOOD-BYE "R$" "N$
9525 PRINT"         WE HOPE YOU ENJOYED PLAYING 'HIGH ANGLE'"
9527 PRINT
9530 PRINT" IF YOU DID, PLEASE TELL YOUR FRIENDS ABOUT IT"
9540 PRINT:PRINT:PRINT"IF YOU WANT TO PLAY ANOTHER ROUND,"
9550 PRINT"TYPE 'RUN' AFTER THE WORD 'READY' APPEARS."
9560 PRINT:PRINT
9600 END
```

FIGURE 10–4 (continued)

```
10000 '
10001 'CHART DATA
10100 'CHARGE
10110 CG=3
10200 'CHART DEFLECTION
10210 CD=2400+RND(1600)
10300 'RANGE
10310 RG=4500+RND(1000)
10400 'SITE
10410 SI$="D/N INC SI"
10500 RETURN
```

FIGURE 10–4 (continued)

Psychological Testing [9] and Risk Analysis [10]

Simulation can be used in psychological investigation. One example of its use is trying to evaluate various strategies for coaching witnesses to make better quantitative estimations. The ability of knowledgeable informants to make acccurate estimates is especially important in risk analysis. [10]

The plan was to set a task for the subjects, use different coaching strategies, and then see what difference, if any, the various kinds of coaching made in their performances.

The task we set was to estimate the number of white squares displayed in a random pattern against a blue background. The display persisted for one second. Each subject got to see 12 different low-density screens (14 to 83 squares) and 12 high-density screens (107 to 879 squares). These are displayed in figures 10–5 and 10–6.

FIGURE 10–5 Low-density screen for the risk-estimation simulator.

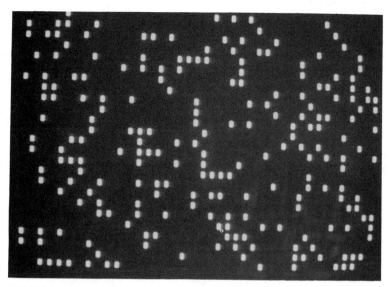

FIGURE 10–6 High-density screen for the risk-estimation simulator.

The patterns were generated with random numbers of squares by a program running on an IBM Personal Computer. The program also gave instructions to the subjects, accepted their estimates of the number of squares, calculated the difference between the subjects' estimates and the number of squares displayed, and formatted the data for transmission to a mainframe computer, where they were processed by conventional statistical packages.

We made four runs. The first was a control run; the subjects were given no help estimating 24 low-density screens and 24 high-density screens except to tell them that the maximum number of squares would be less than 900. In the other runs, the subjects performed half the tests on their own and were coached for the second half.

The first coaching strategy was to ask the subject to estimate the number of squares in one quadrant of the pattern, after which the program multiplied this answer by four. This strategy was called disaggregation.

The second strategy asked the subject to estimate the largest and smallest number of squares that could be in the pattern currently being displayed. The program added these estimates and divided by two. This strategy was called range estimation.

The third strategy was like the second except that the subject was also asked to give the best estimate of the number of squares. The program combined these three estimates as follows:

$$\text{Final-estimate} = (\text{High-estimate} + 4 * \text{Best-estimate} + \text{Low-estimate})/6$$

You may recognize this technique. It is used in the planning of projects and is called the Project Evaluation and Review Technique, or PERT for short.

Our results were interesting, to say the least. The control runs showed no improvement with practice. Disaggregation results were the same as the control runs. This could mean either that disaggregation doesn't work or that subjects mentally disaggregete whether asked to do so or not.

Range and PERT both made performance worse on low-density screens. We rationalized that the subjects who made accurate estimates of the number of squares on low-density screens did so by counting them rapidly and that coaching interfered with their natural strategy while contributing no improvement.

On high-density screens, the range strategy made the subject's performance worse, while the PERT strategy made it significantly better. The psychologist I worked with hasn't as yet developed a theory to explain these results. Pragmatically, however, we know that PERT has a good track record for helping people come up with accurate estimates of various things (but usually of time needed to complete a job). We wondered why range was so bad; what successful strategy was it displacing? We questioned some of the subjects, and they told us that although they couldn't count the squares on high-density squares, they could count the places where squares should have been but weren't—if the screen was sufficiently dense.

Manufacturing Synthetic Text [11] and Classified Files [12]

Many times you need a body of text (corpus) having certain characteristics with respect to content or format. It may be inconvenient or expensive to put the desired corpus into machine-readable form and a suitable corpus may not be readily available as a by-product of other operations such as word processing. One answer is to create synthetic text by simulation.

I developed this system when a very snarky lady at the National Science Foundation said they were not going to spend any money keypunching text for somebody like me. I have used it in two projects. The first was to select the best mathematical criterion for identifying key words for the automatic indexing of documents. The second was to evaluate the consequences of using cryptography to enforce a multi-level security regime on a relational data base. Multi-level secure systems rely on the hardware and/or software of a trusted computing base to handle information having two or more levels of classification [12].

In the key-word selection study, we faced the problem that when one uses real text, reviewers tend to question the judgmental decisions as to what are key words. Using totally synthetic text circumvents some of these arguments.

We posited that documents are made up of three kinds of words: (a) common words, (b) uncommon words, and (c) key words. Moreover, there are three kinds of key words: high-frequency, medium-frequency, and low-frequency.

We created several hundred documents, each having about 1,100 words.

Common words make up roughly 80 percent of a document. To choose them we listed the 200 most common words in order of their normalized-occurrence frequencies and made a cumulative frequency distribution of those frequencies. All we then had to do was to make 800 random draws from the distribution and add the common words thus selected to our synthetic document.

Uncommon words make up about 20 percent of a document. Here we created synthetic words. We used the cumulative-occurrence frequency of letters of the alphabet as initial characters of words to choose the initial letters of our 200 uncommon words. Then we used a table of cumulative digraphic-occurrence frequencies to choose the remaining letters. This can be regarded as a Markov process. Once you choose the initial character, you make a random draw, enter the digraph table in the column corresponding to the initial letter, and find out which letter (or space) follows it. Of course, the resulting product is gibberish, but it looks a lot like English, and the words most assuredly are very uncommon.

Key words were chosen by a double Poisson process. We made random draws from a list of 500 key words appropriate to the desired subject matter (say, descriptors chosen by the Association for Computing Machinery). To find out how many key words to select in each subclass, we made random draws from each of three Poisson distributions having different means (high-frequency mean = 16; medium-frequency mean = 8; low-frequency mean = 4). Note that the Poisson means are geometrically distributed. We determined how many times each of these key words should occur by sampling from one of three Poisson distributions (high-frequency mean = 8; medium-frequency mean = 4; low-frequency means = 2). On average, our synthetic documents contained 1,131 words.

We selected the top N words recalled by our mathematical selection criterion and called them key words. We picked out the K actual key words on this list and computed the recall/precision ratio: K/N. The effectiveness of the selection criteria tested ranged from .23 to .72.

CONCLUSIONS

The foregoing examples are representative of applications of simulation that I have published during more than 20 years of practice. Unpublished work included designing a quality-control (QC) system for a new TV factory in Tennessee (the QC system worked very well, but the plant closed after two years because wage costs couldn't match those in East Asia): simulating 400 years of propagation of plant species on the shoreline of Lake Huron; simulation of various tank attacks over a particular piece of terrain, given several different defense strategies; simulation of target detection by hunter-killer submarines, given several different distributions of hydrophones on and around the hull; bottling of beer; inventory of a hardware distributor; an epidemic model depicting the spread of a venereal disease; and a competitive-species model showing the results of coexisting trout and whitefish populations in a Manitoba lake; and many more.

My conclusion is simply that simulation works: It is often the quickest way to converge on a solution that will save your client money. Furthermore, most simulations can be skeletonized so that they easily run on a personal computer. My early work was done on a mainframe computer with 8,000 words of memory and four tape handlers. I'm writing this on a micro with 256,000 words of memory and 5,360,000 words of disk storage; and I have a machine in the office with twice the main memory, more than four times the disk space, and graphical capabilities I never dreamed of twenty years ago.

REFERENCES

1. J. M. CARROLL, "Estimating Errors in the Inspection of Complex Products," *AIIE Transactions* (September 1969), 229.
2. J. M. CARROLL, "Predicting Product Failure," *Industrial Engineering* (December 1973), 26.
3. J. M. CARROLL and P. G. LAURIN, "Using Simulation to Assign Police Patrol Zones," *Simulation* (January 1981), 1.
4. J. M. CARROLL, "Digital Simulator for Allocating Firefighting Resources," *Simulation* (January 1982), 1.
5. J. J. CARROLL and O.-L. WU, "Simulation of Urban Hospital Emergency Room Activities, *Computer Simulation in Emergency Planning*, SCS Simulation Series, 11, no. 2, 20.
6. J. M. CARROLL and A. MADAN, "Microsimulation of Households," Proceedings of the Association for the Advancement of Simulation and Modeling in Enterprises Conference, Storrs, CT, July 3, 1985.
7. J. M. CARROLL, "How to Turn an Emergency Simulation into a 'Video Game' for Training," *Computer Simulation in Emergency Planning*, SCS Simulation Series, 11, no. 2, 83.
8. J. M. CARROLL, Digital Simulator for Training Artillerymen, *All About Simulators*, SCS Simulation Series, 14, no. 1, 56.
9. J. M. CARROLL and L. M. JACKSON, "Simulation of Human Risk Estimation," *Computer Simulation in Emergency Planning*, SCS Simulation Series, 15, no. 1, 7.
10. J. M. CARROLL, "A Generalized Risk-Analysis Model for Microcomputers," *Computer Simulation in Emergency Planning*, 15, no. 1, 37.
11. J. M. CARROLL, Use of Synthetic Text in the Evaluation of Statistically Based Keyword-Selection Strategies, *Journal of the American Society for Information Science* (July–August 1975), 261.
12. J. M. CARROLL and H. JUERGENSEN, Design for a Secure Relational Data Base, Proceedings of the International Federation for Information Processing Security Conference, Dublin, Ireland, August 12, 1985.

BIBLIOGRAPHY

ADKINS, G., and U. W. POOCH, "Computer Simulation: a Tutorial," *Computer*, 18, no. 4 (April 1977), 12–17.

BAILEY, N. T. J., *The Elements of Stochastic Processes.* New York: John Wiley & Sons, Inc., 1964.

BURINGTON, R. S., and D. C. MAY, *Handbook of Probability and Statistics With Tables.* Sandusky, OH: Handbook Publishers, Inc., 1958.

CHATTERGY, R., and U. W. POOCH, Integrated Design and Verification of Simulation Processes, *Computer*, 10, no. 4 (April 1977), 40–45.

EMSHOFF, J. P., and R. L. SISSON, *Design and Use of Computer Simulation Models.* London: Macmillan & Co. Ltd., 1970.

GORDON, G., *Systems Simulation* (2nd ed.). Englewood Cliffs, NJ: Prentice-Hall, Inc., 1978.

HALL, A. D., *A Methodology for Systems Engineering.* Princeton, NJ: D. Van Nostrand Co., Inc., 1962.

HILLIER, F. S., and G. J. LIEBERMAN, *Introduction to Operations Research.* San Francisco: Holden-Day, Inc., 1967.

KORN, G. A., *Random Processes and Measurements.* New York: McGraw-Hill Book Co., 1966.

MAISEL, H., and G. GNUGNOLI, *Simulation of Discrete Stochastic Systems.* Chicago: Science Research Associates, 1972.

MEYER H., *Symposium on Monte Carlo Methods.* New York: John Wiley & Sons, Inc., 1954.

MILLER, I., and J. E. FREUND, *Probability and Statistics for Engineers.* Englewood Cliffs, NJ: Prentice-Hall, Inc., 1966.

NAYLOR, T. H., J. E. BALINTFY, D. S. BURDICK, and K. CHU, *Computer Simulation Techniques.* New York: John Wiley & Sons, Inc., 1966.

Reference Data for Radio Engineers. New York: ITT Inc., 1964.

SHANNON, R. E., *Systems Simulation.* Englewood Cliffs, NJ: Prentice-Hall, Inc., 1975.

TOCHER, K. D., *The Art of Simulation.* Princeton, NJ: D. Van Nostrand Co., Inc., 1963.

Index